RELIGION IN THE AMERICAN NOVEL

The Search for Belief, 1860-1920

Leo F. O'Connor

UNIVERSITY
PRESS OF
AMERICA

LANHAM • NEW YORK • LONDON

Copyright © 1984 by

University Press of America,™ Inc.

4720 Boston Way
Lanham, MD 20706

3 Henrietta Street
London WC2E 8LU England

Library of Congress Cataloging in Publication Data

O'Connor, Leo F.
  Religion in the American novel.

  Bibliography: p.
  1. American fiction–History and criticism. 2.
Religion in literature. 3. Sects in literature. I. Title.
PS374.R47O26   1984   813'.4'09382   83–21842
ISBN 0–8191–3683–2 (alk. paper)
ISBN 0–8191–3684–0 (pbk. : alk. paper)

To Karen

ACKNOWLEDGEMENTS

Over a period of years many individuals-in many ways-have given support and direction to my efforts in preparing this book. I am particularly grateful to the following: to Gay Wilson Allen for his early guidance, to Leonard Fleischer for his enthusiastic encouragement, to Stanley Crane of the Pequot Library for his assistance in helping me gain access to forgotten novels, to James Tuttleton for his meticulous criticism, to William Gibson for his thoughtful and valued suggestions, to my colleagues Arthur Anderson and Nicholas Rinaldi for their counsel and concern, and finally to my students at Fairfield University, the American College Graduate School (Bryn Mawr), the University of Connecticut, and the NAMSB Executive Development Program who have aided me by their interest in this subject matter.

As the manuscript passed through its various stages, I have been indebted to the patience and good-will of many able hands. First and foremost, I thank my wife Karen D. O'Connor for her impeccable editorial skills. Helping me insert the endless addenda for the final copy, I am indebted to Margaret Otzel, Mary Westwood, and Margie Beam who expeditiously and cheerfully carried out this tedious task. I am also indebted to the considerable editorial skills of Stephanie Knowles and Andrea Moody in realizing the final copy. Needless to say, any errors in the present text are solely my responsibility.

Finally, I wish to acknowledge the extraordinary support which I have received over the years from my beloved mother Helen Sullivan O'Connor. Early on in life, she taught me a love of literature by her respect for books, later on she taught me fortitude in the face of adversity. This book is rooted in the education which she gave me.

Fairfield University
Fairfield, Connecticut

CONTENTS

Contents

INTRODUCTION

The purpose of this study is to examine the treatment of religious sectarianism by selected American novelists during the period 1860-1920. Whenever religious sects showed tolerance of immoral conduct (e.g., slavery, the exploitation of the working classes, avarice, physical violence) either by direct act or by the irrelevance of their teachings, the novelists of the period made an effort to educate their readers through the art of fiction. Their motivation was not to preserve any variety of formalized belief, but rather to revitalize the human spirit. An earlier pattern had been observed by A. N. Kaul in *The American Vision* when he commented upon this phenomenon in the American novels written during the first sixty years of the nineteenth century, noting that the novelists of this period shared

> . . . the general feeling that America was the land of social experimentation, and, while practical men battled over new political and economic institutions, they sought in their work the moral values necessary for the regeneration of human society.[1]

This search for moral values did not cease in 1860, but rather accelerated after the Civil War because of social problems arising from industrialization, urbanization, and increasing immigration. When the serious novelist turned his attention to the activities of the various religions, he found them all too frequently inadequate to the challenges of the age.

This dissatisfaction with religious institutions was consistent with the Protestant tradition in which the overwhelming majority of nineteenth-century American novelists were educated.[2] When the novelist expressed his disapproval with the failure of a particular religion to live up to its ideals, he was carrying out with historical inevitability the Protestant tradition of dissent. In effect, the novel of righteous indignation was, and continues to be, a religious motif in American literature. William G. McLoughlin, the historian of American religious experience, has observed that pietism is a quintessential aspect of the American character and finds its expression throughout American literature. "The temper of our best literature can be stated in pietistic-perfectionist terms as anguish, frustration, despair, anger, intensity—anguish over the impurity of man in an impure world; anger at the corruptions and corrupters of human conscience; frustration at man's inability to come to terms with himself or his universe." McLoughlin concludes that the theme of pietism "has been more pervasive and more consistent in American literature than in that of any culture in modern Christendom or post-Christendom. It is not just *one* theme of our literature, it is *the* theme."[3]

The notion of the artist as preserver and purveyor of the Christian tradition is articulated by several of the novelists in this study. Twain wrote that the average American derived his Christian sensibility from art rather than religion. When a New York City minister refused the use of his church for the funeral of George Holland, an actor, Twain wrote:

2

It is almost fair and just to aver (although it is profanity) that nine-tenths of all kindness and forebearance and Christian charity and generosity in the hearts of the American people today, got there by being filtered down from their fountainhead, the gospel of Christ, through dramas and tragedies and comedies on the state, and through the despised novel and the Christmas story . . . *NOT* from the drowsy pulpit.[4]

As well as reflecting his own understanding of the writer's function, Twain's statement may be appropriately applied to most serious novelists of his generation. Whether it be the implicit matter of the novels or expressed theories of literature (e.g. Howells' theory of complicity or Norris' "The Responsibilities of the Novelist"), there is considerable evidence that the novelists of the Post-Civil War period committed their creative lives to the moral use of literature, and this commitment frequently led to conflict with institutional religions. More recently, Amos N. Wilder in his *Modern Poetry and the Christian Tradition* further extended this concept of the artist's moral vision when he asserted that the custody and very future of the Christian tradition had passed from the exclusive custody of the clergy into the keeping of secular artists.[5]

Most of the novelists included in this study can be broadly classified as realistic artists committed to the description of social actualities. Many of these novelists have given explicit statements of their commitment to a socially realistic aesthetic. Edward Eggleston recognized that his novels were distinguished

3

by "the prominence which they give to social conditions;
. . . the individual characters are here [in his
novels] treated to a greater degree than elsewhere as
parts of a study of society."[6] The importance of the
social milieu in shaping the artist's sensibility and in
affecting his creative life was the subject of a
thorough analysis by the novelist Robert Herrick, who
reduced the creative components of the novelists into

> . . . two inescapable elements,--the
> personality of the creator and that
> social environment or peculiar
> segment of civilization into which
> fate has cast him. And inasmuch as
> he himself, together with his
> creation, springs ultimately from
> the social world which his art seeks
> to reflect and interpret, the latter
> is obviously the more inclusive of
> the two.[7]

When a writer emphasizes his commitment to giving a true
portrait of society, it argues for the reliability of
his fiction as a primary source for social data.

Although literature has long been used as a
primary source for social and historical data, there are
hazards to be avoided. Rene Wellek and Austin Warren
have noted that literature can be made to yield the
outlines of social history, but they also caution
against the indiscriminate use of literature simply as a
mirror of life in any age. Such studies, (write Wellek
and Warren)

> . . . make sense only if we know the
> artistic method of the novelist
> studied, can say--not merely in
> general terms, but concretely--in
> what relation the picture stands to

4

the social reality. Is it realistic by intention? Or is it, at certain points, satire, caricature, or romantic idealization?[8]

The majority of novelists discussed in this study fall by their own definitions and by critical consensus into the realistic tradition, and throughout this study a special effort will be made to verify by historical cross-references the accuracy of their descriptions of religious sects in different regions of the United States at various stages of the nineteenth century.

The specific focus of this study, however, is directed toward the novelist's response to those religions with which they had personal experience. In measuring that response one must keep in mind the novelist's special point of view, and not be misled to an uncritical acceptance of artistic verisimilitude as actuality. Nelson Blake in *Novelist's America: Fiction as History* observes that the novelist

> . . . differs from other people in his creative impulse, his imaginative powers, and his verbal skills. His writing is more like portraiture than photography, because it suppresses less important details to emphasize dominant qualities . . . . Above all, of course, the novelist injects his imagination, and his imagined episodes have a symbolic quality, differing from drab reality.

Having raised these questions regarding the reliability of the artist's view of reality, Blake offers a relatively simple prescription to those who seek historical or social data from novels.

5

They should ask in each case what
kind of person the novelist was,
what his prejudices were, how much
opportunity for observation he had,
and what other people thought of his
accuracy.[9]

Blake's formula does not differ fundamentally from the
critical standards used in measuring any potential
source of information, and it goes without saying that,
in the present study, whenever a question arises
regarding the accuracy of a novelist's perception of a
religious sect, a special effort will be made to
incorporate data which have a bearing on the historical,
biographical, and sociological dimensions of the novels
under discussion.

Most of the novelists included in this study were
serious artists whose commitment to truth was both
intense and conscientious. In 1902, Frank Norris
addressed himself to this very question in his famous
essay, "The Responsibilities of the Novelist." Norris
described the successful novelist as one who

. . . should be careful of what he
says . . . more than all others--
more even than the minister and
editor--he should 'feel his public'
and watch his every word, testing
carefully his every utterance,
weighing with the most relentless
precision his every statement; in a
word possess a sense of his
responsibilities.[10]

During the period from 1860 to 1920, the novel was, by
general consensus, the foremost literary genre in
America, and part of Norris's concern regarding the

6

novelist's role is evident in his recognition of the novelist's particular importance in helping shape popular opinions. The novel, as Norris saw it, was destined to be a primary source for future generations in their understanding of his age. Norris prophesied that ". . . the critics of the twenty-second century, reviewing our times, striving to reconstruct our civilization will look . . . to the novelists to find our idiosyncrasy."[11]

Less than three decades after Norris made these comments, Arthur M. Schlesinger noted that the study of American literature required an awareness of the historical forces operating on the novelists for an understanding of, specifically, nineteenth-century American literature. Schlesinger contended that one must take into account such factors

> . . . as the mechanical improvements
> in printing, the frontier influence,
> and the deeply religious tone of the
> society . . . . The development of
> literature is constantly affected by
> the forces which condition the whole
> course of social growth.[12]

The points of emphasis in the relationship of the novelist to his age differ for Norris and Schlesinger as they differed for Herrick and Blake, but what both novelist and historian recognize is the interdependence between the imagined world of fiction and the realities of a particular society, an interdependence heightened in a literature that proclaims itself as realistic. It is with this interdependence that the current study is basically concerned.

By and large, the novelists in nineteenth-century America anticipated and fulfilled Matthew Arnold's concept of the artist's function.[13] The legacy of the

Judeo-Christian code was to be the basis for the restoration and preservation of a spiritually enlightened culture. Repeatedly, the novelists who wrote between 1860-1920 echoed Arnold's lament over the loss of authentic religious feeling, the kind of religious feeling which could lend depth and dimension to human experience. When Twain, for example, wrote in *Adventures of Huckleberry Finn* that the only ones who go to church because they enjoy it are the hogs, he was implicitly condemning the dearth of any real religious belief. The Grangerfords and Shepherdsons could listen contentedly to sermons on Christian brotherhood while actually rejecting their meaning in the feuding violence of their daily lives. Twain's satire was directed against those who embrace the form but not the substance of religious belief.

In a similar vein, the vacuity of the American religious sensibility prompted Henry James to make some pointed comparisons with the historical importance of religion in England. James saw the absence of a distinguished church architecture in America as symptomatic of America's spiritual impoverishment and natural inclination toward mammonism. For him the New England meetinghouse symbolized American religion.

> Here was no church to begin
> with . . . . One lives among English
> ancientries, for instance, as in a
> world towards the furnishing of
> which religion has done a large
> part. And here [in the
> meetinghouse], immediately, was a
> room vast and vacant.[14]

James and Twain may have looked at similar objects, but where James was struck by a lack of aesthetics, Twain lamented the lack of belief, the failure of the Word to become flesh. The meeting ground for their radically

8

different critiques of religion in America was a general agreement that whether it be form or substance, there were few vital signs in the nineteenth-century American religious experience.

Naturally there have been a number of seminal studies on the subject of religion in American literature; they have not, however adequately assessed the tensions between the artists and the religious sects, which is the central focus of this study. John T. Frederick's *The Darkened Sky* investigated religious tensions in the writings of Cooper, Hawthorne, Melville, Howells, Twain, and James. Frederick contends that there are three major historical forces acting to create religious tension in these writers: (1) the fragmentation of religious sects, (2) the higher criticism of the Bible, and (3) the evolutionary theories of science. The focus of his invaluable study is primarily the impact of these historical forces on the minds of the novelists, rather than on the novelists' disaffection with the religious sects.

Howard Mumford Jones' *Belief and Disbelief in American Literature* is a primary work in the exploration of the religious theme in American literature. Jones describes some of the major concerns in the religious thought of American authors, beginning with Paine's republican religion and concluding with the lonely modern spirit which pervades Frost's poetry. Although Jones brings attention to a much neglected theme in American literature, several of his assertions will be challenged in the present study.[15]

Arnold Smithline's *Natural Religion in American Literature* is an examination of religious sentiments in major American non-fiction writers of the eighteenth and nineteenth centuries. Smithline establishes that the emergence of natural religion was a result of eighteenth-century rational skepticism and that the accompanying reconstruction of religious sentiment outside orthodox limitations was inevitable. He states that natural religion

> . . . evolved out of the need to formulate a new relationship between man, God, and nature based on the realities and novelty of American experience, since the traditional faith no longer fulfilled the needs. The dominant ideals of that new experience were: individual freedom, distrust of authority, and the equality of all men before their Creator. Natural religion appears in American literature as an expression of those ideals.[16]

This analysis is of value in understanding the evolution of religious thought in American literature, although Smithline's failure to acknowledge the importance of the paradigmatic sectarian belief that first created the religious consciousness in Parker, Emerson, and Whitman is an unfortunate omission. He does not examine any novelists in this study, and his references to religious sects serve only as background material for his thesis of an evolving natural religion.

Randall Stewart's *American Literature and Christian Doctrine* examines the Christian vision implicit in the works of most American writers. Stewart limits himself to general observations and limits the documentation of his thesis to a few American authors, especially Hawthorne. He is primarily concerned with verifying the Christian viewpoint of the representative American writer, and does not concern himself with sectarian distinctions. It is Stewart's opinion that the best American writing rests on the common ground of Christian belief and that this religious foundation perceives man as a moral agent and a tragic figure.[17]

The selection of novels for this study has in many ways been problematic, yet an attempt has been made to choose representative novels for their various attitudes toward sectarianism. Where a choice between novels was necessary, the more historically interesting work was selected. A number of novels in this study have unfortunately been ignored by the critics. Several of these works such as Arlo Bates' *The Puritans*, Sidney Luska's *The Yoke of the Thorah*, and Robert Herrick's *The Memoirs of an American Citizen*, deserve a better fate than the relative oblivion they presently share.

Basically, it is the contention of this study that the primary religious tension in the novels under consideration is found in the failure of religious institutions to live up to their own proclaimed ideals. The novelist's expression of dissatisfaction with his church is a fulfillment of the Protestant imagination in quest of moral perfection, and the novelist's repudiation of this failure represents the continuance and revitalization of the Protestant sensibility. The organizational principle of this study is thematic, and the treatment of religious sects has been divided into four units. Chapter I "The Novelist and the New England Religious Tradition" examines the novelist's attitude toward the decline of orthodoxy during the nineteenth century. Chapter II "Frontier Religion and the Novelist" focuses primarily on the novelist's treatment of Methodism as a civilizing influence in settling the West. Chapter III "The New Religions: American-Made and Immigrant" surveys the fictional portraits of such American religious movements as Christian Science, Shakerism, and spiritualism, as well as Judaism and Roman Catholicism, which were becoming increasingly more visible due to massive immigration. Chapter IV

11

"Religion and Reform Literature" surveys the impact of Social Gospel theology on the fiction of protest, especially the proliferation of utopian novels from 1880-1910.

The time frame for this study (1860-1920) of religion in the American novel is neither arbitrary nor accidental. This volatile period in American history contains events which would permanently alter America's social and cultural institutions. The manner in which clergymen and artists responded to the forces flowing from these events was critical in resolving the inevitable conflicts which later emerged. The problems of an increasingly heterogenous society haunt us to the present day. The dark side of a pluralistic society is an absence of order which is not resolved by the "civil religion" concept invoked by Robert N. Bellah.[18] To identify certain American institutions and traditions as possessing a religious/mythic component, as Bellah and others have, is fair and accurate, but the absence of a prescribed ethical element with a supporting institutional apparatus reduces serious claims for civil religion to little more than a vague set of values. If Twain and James found failings in the vapidity of nineteenth-century Protestant latitudinarianism, one winces at their likely response to the twentieth century concept of civil religion.

The unique role of religious institutions in forming a truly human society appears to be one of the *a priori* assumptions shaping the critical vision of the nineteenth-century American novelists as they sought from various religious sects a reaffirmation of the Judeo-Christian tradition in a world they found increasingly confusing. The search for meaning manifest in the novels examined in this study has become the commonplace for the modern sensibility. Although the quest for an ordered world may find resolution in the "leap of faith" evident in the recent successes of various fundamentalist sects, the modern temper is more likely to find a kindred spirit in the persons of Eggleston, Howells, Twain, and others whose various critiques of religious institutions were less a denunciation than a prayer of hope.

CHAPTER I

THE NOVELIST AND THE NEW ENGLAND RELIGIOUS TRADITION

The novelists discussed in this chapter all deal with
the disintegration of religious orthodoxy in New England
during the nineteenth century, and each of the examined
novels explores this phenomenon from a different
perspective. Harriet Beecher Stowe gives a warm and
sympathetic portrait of an orthodox minister in *The
Minister's Wooing*, while Oliver Wendell Holmes satirizes
orthodox doctrinal rigidity in *Elsie Venner*. Henry
Adams' *Esther* presents the ideological conflict between
belief and disbelief in the context of a love story, and
Margaret Deland, in *John Ward, Preacher*, uses a marriage
as the vehicle for similar conflicts with more tragic
results. In *The Puritans*, Arlo Bates presents a
dramatic analysis of the clash between liberal and
conservative theologies in New England Protestantism at
the end of the nineteenth century. The other novels
covered in this chapter--*Kavanagh, A Modern Instance,
The Minister's Charge,* and *Annie Kilburn*--all give
further dimension to the fictional image of religion in
New England during the period 1860-1920.[1]

Although most of Nathaniel Hawthorne's fiction
falls outside the limits of this study, he is in many
respects the archetypal New England novelist; the
tensions found in his work are echoed in the novels
discussed in this chapter. Hawthorne was fascinated by
the impact of seventeenth-century Puritan orthodoxy on

the New England temperament, and the Puritan attitudes toward sin and human imperfection had a particularly hypnotic effect upon him. As A. N. Kaul noted in *The American Vision*, what most troubled Hawthorne and other nineteenth-century novelists were the psychological inconsistencies found in traditional Puritan orthodoxy. "If sin is the universal destiny of mankind, its manifestation should occasion sympathy, understanding, and compassion rather than pietistic arrogance and blindness."[2] Although Hawthorne felt that the fixation on sin was destructive to a person's humanity (e.g., *The Scarlet Letter*, "Young Goodman Brown," and "The Minister's Black Veil"), he likewise disapproved of the more fashionable and flexible doctrines which were being proposed by the churches during his lifetime. His hostility toward religious liberalism is given explicit statement in "The Celestial Railroad," a story considered so devastating in its day that "advocates of more rigorous systems pirated the tale and circulated it in pamphlet form as a tract."[3]

Miles Coverdale in *The Blithedale Romance* is the fictional persona for another convincing attack on the nineteenth-century liberal visionary temperament. When Coverdale leaves the Blithedale community to return to civilization, he disavows the experimental-innovative approach to life and affirms a conservative-traditional viewpoint.

> It was now time for me [Coverdale], therefore, to go and hold a little talk with the conservatives, the writers of the North America Review, the merchants, the politicians, the Cambridge men, and all those respectable old blockheads who still, in this intangibility and mistiness of affairs, kept a death-

16

> grip on one or two ideas which had
> not come into vogue since yesterday
> morning.[4]

Hawthorne's repudiation of orthodox Puritanism in his earlier fiction seems to be contradicted by this later almost instinctive reaction against change found in *The Blithedale Romance*. This tension between an empathy for the conservative values implicit in Puritanism and a repugnance for the excesses of Puritan dogma is characteristic of those nineteenth-century writers nurtured in the traditions of New England.[5]

It is a mistake, however, to think that the decline of Puritan orthodoxy is a nineteenth century phenomenon, because

> . . . the history of the New England
> theology is the history of a
> degradation. It declined because
> its theocentric character, its
> supreme regard for the glory of God
> and His sovereignty over man, made
> it ill-fitted to give expression to
> the ideals of eighteenth-century New
> England and to meet its immediate
> social needs.[6]

As a result of the growth of liberal secular thought in the eighteenth century, the role of the church began to veer away from pietism toward a more socially useful moralism. The ministers who wished to continue participating in the life of their communities

> . . . turned their energies to the
> problems of moral reform, and the
> 'instituted churches' together with
> their institutions and 'exercises,'
> became means to that end . . . . To

make people good became the supreme
task of the churches, and legalism
followed as a matter of course.
Thus the Word of God became restated
by the humanitarianism of the age.[7]

The career of Cotton Mather illustrates this ministerial
accomodation to the reality of declining religious
orthodoxy in eighteenth-century New England. In
Magnalia Christi Americana published in 1702, Mather had
issued a plea to the third and fourth generation New
Englanders for a return to "the *Greatness*, and the
Goodness which was in the *first Grain*." His quixotic
appeal was greeted with indifference, but a decade
later, when he had softened his gospel to the more
agreeable and secular tenets in his *Essays to Do Good*,
an interested readership responded to this new vision of
how Christian prudence could be employed as a valuable
asset for business success.

The liberal trend in New England Congregationalism
did not, however, go unopposed. One of the most
dramatic attempts to reverse the ideological tide was
conducted by Jonathan Edwards during the Great
Awakening. The success of this revival lingered in
Western Massachusetts for another century, but it failed
dismally in the more cosmopolitan congregations centered
around Boston, and toward the end of the eighteenth
century liberal ideas were central to the new
Congregationalism. Ironically, the process of
assimilating secular ideas was accelerated by the Great
Awakening, a development observed by Clifton E.
Olmstead in *Religion in America.*

Many ministers in Eastern
Massachusetts, particularly those
who had opposed the revival, began
to espouse a rational religion
devoid of Trinitarian concepts. The

18

estrangement between them and their orthodox colleagues became steadily more pronounced after the election of a liberal candidate, Henry Ware, to the divinity professorship at Harvard in 1805. According to conservatives, the liberals held to the mere humanity of Christ. In reality they held to an Arian or supernatural position, while rejecting the doctrine of the Trinity.[8]

The liberal drift in theological doctrine which conservatives found abhorrent, was codified by William Ellery Channing in his 1819 ordination sermon in which he gave definition to Unitarianism. During the next three decades, the old orthodoxy was subjected to increasing attacks from liberal spokesmen: Ralph Waldo Emerson's "Divinity School Address," Theodore Parker's sermons on Moralism, and Horace Bushnell's *Christian Nurture* (1847), all of which helped to undermine the credibility of the conservative viewpoint in New England.

The successful assault upon orthodoxy created another set of problems. As we have already observed in Hawthorne's experience, the narrow doctrines of Puritan orthodoxy were unsatisfactory sources of inspiration and thoroughly inadequate as sources of human comfort. But Hawthorne and many other New Englanders were equally appalled with new ideas which seemed to ignore the tragic dimensions of the human condition. Orthodoxy had cultivated a destructive preoccupation with sin, while the new dogma refused to acknowledge sin. Emily Dickinson, living in Amherst, Massachusetts, the center of New England conservatism, rejected the narrow religious doctrines which prevailed in her community, but by 1882 she too was disturbed by the social and psychological consequences of disbelief, as can be seen in her poem #1551.

Those—dying then,
Knew where they went—
They went to God's Right Hand—
That Hand is amputated now
And God cannot be found—

The abdication of Belief
Makes the Behavior small-
Better an ignis fatuus
Than no illume at all—

This poem has no trace of nostalgia for the righteousness of times past, when after death, one "went to God's Right Hand;" still there is anxiety in the speaker's concern for people without belief. The speaker feels that even an *ignis fatuus* (i.e., an unsteady light) serves to influence behavior, and this notion of religion as a socially useful institution echoes the regional novelists' utilitarian attitude toward religion. Both Hawthorne and Dickinson, who were representative New England artists, repudiated the orthodox dogma of conservative theology, but they nevertheless absorbed the moral values of the New England tradition. This is the symptomatic paradox in the treatment of religion by the New England artist, and no matter how severe the novelist's alienation from the doctrines of the old orthodoxy, he never does repudiate the moral preoccupations which were so characteristic of that orthodoxy.[9] Not surprisingly, one of the major themes to which the New England novelist addresses himself, is the problem of how to preserve the moral values of the dying culture without the restraints of religious belief.

Although Henry Wadsworth Longfellow is not remembered for his prose, his novel *Kavanagh* (1865) provides a good example of how the New England writers of the mid-nineteenth century perceived the future of religious sectarianism. As Cecil Williams observed: "There are numerous hints at [Longfellow's] religious beliefs throughout his poetry, but perhaps his most forthright treatment of religion is in *Kavanagh*."[10] Reverend Arthur Kavanagh, born a Roman Catholic, is educated by Jesuits, but is eventually converted to Unitarianism. His spiritual journey tempers his religious feelings with a tolerance not usually found in sectarian thought. In his critical biography of Longfellow, Edward Wagenknecht notes that:

> Kavanagh takes his text from the Gospels, denounces vice less than he praises virtue, practices open communion, and defies sectarianism. In much of this he is in harmony with Channing's teaching, for the great Unitarian maintained 'that he did not belong to any one sect but rather to the community of those free minds who loved the truth.'[11]

As a Unitarian with latitudinarian inclinations, Kavanagh is a spokesman for Longfellow's own religious sentiments, which emphasized the virtuous life rather than a body of religious doctrine.

Kavanagh begins his ministry as a replacement for a conservative Congregationalist, the Reverend Mr. Pendexter. The departure of the orthodox Pendexter in favor of the liberal Kavanagh is symbolic of the changes occurring throughout nineteenth-century New England.

21

Pendexter interprets his failure to retain the support of his congregation as symptomatic of a growing hedonism and a decline of *true* religious feeling. His orthodox Calvinist theology has become so repugnant to his congregation that its members will no longer make contributions to support his ministry. Consequently, he is forced to resign. In his valedictory sermon, he sarcastically apologizes to the members of his congregation

> . . . for having neglected his own
> business, which was to study and
> preach, in order to attend to that
> of the parish, which was to support
> its minister,—stating that his own
> shortcomings had been owing to
> theirs, which had driven him into
> the woods in winter and into the
> fields in summer;—and finally by
> telling the congregation in general
> that they were so confirmed in their
> bad habits, that no reformation was
> to be expected of them under his
> ministry.[12]

Pendexter's words recall Jonathan Edwards' "Farewell Sermon" at Northampton (1750) in that both men were convinced that the rift between minister and congregation was rooted in the ungodly attitudes of the people rather than any failure of their respective ministries.

Churchill, the local schoolmaster, is the only character in the novel who appears to understand the historical forces which have victimized the well-meaning Pendexter, and Longfellow uses Churchill to deliver a panegyric to the minister and the passing culture he represents.

Farewell, poor old man! We are not worthy of thee, or we should have had thee with us forever. Go back again to the place of our childhood, the scene of thine early labors and thine early love; let thy days end where they began, and like the emblem of eternity, let the serpent of life coil itself round and take its tail into its mouth, and be still from all its hissings evermore! I would not call thee back; for it is better thou shouldst be where thou art, than amid the angry contentions of this little town.[13]

Churchill sees Pendexter's religious character as unsuitable to the age. What is most interesting about Pendexter's retreat in the face of the people's indifference to his ministry, is that Longfellow never delves into the reasons for the congregation's attitudes toward traditional modes of religious expression. He is apparently expressing disapproval with the decline of orthodoxy through Churchill's sentimental speech about Pendexter, but this attitude toward orthodox Calvinism is not borne out in the remainder of the novel. The Unitarian Kavanagh is given a most favorable treatment as he successfully reawakens the religious spirit among the townspeople. Longfellow's unwillingness to deal more precisely with the failings of the old orthodoxy is traceable to a disposition unwilling to give offense—a rare case in literature of a critical vision being tempered by sensitivity to the beliefs of others.

The Reverend Mr. Kavanagh awakens interest in religious questions because the emphasis of his Unitarian belief is focused on moral conduct and its relationship to each man's life, rather than on the pietistic doctrines of Pendexter. Kavanagh's success as a preacher is almost instantaneous, because his ministry is synonymous with Christian witness and the virtuous life reminiscent of Cotton Mather's modified theology in his *Essays to Do Good*. Longfellow informs the reader that Kavanagh

> . . . preached holiness, self-denial, love; and his hearers remarked that he almost invariably took his texts from the Evangelists, as much as possible from the words of Christ, and seldom from Paul, or the Old Testament.[14]

The break with New England orthodoxy is clear; Kavanagh's theology is representative of the Christocentric belief which came to dominate Protestant theological centers by the end of the nineteenth century.

Kavanagh is more than a liberalizing catalyst for a new theology. He is the symbol of a new religious sensibility, as he attempts to put aside the divisive spirit of doctrinal disputes and replace it with understanding and compassion for mankind. In one passage, Longfellow describes the ascetic Kavanagh sitting in his study dreaming of the coming brotherhood.

> [He] meditated the great design and purpose of his life, the removal of all prejudice, and uncharitableness, and persecution, and the union of all sects into one church universal. Sects themselves he would not destroy, but sectarianism; for sects were to him only as separate converging roads, leading all to the same celestial city of peace.[15]

24

How Kavanagh will unite the Christian world and destroy sectarianism without destroying the denominations themselves is never clarified by Longfellow, and his fogginess on this theme is, once again, probably rooted in an unwillingness to offend readers.

Longfellow attempts to resolve the distinctions between sects and sectarianism by making sectarianism a synonym for religious fanaticism, personified in this novel by the Millerites. The reader is told that religious sects are acceptable when they are informed by a moderation which encourages toleration of other sects, and where such moderation exists, Christian unification is a real possibility for the future. The evolution of Congregationalism into Unitarianism is seen as a movement away from narrow doctrinal distinctions toward an open and universal Christian morality. Kavanagh, whose liberalism succeeds where Pendexter's orthodoxy failed, seems to represent this wave of the future.

Although Longfellow is never explicit in describing how Kavanagh will succeed in his mission, the longing for Christian brotherhood is a dream which the author shared with his protagonist. It is the very same hope which interfered with Longfellow's perception of religion. Hyatt H. Waggoner observes in his *American Poets* that the price of comfort in Longfellow's poetry is the shutting off of thought, and this is the principal flaw in *Kavanagh*. As Longfellow begins to describe the decline of orthodox Congregationalism in New England, he perceives the apathy of the people without explaining the cause. Kavanagh's moralism is presented as a religious panacea, but Longfellow never attempts to explain why Kavanagh's religion is so agreeable to the same congregation which rejected Pendexter. More importantly, Longfellow fails to deal with Kavanagh's moralism as a non-religious response to a dying religious tradition. He implies that the decline of doctrinal pietism could be the prelude to the

25

breakdown of sectarian consciousness and a new universal brotherhood of man, but he does not examine another possibility, that the collapse of religious sectarianism might actually be the prelude to religious indifference.

The apparent optimism in Longfellow's work is seen in a different light by Hyatt Waggoner, who observed that Longfellow "did what he could to cheer himself and reassure his age by repeating the cliches about Progress and Enlightenment. But though his words of cheer convinced many . . . he himself remained unconvinced."[16] If this interpretation is valid, one may read *Kavanagh* as a fictional work born of a desire to harness harsh realities into a dream vision. Indeed, there was precious little evidence in Longfellow's America to support a belief in the immanence of a universal Christian brotherhood leading all "to the same celestial city of peace." Kavanagh's musings in his study are reflections of his creator's own hopes, but neither the character nor his creator understood the revolutionary transformation taking place in the New England faith. One may read *Kavanagh* as Longfellow's imaginative palliative in which he attempted to provide a sense of historical orderliness to events which did not lend themselves to such neat prescriptions.

Oliver Wendell Holmes: Humanism vs. Sectarianism

The impact of converging religious sects in New England may also be observed in Oliver Wendell Holmes' *Elsie Venner*. This romance is set in the typical New England town of Rockland, which has three churches within its limits: Congregational, Unitarian, and Roman Catholic. Two miles outside of town is the Episcopal church. The ministers and parishioners of each sect are isolated from each other, and the very churches in which

26

they worship are embodiments of their differences. Holmes' descriptions of the differences between the various sects are considerably less romantic than were Longfellow's in *Kavanagh*, for as Holmes perceived it, the uniqueness of each sect had the long-term effect of alienating Christians from each other because sects by their very nature foster suspicion and intolerance for those who do not share the same body of doctrinal "truths."[17]

The first religion described in *Elsie Venner* is the traditional New England Congregationalism, which in the town of Rockland is presided over by the Reverend Mr. Pierrepont Honeywood. His ministry is punctuated by an occasional sermon

> . . . which was considered by the hard-headed theologians of his parish to have settled the whole matter fully and finally, so that now there was a good logical basis laid down for the millenium, which might begin at once upon the platform of his demonstrations.

In the same passage, Holmes notes that Honeywood had no natural propensity for doctrinally rigid sermons; rather, he was fonder of "preaching plain practical sermons about the duties of life, and showing his Christianity in abundant good works among his people." He is ideologically orthodox, but he never allows orthodoxy to subvert his humanity because he is a

> . . . man of a very warm, open, and exceedingly human disposition . . . he exercised his human faculties in the harness of his ancient faith with such freedom that the straps of it got so loose that they did not

27

interfere greatly with the
circulation of the warm blood
through his system.[18]

For Holmes, Mr. Honeywood is a good man in spite of his
professed orthodoxy.

Across the town square from the Congregational
church stands the Rockland Unitarian Church, more modern
in style and doctrine. Holmes describes it with a touch
of irony:

> The new building was in what may be
> called the florid shingle--Gothic
> manner. Its pinnacles and crockets
> and other ornaments were, like the
> body of the building, all of pine
> wood--an admirable material, as it
> is very soft and easily worked, and
> can be painted of any color desired.
> Inside the walls were stuccoed in
> imitation of stone.[19]

The ironic dimensions of this description suggest that
Unitarianism is too flexible a faith, of "soft and
easily worked" materials which only imitate the real
religion. There appears to be some confusion in Holmes'
attitude toward the two major religious positions of
nineteenth-century New England. If the old
Congregational orthodoxy was too rigid, one would expect
to find Holmes more receptive to the more flexible
doctrines of Unitarianism, but he had little sympathy
with this liberal theology and, like Nathaniel
Hawthorne, had a grudging admiration for traditional
Puritan belief even though he could not intellectually
accept it.

The Rockland Unitarian Church is presided over by the Reverend Mr. Chauncey Fairweather, who is himself dissatisfied with the doctrines which he preaches. Unlike Kavanagh, Mr. Fairweather is not pleased with his ministry; he sees himself presiding over a religion without any supernatural beliefs. What is most interesting in *Elsie Venner* is that the agnostic Holmes has considerably less tolerance for Unitarianism than for traditional Calvinist Congregationalism. He describes Fairweather's ministry as one

> . . . attended with decency, but not
> followed with enthusiasm. 'The
> beautyof virtue' got to be an old
> story at last. 'The moral dignity
> of human nature' ceased to excite a
> thrill of satisfaction, after some
> hundred repetitions.[20]

As Holmes implies, the rationalization of moral conduct is at last ineffective, for the rhetoric of ethics is less moving than the poetry of biblically inspired sermons. The enervating impact of moralism causes increasing dissatisfaction for Mr. Fairweather because his ministry has become

> . . . a dull business, with its
> preaching against stealing and
> intemperance, while he knew that the
> thieves were prowling round orchards
> and empty houses, instead of being
> there to hear the sermon, and that
> the drunkards, being rarely
> churchgoers, get little good by the
> statistics and eloquent appeals of
> the preacher.[21]

Holmes' final fillip is that the very people who need such guidance are not to be found in church. A religion addressing itself primarily to propriety and the bourgeois virtues of honesty and temperance not only fails to provide a spiritual experience for its congregation, but it is also trapped into echoing values already embraced by that congregation.

Fairweather suffers spiritual atrophy in his rational faith, and one way in which he expresses his anxiety is by envying the devotional worship of those who attend Mass at the Rockland Roman Catholic Church. Fairweather

> . . . could never look on the thronging multitudes that crowded its pews and aisles or knelt bare-headed on its steps, without a longing to get in among them and go down on his knees and enjoy that luxury of devotional contact which makes a worshipping throng as different from the same numbers praying apart as a bed of coals is from a trail of scattered cinders.[22]

In Holmes' portrait, Unitarianism had failed to provide the necessary emotional and sensual dimension of religious experience, which is what Fairweather seeks; his attraction for the Roman Catholic experience is more a measure of his own spiritual and emotional desperation than a particular affirmation of Catholicism.

The fourth church portrayed in *Elsie Venner* is an Episcopalian church located two miles outside of Rockland and presided over by a pompous Anglophilic preacher who reads

> . . . the service with such ventral depth of utterance and RRReduplication of RRResonant

30

letter, that his own mother would
not have known him for her son, if
the good woman had not ironed his
surplice and put it on with her own
hands.[23]

It is significant that Holmes locates the Episcopalian
church outside of town, for it symbolizes the status of
Episcopalian churches in New England life since its
alliance with Toryism during the American Revolution.
The rector's affected speech, so totally foreign to the
Rockland vicinity, provides comic emphasis for Holmes'
thinly disguised bias against Episcopalianism.

Each of the Rockland sects has its limitations,
but Holmes' grudging sympathy is with traditional
Congregationalism--as long as it is tempered by
humanism. It appears to be the congenital kindness of
Honeywood which mutes his Calvinism into a compassionate
form. Mr. Soper, the Deacon of Honeywood's church, is
the spokesman for orthodox Calvinism priding himself on
his rigidity in matters of faith and morals, but after a
few drinks, even Soper's inflexibility gives way to a
less austere world view.

The Deacon's theology fell off
several points toward latitudinarianism . . . . He had a deep inward
sense that everything was as it
should be, human nature included.
The little accident of humanity,
known collectively to moralists as
sin, looked very venial to his
growing sense of universal
brotherhood and benevolence.[24]

Holmes considered religion and the moral doctrines
fostered by religionists as primarily destructive to the
processes of human understanding.[25] The concept of evil

31

was unacceptable to this true son of the Enlightenment who had been educated for a career in medicine. His views surface in his treatment of the character Elsie Venner whose strange behavior comes under the scrutiny of the Rockland town teacher, Bernard Langdon. He is so bewildered by her behavior that he seeks help from his former college professor, whose advice is a thinly disguised Holmesian homily: "I will tell you my rule in life, and I think you will find it a good one. *Treat bad men as if they were insane.* They are insane, out of health, morally . . . . Avoid collision with them, so far as you honorable can."[26] The measure of a man's mental state is his capacity for virtuous behavior. Curiously enough, this method of diagnosis seems more closely allied to Unitarian notions of human behavior than to orthodox Congregational beliefs.

The only prescription for Elsie Venner's sickness is a compassionate understanding. In the second half of this novel, Langdon, Honeywood, and Kittredge, the town doctor, try to help the ailing Elsie. These three men are brought together by their common humanity and desire to relieve suffering. Holmes tells us that this is most difficult for Honeywood, whose religious education has tended to produce an abstracting quality in his mind. But the minister has, in effect, managed to overcome his religious training. He was as

> . . . kind-hearted as if he had never groped in the dust and ashes of those cold abstractions which have killed out so much of the world's life and happiness . . . a man's love is the measure of his fitness for good or bad company here or elsewhere. Men are tatooed with their special beliefs like so many South-Sea Islanders; but a real human heart, with Divine love in it,

> beats with the same glow under all
> the patterns of all earth's thousand
> tribes.[27]

Honeywood's capacity to love enables him to transcend sectarian doctrine. As Holmes notes later in the novel: "The truth was, the good man Honeywood had got so humanized by mixing up with other people in benevolent schemes, that, the very moment he could escape from all of his old scholastic abstractions, he took the side of humanity instinctively."[28]

Throughout the remainder of the novel, Holmes continues to attack religious sectarianism as something to be overcome because it is an impediment to reason and understanding. He describes it as a destructive force in the lives of the Rockland townspeople because it nurtures both divisiveness and a bastardized Christianity whose success is measured by its capacity to formulate syllogisms that will destroy another man's idea, or even better, another man's syllogism. It is because the Reverend Mr. Honeywood sublimates dogma in good works that Holmes favors him above the other ministers; Mr. Fairweather's intellectual preoccupations are used as a counterpoint to Honeywood's instinctive goodness. Fairweather does not seek to sublimate his dissatisfaction with Unitarianism in good works, but rather he seeks out personal spiritual gratification in his attraction to the Roman Catholic Church.

> He yearned especially towards the
> good unquestioning, authoritative
> Mother Church, with her articles of
> faith which took away the necessity
> for private judgment, with her
> traditional forms and ceremonies,
> and her whole apparatus of
> stimulants and anodynes.[29]

33

In his unsympathetic portrait, Holmes is expressing in fictive form his grievance with some of the notable Unitarians (e.g., Orestes Brownson and Isaac Hecker) who had converted to Roman Catholicism. As Holmes suggests, Fairweather is representative of an intellectual religiosity preoccupied with its own narcissistic needs, while Honeywood is orthodoxy infused with an altruistic need to serve others. For Holmes, humane and compassionate behavior is the singular measurement to validate the relevance of a belief.

Elsie Venner should not be read as a tract against Episcopalianism, Unitarianism, or Roman Catholicism. Holmes was quite simply indifferent to all forms of sectarianism except in terms of its negative influence on the spirit of its followers. Fairweather's preoccupation with theological matters is presented as nonsensical because these diversions keep Fairweather from helping his fellow men. He seeks out Roman Catholicism as a patient seeks a psychiatrist. Dr. Kittredge, who is a thinly-disguised persona for Holmes, gives this analysis of sectarianism:

> Everybody knows that Catholicism or Protestantism is a good deal a matter of race. Constitution has more to do with belief than people think. I went to a Universalist church, when I was in the city one day, to hear a famous man whom all the world knows, and I never saw such pews--full of broad shoulders and florid faces, and substantial, wholesome-looking persons . . . . Either their creed made them healthy, or they chose it because they were healthy.[30]

There are two ideas in Kittredge's observation: first, it is an accident of history whether a Christian is Protestant or Catholic, and second, individuals seeks out forms of worship which correspond to and complement their daily life. In either case, the impression Kittredge conveys is that religious sectarianism, and particularly Christian sectarianism, is intrinsically meaningless.

Howard Mumford Jones interprets *Elsie Venner* as a frontal assault on the Calvinist theories of sin. To support his case, Jones cites Holmes' own introductory remarks in the preface to the novel:

> The real aim of the story was to test the doctrine of 'original sin' and human responsibility for the disordered volition coming under that technical denomination. Was Elsie Venner, poisoned by the venom of a crotalus before she was born, morally responsible for the volitional aberrations, which translated into acts become what is know as sin, and it may be, what is punished as crime? If . . . she becomes by the verdict of human conscience a proper object of divine pity and not of divine wrath, as a subject of moral poisoning, wherein lies the difference between her position at the bar of judgment, human or divine, and that of the unfortunate victim who received a moral poison from a remote ancestor before he drew his first breath?[31]

The case of Elsie Venner is for all its exotic metaphoric trappings just another exploration of human culpability in the context of Calvinistic predestination. There is no doubt that Holmes shared with Hawthorne an aversion for the cruel aspects of New England's Calvinist heritage, and specifically to the intellectual and spiritual isolation produced by this tradition. The ultimate indictment made by Hawthorne and Holmes is that the destructive nature of Puritanism resulted from its failure to synthesize Christian humanism within its doctrinal structure. Throughout *Elsie Venner*, the healing powers of science tempered by human compassion are in marked contrast to the narrow soul-stifling tenets of religious sectarianism. Unlike Longfellow, Holmes found little comfort in the new doctrines of Unitarianism, and as a result, his humanistic critique is more pointedly anti-religious. Using essentially pragmatic criteria, Holmes demonstrated how various beliefs affected human behavior, and it was in this context that he championed his own predilection for scientific humanism as the most useful of all ideologies.

Harriet Beecher Stowe: The Compassionate Belief

In writing *The Minister's Wooing*, Harriet Beecher Stowe presented in a fictional mode her own journey away from traditional Calvinism. The events of the novel take place in the first decade of the nineteenth century in Newport, Rhode Island. Using the form of an historical romance, Mrs. Stowe describes an archetypal Puritan minister, the Reverend Mr. Hopkins, whose sermons against slavery are echoes of her own father's sermons. Hopkins is an heir to the uncompromising theological orthodoxy of Jonathan Edwards, and as Percy H. Boynton has observed:

Mrs. Stowe believed stoutly that the old Puritan discipline of mind and conduct, and the old integreties which it had fortified, formed the best of foundations for a new order, in which monarchy, aristocracy, and theocracy with their peculiar train of ideas, were passing away, and New England was coming within the sweep of pure republican influences, in which the individual is everything.[32]

In spite of her obvious sympathy for the discipline and integrity of her father's faith, Harriet Beecher Stowe eventually repudiated Calvinism in 1857. Two years prior to the publication of *The Minister's Wooing*, she converted to Episcopalianism after her son Henry had drowned, because she refused to accept the doctrinal implications of his dying in an unregenerate state. Her own personal tragedy provided the dramatic structure for this novel.

The Minister's Wooing is concerned with the moral and personal grace which a hard religious vision develops in its followers. Adversity and hardship are endured with dignity, but the cultivation of the stoic sensibility handicaps the development of other human qualities--compassion, understanding, tenderness, and joy. Mrs. Stowe remarks at the very beginning of the novel:

The rigid theological discipline of New England fitted to produce rather strength and purity than enjoyment. It was not fitted to make a

sensitive and thoughtful nature
happy, however it might ennoble and
exalt.[33]

The stoic soul is capable of not only enduring pain, but
of feeding on pain through discipline. Throughout *The
Minister's Wooing*, the Reverend Mr. Hopkins
demonstrates, in his response to personal duress, that
his faith has conditioned him to suffering, and his
willing surrender of happiness at the end of the novel
might be interpreted as the fulfillment of his stoical
need for pain.

The Minister's Wooing presents a vivid portrait of
the changing attitudes toward religious belief in New
England during the first two tumultuous decades of the
nineteenth century. Simeon Brown, a successful slave
trader and a loyal church member, fancies himself a
theologian. His reading of Scripture is more a search
for personal justification than an inquiry into either
the meaning or the spirit of the text. In contrast to
Brown there are the conventional orthodox believers,
such as Katy Scudder and her niece Mary, whose everyday
lives are models of decorum and virtuous activity. The
new, independent mood in New England religious thought
is represented by Katy's adventurous son, James, who
writes a letter to his beloved cousin Mary before
shipping out to sea, explaining in the letter why he
rejects religious forms and theological disputes:

> I see no sense in it, and can't take
> the trouble to put it together. But
> then he [Hopkins] and you have
> something in you that I call
> religion,--something that makes you
> *good*. When I see a man working away
> on an entirely honest, unworldly,
> disinterested pattern, as he does,
> and when I see you, Mary, as I said

38

before, I should like at least to be
as you are, whether I can believe as
you do or not.[34]

James Scudder acknowledges the beneficence of orthodox
belief in the impact it has upon the lives of two people
whom he admires, yet he realizes that an intellectual
affirmation of that faith is impossible for him.

Mrs. Stowe was sympathetic with many of Oliver
Wendell Holmes' ideas on religious matters; they both
shared a repugnance for those doctrinal minds which lose
sight of common decency, and the portrait of Hopkins
bears many resemblances to Holmes' portrait of the
Reverend Mr. Honeywood--both men are valued for their
human decency rather than for the doctrines they
articulate. Mr. Hopkins rejects slavery as a practice
inconceivable for a Christian, and he does so as Mrs.
Stowe's father had, at a time when few ministers
concerned themselves with applying Christian values to
the social environment. In his revulsion against
slavery Hopkins is a clerical maverick, and as he tells
Katy Scudder:

> What a shame it is . . . what a
> scandal and disgrace to the
> Protestant religion, that Christians
> of America should openly practice
> and countenance this enslaving of
> Africans! I have for a long time
> holden my peace,--may the Lord
> forgive me!--but I believe the time
> is coming when I must utter my voice
> . . . I must testify.[35]

In bearing witness to his Christian ministry, Hopkins is
running against the grain of the established and
accepted morality of slave trading; he is launching an
attack on the economic roots of major financial

supporters of his parish such as the slave trader Simeon
Brown. In so doing this, Hopkins is acting out the
historical role of the Christian outsider in a corrupt
society, and he achieves moral stature by rejecting the
values of influential church members who would support
him in order to control him.

The predictable confrontation between the Reverend
Mr. Hopkins and Simeon Brown occurs when the minister
castigates Brown for his profiteering in slavery. Brown
answers these accusations with an easy pragmatism:

> You are not a practical man. You
> are good in your pulpit;--nobody
> better. Your theology is clear;--
> nobody can argue better. But come
> to practical matters, why, business
> has its laws, Doctor. Ministers are
> the most unfit men in the world to
> talk on such subjects; it's
> departing from their sphere; they
> talk about what they don't
> understand.[36]

Brown's reply to Mr. Hopkins contains a predominant
notion of religion as an abstraction, a Platonic ideal,
a dream reverie of the world as it should be; Sunday is
the day on which the Simeon Browns go to church to hear
and dream of this ideal state. For the pleasures of
such reveries and the consolations of rewards in an
afterlife, Brown contributes handsomely to the support
of the minister and his church, but rejects any attempt
to bring the Gospel into his market place. He pays
tribute to be comforted not criticized. Brown also
resents that Hopkins does not recognize his proper
place, especially since Hopkins' ministry is a luxury
supported by the very profiteering which he finds so
sordid.

40

Hopkins persists by attempting to introduce moral concepts into the "real world" of slave trading, and Brown informs him that he had better be prepared to pay the price for his moralizing:

> ... if you have the most theology, I flatter myself I have the most common-sense . . . . All men are not like you; men are men, and will be, till they are thoroughly sanctified, which never happens in this life,--and [if Hopkins persists in harassing those who are connected with the slave trade] there will be an instant and most unfavorable agitation. Minds will be turned out,--and you know, Doctor, you are not appreciated as you ought to be, and it won't be easy for you to get a new settlement; and then subscriptions will drop off your book, and you won't be able to get that out; and all this good will be lost to the world just for want of common sense.[37]

Not only is Brown threatening Hopkins' security, he is also suggesting that any good which the minister might accomplish by working within the existing order would be forfeited by his possible banishment. In this temptation scene, Mrs. Stowe provides a dramatic confrontation between a religiously inspired moral vision and a materialistic society which does not wish to have religious idealism disrupting the daily, sometimes sordid, realities of economic life.

Simeon Brown fails in his threat, and Mr. Hopkins delivers a rebuttal in the form of a sermon addressed to the entire community of Newport and all parts of New

41

England which have been even remotely connected with the slave trade. He tells his congregation:

> Not only the merchants who have been engaged in this trade, and the captains who have been tempted by the love of money to engage in this cruel work, and the slaveholders of every description, are guilty of shedding rivers of blood, but all the legislatures who have authorized, encouraged, or even neglected to suppress it to the utmost of their power, and all the individuals in private stations who have in any way aided in this business, consented to it, or have not opposed it to the utmost of their ability, have a share in this guilt.[38]

With this sermon, Hopkins has completed his transformation from a congregational minister with a theology of personal redemption to one whose doctrinal concerns are primarily social. Both the tone and substance of Hopkins' new found theology anticipates the emergence of Social Gospel theology at the end of the nineteenth century.

Mrs. Stowe appears to have written *The Minister's Wooing* as a panegyric to a disappearing species--the Calvinist minister. Perhaps nostalgia or totem worship can provide the explanation for the apparent contradiction between her private beliefs and what she wrote. When she praises this ministry, she is celebrating its historical role rather than anything connected with her own times. She noted that:

. . . the spectacle of the early
ministry of New England was one to
which the world gives no parallel
. . . . They had accustomed
themselves boldly to challenge and
dispute all sham pretensions and
idolatries of past ages,--to
question the right of kings in the
State, and of prelates in the
Church; and now they turned the same
bold inquiries toward the Eternal
Throne, and threw down their glove
in the lists as authorized defenders
of every mystery in the Eternal
Government.[39]

Hopkins' ministry is part of this noble heritage, but
Mrs. Stowe saw, as others had, that the status of this
belief system had eroded considerably with the passing
of years, and that the social and historical forces
which gave authority to that ministry had long since
vanished.

Mrs. Stowe does not avoid presenting some of the
intrinsic problems of New England orthodoxy. When James
Scudder is reported lost at sea, Mr. Hopkins can provide
little solace to either Mrs. Scudder or Cousin Mary;
according to Hopkins' belief, it is a double tragedy
because James is not only dead but must also burn in the
everlasting fires of hell because he never converted to
the faith. Candace, the Negro servant, instinctively
perceives that Hopkins is "a mighty good man, an'
larned,--an' in fair weather I ha'n't no 'bjection to
yer hearin' all dese yer great an' mighty ings he's got
to say." But as Candace sees it, there are limits to be
placed on rigid doctrines such as Hopkins espoused, and
she rejects his harsh dogma with a simple statement of
her faith in Christ.

I'm clar Mass'r James is one o' de
'lect; and I'm clar dar's
consid'able more o' de 'lect dan
people tink. Why, Jesus didn't die
for nuthin',--all dat love a'n't
gwine to be wasted. De' lect is
more 'n you or I knows, Honey!"[40]

The simple compassionate faith expressed by Candace is a
dialect rendering of the belief which Mrs. Stowe
embraced following the death of her son. The
unrelenting legalistic harshness of orthodox Calvinism
provided little comfort for a grieving parent, and this
was one of its great failings.

Central to this novel are the questions raised by
the contradictions in the portrait of Hopkins as a
personally decent man who is nevertheless capable of
great cruelty because of his doctrinal commitment. The
confusion in the novel's narrative can be traced to Mrs.
Stowe's own ambivalence on the subject. While she
obviously favors the personal moral character which
Hopkins' strong belief fostered, she also despised the
narrowness of its doctrines. Candace's gospel of love
is much more attractive in human terms than are Hopkins'
theories of damnation. Stowe resolves her dilemma by
putting aside the rigid aspects of the minister's
character in order to give a favorable image of moral
strength conferred on him by his religious beliefs.

As the tale unfolds, Mary becomes engaged to the
aging Hopkins because her beloved James has apparently
died at sea. As one character remarks, "Mary, it is
like a marriage with the altar, like taking the veil, is
it not?"[41] Mary dismisses this chilling image by
stating that she has merely made the selection of a
reasonable life with a "kind, noble friend." In the
midst of the preparations for the marriage, James
reappears, a survivor of the shipwreck which was

supposed to have taken his life. Hopkins responds nobly, releasing Mary from her engagement so that she will be free to marry young James, and he does so without revealing his own deep feelings and the enormity of the sacrifice he is making. His stoical carriage is described as an essential aspect of his personality. "Hopkins considered sacrifice as the foundation of all existence . . . . [He] smoothed the asperities of a temperament naturally violent and fiery by a rigid discipline which guided it entirely above the plane of self-indulgence."[42] Part of Hopkins' code is that the world will never know his torment; the truncated emotional life is sublimated in the religious values he asserts. Hopkins stifles the natural impulse to fight for Mary's hand and fortifies himself instead with his religious vision. In fact, in a silent sermon he chastises himself for seeking human happiness.

> What is it that thou art fretting
> and self-tormenting about? Is it
> because thou are not happy? Who
> told thee that thou was to be happy?
> Art thou nothing but a vulture
> screaming for prey? Canst thou not
> do without happiness?[43]

Cruel doctrines forge a tough spirit, and Hopkins survives his personal anguish because his spirit has been hardened by uncompromising dogma.

Calvinism was a faith which produced toughminded people who, having adjusted themselves to the terrors of its doctrine, were prepared for any hardship, physical or emotional, which the world could offer. As Emily Dickinson wrote: "Power is only Pain--/Stranded, thro' Discipline." The great failure of Calvinist doctrine was its lack of humanity and its unyielding rigidity in dealing with the more tender aspects of the human spirit (e.g., a mother's need to be comforted at the loss of

45

her son, and not to be informed that he will burn for all eternity). James Scudder resolves the religious theme of the novel by finally affirming a simple belief in Christ as redeemer, rejecting Hopkins' stern orthodoxy in favor of Candace's sweet piety. In the opinion of Willard Thorp, *The Minister's Wooing* is "one of the best treatments in fiction between orthodoxy and the new liberal views . . . . Many critics think it her greatest artistic success. After *Uncle Tom's Cabin* it is probably her greatest work."[44] The failings of orthodox Calvinism are given a more humane critique in Stowe's novel than in the previously reviewed works of Longfellow and Holmes; however, her narrative is fundamentally a variation on the theme of alienation from a bankrupt religion.

Margaret Deland: The Isolating Effect of Calvinism

In *John Ward, Preacher* (1888), Margaret Deland examines the tensions which beset an orthodox Presbyterian minister when his wife rejects his religion. The roots of John Ward's personality may be, once again, traced back to that paradigmatic figure Jonathan Edwards, whose collected writings are prominently displayed in Ward's library. The similarity in names, John Ward and Jonathan Edwards, is substantive as well as nominal. Mrs. Deland's interest in the decline of orthodoxy had autobiographical origins.

> This novel is connected in a personal way with Mrs. Deland's early life. Her father was a Presbyterian, her mother an Episcopalian, so both forms of belief were familiar to her. Before *John Ward* was published, it was read

46

in the household of the author's
youth, which was strongly
Presbyterian. The head of the
family regarded it with disfavor and
offered the author money in place of
her royalties if she would refrain
from publishing it.[45]

To settle the dispute Mrs. Deland called upon her
favorite uncle, Dr. William Campbell, who was a
clergyman and former president of Rutgers University.
He supported his niece and insisted that she publish the
novel at once.

John Ward is a paradoxical figure whose unyielding
Presbyterianism runs counter to his inherent gentleness,
a paradox already noted in the characters of Honeywood
in *Elsie Venner* and Hopkins in *The Minister's Wooing*.
Ward differs from these ministers by the intensity of
his commitment to doctrinal matters, and he never
achieves a successful *detente* between the ideal world of
religious concepts and the everyday realities of human
interaction. He is described by one character in the
novel as

. . . a blue Presbyterian, through
and through. He didn't have much to
say for himself, but what he did say
made me believe he was consistent;
he doesn't stop short when his creed
ceases to be agreeable, and you know
that is unusual.[46]

Ward marries Helen Jeffrey, whose religious
beliefs are vaguely Episcopalian, but he is convinced
that she will eventually convert to Presbyterianism once
she has had sufficient exposure to its truth. What he
does not anticipate is Helen's failure to see the light
after their marriage. Not only does she fail to

47

convert, but her patience with both his religion and his
congregation begins to wear thin, and she refuses to
attend any of his religious services. She makes quite
clear to her husband the cause of her growing
disenchantment with Presbyterianism, when she tells him

> . . . it is worse than useless for
> me to go and hear Elder Dean or old
> Mr. Smith; they either annoy me or
> amuse me, and I don't know which is
> worse . . . . Mr. Smith thank[s]
> the Lord that we are not among the
> pale and sheeted nations of the dead
> . . . . And Elder Dean's pictures
> of the eternal torments of damned'
> souls wreathing in sulphurous
> flames' and then praising God for
> his justice (his justice!) . . . I
> cannot stand it . . . . I do not
> believe in hell, such a hell, and so
> it is absurd to go and listen to
> such things.[47]

While Helen desires to be left to her own casual
religious beliefs, John is driven by what he perceives
as a moral imperative to convert his wife to the truth
of Presbyterianism, for the sake of her immortal soul.
The very casualness of her attitude toward religion is
exasperating to the intensely committed Ward, as when
she tells him that "you were born a Presbyterian, dear;
you can't help it. Perhaps you need the sternness and
horror of some of the doctrines as a balance for your
gentleness."[48]

When the local wastrel, Tom Davis, dies, the
Reverend Mr. John Ward can give no comfort to the Davis
family because he is convinced that Tom has gone to

eternal damnation. Helen is moved by the family's plight, and in attempting to comfort them, she dismisses some of Presbyterianism's basic tenets:

> I cannot believe that God punishes people eternally; for if He is good, He could not be so cruel. Why, no human being could be so cruel as that, and do you think we ought to believe that men are better and kinder than God?[49]

Helen's words echo those spoken by Candace in *The Minister's Wooing*, but as a minister's wife her sentiments carry social consequences which Candace's did not. Helen is attacking one of the pillars of her husband's faith--hell and eternal punishment for the unregenerate. John Ward is no liberal theologian presiding over a comfortable and slightly indifferent congregation; his orthodoxy mirrors that of his congregation, who thrive on a steady diet of eschatological terrors. As one observer notes:

> I doubt if he could say anything on the subject of hell too tough for the spiritual digestion of his flock. They are as sincere in their belief as he is; though they haven't his gentleness; in fact they have his logic without his light.[50]

As Helen's heretical beliefs become known to her husband's congregation, she is perceived as a child of the devil. Ward attempts to cushion the conflict developing between Helen and Elder Dean, but he finds that Elder Dean is not to be placated. As he tells Ward: "There is some folks as would take, 'God is Love' out of the Good Book, and forget 'Our God is a consuming fire.'"[51] Elder Dean worships a wantonly cruel deity who is, perhaps, a convenient extension of his own sadistic cravings to inflict punishment. His quotation is amusing to a modern reader, but Margaret Deland's intention is to deal with the real and terrifying consequences of such beliefs as they affected people in the world in which she had been raised. Ward is torn between the irreconciable needs for dogmatic consistency and the love of his wife.

Helen's effect upon John is to strengthen his basic gentleness, and in a conciliatory manner, he repudiates the doctrine of damnation for unbaptized children. But despite his wife's influence, John is no candidate for conversion to Helen's latitudinarian beliefs. One of the novel's difficulties is its failure to explain how so gentle a soul as John Ward ever found himself presiding over a congregation personified in the harsh character of Elder Dean. As Helen comes to reject every premise of John's religious belief, he becomes aware that the doctrinal chasm cannot be reconciled. Helen too perceives the extent of their differences, as she tells John:

> You take all this from the Bible, because you believe it to be inspired. I do not believe it is. So how can we argue? If I granted your premise, all that you say would be perfectly logical. But I do not, John. I cannot.[52]

There is no turning back; Ward is faced with an explicit challenge to his faith, and his response is an ideological one. He reasserts the primacy of his belief even over his personal feelings, and he turns Helen out of his house because she gives offense and scandal to his beliefs and those of his congregation. Dr. Howe, a liberal Episcopalian clergyman, is dumbfounded by what he interprets as the monstrous absurdity of Ward's action. Howe cannot appreciate a religious belief which is the sole reality of one's consciousness. The degree to which one submits his humanity to an ideology marks the difference between the religiously inspired person such as Howe, and a religious ideologue such as Ward.

As Ward is caught up in the consequences of his belief and the actions which flow from it, Helen becomes the objective observer in the novel. She is stunned into a detached awareness of what is happening to her husband. She notes

> . . . how narrowness and intolerance seem to belong to intense belief. Some of these elders in John's church . . . believe in their horrible doctrines with all their hearts, and their absolute conviction makes them blind to any possibility of good in any creed which does not agree with theirs.[53]

John Ward is the most tragic victim of such intolerance, for he is committed to subordinating his own needs to the demands of his Presbyterianism. He dies attempting to live according to his beliefs, still suppressing his natural desire for a reunion with Helen. Shortly before Ward's death, Dr. Howe admonishes him for mistreating his wife: "The way in which you pride yourself upon devising the most exquisite pain for your wife is inhuman,--it is devilish!"[54] What Howe does not perceive is that Ward had contrived a punishment that he feels even more intensely than his wife. His death is symbolic of the death of orthodoxy, while Helen survives as the representative of the rising religious liberalism. Toward the end of the novel, Helen is advising some young relatives on the gospel of love as a redemptive faith: "The main thing is to have the realization of God in one's own soul." For Helen, the old orthodoxy is as dead as her husband because it had failed to assimilate the needs of the heart. Ward's intellectual pride in his orthodoxy unites him with the tragic figures in Hawthorne's fiction who suffer a similar fate of isolation and alienation from their own humanity.

Henry Adams: Celebrant of Spiritual Independence

The conflicts between orthodoxy and nineteenth-century liberalism once again provide the narrative spine to Henry Adams' *Esther* (1884), and although the novel is set in New York City, Adams is writing from a distinctly New England perspective. In this novel, Reverend Mr. Stephen Hazard is the embodiment of traditional religious orthodoxy while Esther Dudley is his educated, skeptical, liberal adversary. Adams places the conflict in the context of a romance which will result in marriage on the condition that Esther submits herself to Hazard's religious beliefs. In this novel, religion becomes an arena for the battle of the sexes. Hazard demands adherence to his religion, although his religion seems more an act of the will than a supernatural belief. Esther is not a shy maiden who will quietly submit herself to the whims of another--even if it is the man she loves. She certainly wants to marry Hazard, but she resists the price he demands.

What Hazard finds most attractive in Esther--her freedom of thought, her artistic interest, and the independent tone of her conversation--are the very things which he wishes to bring under his control. The uniqueness of her personality represents a challenge to his ministry. If Esther is the Dionysian force, Hazard is the Apollonian who will glorify himself by breaking

52

her will. After his first meeting with the Dudley
family, Hazard reflects on the challenge presented by
these intellectual and cultivated people, who are so
markedly different from his own parishioners:

> . . . it was small triumph to draw a
> procession of followers from a class
> who took their opinions, like their
> jewelry, machinemade. He felt that
> he must get a hold on the rebellious
> age, and that it would not prove
> rebellious to him. He meant that
> Miss Dudley should come regularly to
> church, and on his success in
> bringing her there, he was half-
> ready to stake the chances of his
> mission in life.[55]

Having established Esther as the personification of the
modernist temper, Hazard embarks upon her spiritual
seduction. Her conversion to religious orthodoxy will
confirm for Hazard his ability to deal with the
challenges of modernism, and it will also reassure him
that he is masculine enough to gain dominance over so
exotic a creature.

The initial setting for the siege on Esther's soul
is St. John's Episcopal Church, which is Hazard's
fashionably-located parish in New York City.[56] He
engages Wharton, an artist, to complete the interior of
the church by painting wall and ceiling murals based
upon biblical episodes. Esther is invited to contribute
to the work and to gain valuable experience by her
temporary apprenticeship to Wharton. While Esther
paints, Hazard launches his campaign to convert her. As
she becomes aware of his increasing attentiveness,
Esther anticipates the problems of a serious
relationship because, although she finds Hazard
attractive, she also knows that she could never be a

minister's wife. What she doesn't realize is that Hazard has no intention of allowing her to remain in a state of disbelief. Unlike Helen Ward, Esther is not naive about the consequences of such a marriage, and, unlike John Ward, Hazard will not marry a woman and expect to convert her later.

Hazard underestimates how formidable an adversary Esther is. She has developed great strength of character from the influences of her agnostic father, who on his deathbed tells his tearful daughter to "laugh, Esther, when you're in trouble. Say something droll! Then you're safe. I saw the whole regiment laugh under fire at Gettysburg."[57] After such a gentle admonishment, Esther brings herself under control. When Hazard arrives, half anticipating a deathbed conversion, he finds that he is not even requested to say a few prayers. Instead, he is impressed by the Dudleys' stoicism in facing death without the support of any religious belief. He reflects that perhaps Esther "could give a lesson in strength to me. It seems rather unnecessary, my offering to give one to her."[58] Esther greatly appreciates Hazard's kindness, and when her father dies the young minister becomes even more important to her. Out of gratitude and growing affection, she agrees to accept Hazard's invitation to attend services at St. John's.

At St. John's, Esther enjoys sitting amidst the beauty Wharton has created. She also enjoys the music as a sweet background for her own reveries, but her appreciation is shattered by the voice of the Reverend Mr. Hazard. His sermon on doctrine interrupts Esther's aesthetic contemplation and brings her back to the substance of this church worship. It becomes apparent to her that she is an alien in this church, that she rejects everything about it--its service, its congregation, and finally its minister.

She began to take a bitter pleasure
in thinking that she had nothing,
not even a religious idea, in common
with the people who came between her
and her lover. Her fatigue steadily
worked on her nerves. By the time
the creed was read, she could not
honestly feel that she believed a
word of it, or could force herself
to say that she could believe it.[59]

To provide some objectivity to the romantic-
ideological conflicts, Adams introduces the character
George Strong, a cousin of Esther's who is a geologist
by profession and an agnostic by inclination. Strong is
amused that Hazard could ever have thought himself
capable of converting Esther. He sees the minister as
the victim of his own vocational miasma.

Hazard is a priest at heart. He has
the qualities and faults of his
class . . . . He sees nothing good
in the world that he does not
instantly covet for the glory of God
and the church, and just a bit for
his own pleasure. He saw Esther
. . . so he fell in love with her
himself and means to turn her into a
candlestick of the church . . . .
Now he will see whether he has met
his match.[60]

Strong's analysis of Hazard's personality and the
impending intellectual conflict between Hazard and
Esther is perceptive, but he never does understand the
emotional aspects of their relationship which provide an
added dimension to their struggle. Esther is not simply
Hazard's intellectual antagonist, for she is willing to
give him anything but the integrity of her own mind.

55

Strong underestimates the extent of her feelings and the tensions she suffered from her conflicting emotional and intellectual drives.

As Hazard's romantic attachment to Esther becomes obvious, many members of his congregation become alarmed. Esther is stigmatized both by her infrequent attendance at services and by her father's reputation as a non-believer whose notion of religion was that it contributed to providing a stable and orderly society. Based on this social service he

> . . . paid for a pew at St. John's because, he said, society needs still that sort of police. But he had told me a dozen times that he could get more police for his money by giving it to the Roman Catholics. He never entered his pew.[61]

Mr. Dudley understood religion to be a bromide which kept people in their place, complementing the forces of law and order; implicit in that passage is the Marxist idea of religion as an institution to preserve the status quo by cultivating docility in the lower classes, and thereby providing a valuable service to the ruling classes. Thus, Roman Catholicism in the late nineteenth century yields the best social return for monies contributed, because in Dudley's judgment, it is the most effective controlling agent over the poorest and potentially most dangerous elements in American society, the disenfranchised immigrants of the new industrial society.

Hazard comes to view Esther's disbelief more and more as a symbolic challenge to his entire life as a minister. He perceives the conflict which faces him as

> ... not a selfish struggle. It is
> a human soul I am trying to save,
> and I will do it in the teeth of all
> the powers of darkness. If I can
> set right this systematically
> misguided conscience, the task is
> done. It is the affair of a moment
> when once the light comes;—a flash!
> A miracle! If I cannot wield this
> fire from heaven, I am unfit to
> touch it. Let it burn me up![62]

This messianic self-concept reflects an obsession that approaches madness, but Hazard's need to convert Esther in order to validate his own vocation can be read as simply a battle for ego-domination taking place within a religious framework.

When Esther finally bolts from her spiritual seducer (an interesting inversion of villainy in nineteenth-century fiction), she goes to Niagara Falls. The Falls are to her a splendid natural force whose energy and beauty give her strength to cope with the decision to break with Hazard and avoid the marriage which would compromise her integrity. Esther sits awed by the sights and sounds of the rushing water, her thoughts drifting to the man she both loves and fears: "If only he could hear it as I do . . . how much he would feel it." Her own feelings toward the majestic Falls *are* religious, and she cannot help but contrast this experience with her feelings of constriction and repression when sitting in St. John's Church. Esther reflects that "to have Niagara for a rival is no joke. Hazard spoke with no such authority; and Esther's next idea was one of wonder how, after listening here, any preacher could have confidence to preach again." Once she has been calmed by the beauty of the Falls, Esther perceives Hazard's schemes to convert her as absurd. In

the afterglow of resolution she comes to perceive
churches as nothing but "flesh--flesh--flesh, at every
corner."

To the astonished Hazard, she later reveals the
depths of her disaffection with what he calls religion:

> I can see nothing spiritual about
> the church. It is all personal and
> selfish. What difference does it
> make to me whether I worship one
> person or three persons, or three
> hundred, or three thousand. I can't
> understand how you worship any
> person at all.[63]

Hazard predictably shocked at the intensity with which
she rejects both him and his religion, appeals to her
need for the consoling doctrines of immortality, and
Esther lashes out at him for trying to intimidate her
into belief. Ungracious in defeat, Hazard leaves her
with this:

> I am beaten. You have driven me
> away, and I will never trouble you
> again, till in your days of
> suffering and anguish you send to me
> for hope and consolation. Till
> then--God bless you![64]

This twisted hope reveals the depths of Hazard's
anguish; his failure to convert Esther forces him to
acknowledge for the first time that his ministry may not
be adequate to the challenges of modernism. Esther is
not triumphant in her repudiation of the minister, for
she tells George Strong that she still loves Hazard in
spite of all which has occurred between them.

In *Symbol and Idea in Henry Adams,* Melvin Lyon
summarizes the novel as emphasizing

> . . . the tragic consequences for
> Esther and Hazard of the struggle
> between a vital expression of truth
> and an outworn view. As usual in
> Adams' work, the two basic elements
> are antithetical and irreconcilable.
> As in *Chartres,* art is a means of
> reconciling or at least escaping
> their conflict . . . . Adams in
> *Chartres* and his characters in
> *Esther* care more for truth than for
> beauty, and thus are forced to look
> for answers to their problems, not
> in art, but in that arena where
> illusion and reality, religion and
> the truth which science struggles
> toward, wage what Adams views as
> inevitable and irreconcilable
> warfare.[65]

Several critical biographers have observed that
Esther Dudley was closely modeled on Adams' own wife,
Marian Hooper, whose disaffection with religious
institutions was characteristic of her individualism.[66]
The year after Adams published this fictional tribute to
his independently minded wife, Marian was so aggrieved
by her father's death that she entered a period of
depression from which she never emerged, and she
committed suicide by poisoning herself on December 6,
1885. This all took place approximately one year after
the publication of *Esther,* a fact which adds a ghoulish
footnote to Adams' heroic fictional portrayal of his
wife's independent spirit. One can easily imagine how
the novel must have haunted him; even though it had been
published anonymously, he tried to halt its further

distribution. Adams once described his feelings about this novel in a letter to Elizabeth Cameron:

> I care more for one chapter, or any dozen pages of *Esther* than for the whole history, including maps and indexes; so much more, indeed, that I would not let anyone read the story for fear the reader would profane it.[67]

In the character of Esther Dudley, Adams had created a woman fairly unique in nineteenth-century fiction because she is intelligent and appreciates her own intrinsic worth apart from the man whom she loves. Esther is willing and able to accept the consequences of her agnosticism, but the fate of Esther's real-life model Marian Hooper Adams introduces a discomfiting feeling regarding Henry Adams' accuracy in presenting Esther's capacity to transcend the comforts of traditional religious belief by relying, solely, upon her own personal resources.

Arlo Bates: The Quest for Moral Order

The most sophisticated fictional treatment of the deterioration in the status of traditional New England religions may be found in Arlo Bates' *The Puritans*. It was Bates' thesis that the Protestant moral tradition was very much alive at the end of the nineteenth century despite the decadent condition of the Protestant institutional churches. Much of the action in *The Puritans* focuses on the church politics concerned with filling a vacant bishopric, and the *ideological* battle which occurs between liberal and conservative elements within the church. Both factions are attempting to meet

60

the challenges of an age when religious belief appears to be on the decline and the former church membership is sliding into spiritualism, Eastern cults, or general indifference . Historical perspective indicates that neither liberalization of church traditions nor rigid adherence to tradition are likely to increase the significance of any church in such an age of transition.[68]

The two episcopal candidates in *The Puritans* are embodiments of liberal and orthodox religious attitudes at the end of the nineteenth century. The implications of their confrontation are well described by Arlo Bates:

> Mr. Strathmore [the liberal] and Father Frontford [the traditionalist] might not unfairly be said to represent the two extremes of modern theology: on the one hand the relaxing of creeds, the liberalizing of thought, the breaking down of barriers which have divided the church from the world, and above all, acquiescence in individual liberty of thought; on the other hand, the conservative element taking the position that individual liberty of interpretation means nothing less than a practical destruction of all standards, and that what is called the liberalizing of thought can result in nothing less than the utter overthrow of the church . . . . If Mr. Strathmore was right, Father Frontford was little less than a medieval bigot, unhappily belated; if the Father was correct, than Strathmore, despite

all his influence, his popularity,
his power of attracting great
congregations, was little better
than a dangerous and pestilent
heretic.[69]

The clash between liberalism and orthodoxy is observed
by the novel's two protagonists, Phillip Ashe and
Maurice Wynne, both of whom are seminarians studying for
the ministry. The pressures brought upon them by the
religio-political confrontation between Strathmore and
Frontford forces both young men to re-evaluate their
relationship to the church and the viability of a career
in the ministry. Maurice finds the venality of church
politics so disturbing that he finally decides against
any sectarian affiliation; Phillip, though offended by
the petty jealousies, still wants a religiously-ordered
existence. He is eventually attracted by what he
perceives to be the stability of Roman Catholicism.

Maurice Wynne's break with the church is hastened
by his developing interest in Berenice Morison, who
nurses him back to health after a train accident
fortuitously places him in the Morison household for
several weeks. The possibility of sharing a
conventional domestic life with Berenice contributes to
Maurice's disillusionment with the ministry. During his
convalescence, he discovers that he is temperamentally
unsuited for the celibate ideal espoused by Father
Frontford, and he is not unsympathetic to the
latitudinarian ways of Mr. Strathmore. Bates describes
Maurice's rapid transformation as follows:

There is nothing more inflammable
than the punk left by the decay of a
religion, and any theology may be
said to be doomed from the moment
when men begin to ask themselves

whether they believe it .... In
the days of his stay at Brookfield
[the Morison home], moreover, he had
been rapidly journeying on the road
to a new life; and the idea of
returning to the Clergy House became
to him well-nigh intolerable.[70]

Despite his new understanding, Maurice finds it a
difficult task to break away from the seminary. He
seeks counsel from Mr. Strathmore, who assures him that
his doubts are quite normal and that he should simply
put them aside and not pay them too much attention.
Although Maurice finds little comfort or wisdom in
Strathmore's flexible platitudes, he gets even less help
from Father Frontford, who wishes to capitalize on
Maurice's friendship with the Morisons in his pursuit of
the bishopric. When Maurice refuses to use his
friendship for political purposes, Frontford chastises
him sanctimoniously:

> You seem to forget your vow of
> obedience. It is in the sacrifice
> of self and our own inclinations
> that we gain the conquest of self.
> Go, my son, and pray to be forgiven
> for pride and insubordination.[71]

Maurice is outraged by Frontford's scheming and self-
deception; his journey toward independence from
religious sectarianism is hastened by the respective
failings of Strathmore and Frontford.

Ambivalent feelings about the relevance of
religion begin to surface in the midst of Maurice's
disillusionment with orthodox and liberal clergymen.
Although his alienation is based primarily on an
intellectual rejection of dogma, religious ceremonies
and art still act as powerful and seductive influences

63

on his soul, just as they had for the agnostic Esther Dudley. Bates reveals the anxieties of this transitional status in a scene where the singing of the "Kyrie" so moves Maurice that he

> . . . lost his anger, he swam in billows of celestial delight; a blessed peace soothed his troubled soul; he knew again some of the old time ecstasy. Yet in all this religious fervor there was some subtle consciousness that it was unreal . . . . He had even a whimsical, momentary irritation that the part of his mind which was acting the devotee could not do it so well that his other consciousness could not detect the unreality of it all.[72]

In order to achieve spiritual freedom Maurice must relinquish the aesthetic pleasures of religious ceremony, and in so doing, he finds that there is an emotional price to be paid for his intellectual decision.

As the events of the novel bring Mr. Strathmore closer to a victory over Father Frontford, the significance of their battle becomes more apparent. Frontford's defeat is another blow against the rapidly disintegrating orthodoxy of New England Protestantism. Strathmore's religious vision is vague and highly flexible, and under his direction, doctrine will continue to be tailored to the needs of the people. As one character observes to Maurice:

> When we come out from any conviction, and most of all from a religious belief, it seems to us a

profound misfortune that any man
should still believe what we have
decided is false. By and by I think
you will see that the chief point is
that a man shall believe. What he
believes doesn't so much matter. It
must be the thing that most suits
his temperament.[73]

The need for belief in something is recognized as a
psychological imperative, but the doctrine affirmed is
important primarily to the person asserting the belief.
In this passage, Arlo Bates, who was a professor of
English at M.I.T., appears to be theorizing about the
nature of belief along the same lines as had his Harvard
neighbor William James in "The Will to Believe."
Neither Bates nor James meant that one could believe
anything without regard to the laws of nature. Both
perceived the psychological distress which accompanied
the loss of faith and James' investigation into the
religious experience had led him to believe that
"everyone had a *right* to adopt a helpful or useful
hypothesis; and if experience confirmed its practical
value, then one might have increasing confidence, or
faith in it."[74] The dramatic resolution of spiritual
conflict in *The Puritans* is an imaginative rendering of
this Jamesian insight. Faced with the declining
viability of nineteenth-century Episcopalianism, the
young protagonists, Maurice Wynne and Phillip Ashe, are
groping for the "useful hypothesis" to give meaning to
life.

Maurice Wynne's gradual disavowal of his religious
heritage is in marked contrast to Phillip Ashe's
portrait of spiritual journey which concludes with his
conversion to Roman Catholicism. Their divergent
courses are not as contradictory as they appear to be.

Toward the end of the novel, Mrs. Staggchase reminds Maurice that his rejection of religion was personal and subjective, and that he had best beware of merely patronizing those who still believe:

> The great fault and danger of this age is that it is all breaking down. It reforms abuses and improves away old errors; but it seems to forget the need of providing something to take the place of what it clears away. Man can no more live without a belief than without air.[75]

Mrs. Staggchase speculates that Phillip sought out Catholicism because it had conviction, and she further observes that his Puritan heritage was excellent preparation for his conversion. Maurice acknowledges the validity of her argument by adding that "I suppose that in this age there are only two things possible for a thinking man. One must go over to Rome and rest on authority, or choose to use his reason, and be an agnostic."[76]

Maurice follows the demands of his intellect into agnosticism; Phillip follows the demands of his temperament into Roman Catholicism. The similarity of their decisions lies in the unyielding and uncompromising nature of their separate conclusions; they are the true Puritans who do not flinch at the emotional demands which proceed from their search for moral and intellectual perfection. One character observes:

> The age isn't greatly given to reverence. I am a Puritan, however, and I must say what I think. I

believe that there is a hundredfold
more devoutness in the infidelity of
New England today than in its
belief.[77]

Implicit in this statement is the need to break from the
spiritless forms of orthodox worship in New England.
Paradoxically, the rejection of conventional religious
expression gives evidence of the characters' continuing
religious vitality. The discontent of Maurice and
Phillip arises from standards of perfection which cannot
be satisfied by Mr. Strathmore's easy doctrines or
Father Frontford's ego-centered authoritarianism.

The Puritans may be interpreted as a novel simply
concerned with revealing the spiritual bankruptcy of New
England Protestantism, but Arlo Bates had also given us
a portrait of two young men who actively seek out a
moral and purposeful existence. In their separate
quests for truth after abandoning the seminary, they are
living embodiments of the Puritan tradition. In the
final sentence of the novel Maurice remarks to Mrs.
Staggchase: "I suppose that if I would give you the
chance you would easily prove that Phil and I are both
merely Puritans more or less disguised."[78] Maurice
suspects what the reader should know—agnosticism and
Roman Catholicism only disguise the quintessential
Puritan character of the spiritual/moral preoccupations
of Wynne and Ashe.

William Dean Howells: The Doctrine of Complicity

In *A Modern Instance*, William Dean Howells
examined the consequences of an exhausted New England
culture, and like Arlo Bates, he saw that the Puritan
sensibility might be driven into agnosticism or even

67

atheism by its revulsion with the institutional churches of nineteenth-century New England. In his description of Equity, Maine, Howells notes that:

> Religion there had largely ceased to be a fact of spiritual existence, and the visible church flourished on condition of providing for the social needs of the community. It was practically held that the salvation of one's soul must not be made too depressing, or the young people would have nothing to do with it. Professors of the sternest creeds temporized with sinners, and did what might be done to win them to heaven by helping them to have a good time here. The church embraced and included the world.[79]

In the world described by Howells, the compromises on the Half-Way Covenant (1662) had dwindled into nineteenth-century absurdities. The spirit of accommodation had led the Equity Congregational Church to assume a social rather than a spiritual role in community life. The church survived at the price of having abandoned its historical mission.

Howells uses Squire Gaylord, father of Marcia, as a spokesman against the vacuous religious establishment, and the Squire's cantankerous skepticism reveals more of the ancient Puritan faith than the modern church of which he so clearly disapproves:

> For liberal Christianity he had nothing but contempt . . . . The idea that souls were to be saved by church sociables filled him with inappeasable rancor; and he

68

maintained the superiority of the
Old Puritan discipline against them
with a fervor which nothing but its
re-establishment could have
abated.[80]

Nominally an atheist, Squire Gaylord's moral rigidity
persists in his retention of the Puritan temperament
which neither the doctrinal nor the institutional
supports.

The disruptive impact of this transitional New
England culture is revealed in the confused life of
Marcia Gaylord, the Squire's daughter. Edwin H.Cady
describes Marcia as a victim of a spiritual-cultural
vacuum which leaves her without ideals or self-
discipline, unprepared to cope with the challenges which
life presents to her.

Marcia has grown up with 'no
principles, no traditions' in
Equity--where, after the death of
rural religion, the withering of New
England village culture, there is
neither equity nor any of the
idealistic promise of the American
small town left.[81]

After marrying Bartley Hubbard and settling in Boston,
the limitations of Marcia's emotional and spiritual
resources become quite evident. She encounters Boston
society *via* the Halleck family and their friends, and as
Howells presents them, we are given a microcosmic image
of the religio-cultural confusion in post-Civil War
Boston.

The elder Hallecks have retained the
village orthodoxy of their youth,
but their daughter Olive has adopted

69

an abrasive Unitarianism, while her
crippled brother Ben, by missing
Harvard to attend a college Down
East, has been deprived of even the
Unitarian compromise between
'radicalism and amateur
episcopacy'.... Then there is
Clara Kingsbury....'She had not
yet found a religion that exactly
suited her.' 'Meanwhile, she had
sponsored the 'Indigent Children's
Surf-Bathing Society,' though less
for her soul's need than for 'social
distinction.' Privately, she has
admitted that 'indigent children
were personally unpleasant to
her.'[82]

The world of the Hallecks is immersed in a confusion of
religious values, but the flighty yet callous Clara
Kingsbury represents an even more serious problem. She
possesses wealth without a commitment to the old Puritan
doctrine of stewardship. Her indifference to indigent
children is symptomatic of her indifference to all
problems beyond the walls of her own drawing room.[83]

In a conversation with Mrs. Halleck, Marcia asks
the old woman's advice about joining a church in Boston
because she wants her daughter to avoid the tragic
consequences of her own upbringing. She perceives
church membership as an entree into the lives of decent
people, so she would like her daughter "to belong to the
church where most of the good people went. I think that
would be the right one, if you could only find which one
it is .... I've been thinking a good deal about this
lately."[84] Implicit in Marcia's pathetic appeal is a
desire for tradition and the re-establishment of some
social order. Howells does not mean that Marcia is to
be taken as a curiosity, for when Mrs. Halleck tells her

70

daughter Olive about the conversation, Olive observes: "We should all be shocked if we knew how many people there were like her, and we should all try to deny it, and so would they. I guess Christianity is as uncommon as civilization--and that's very uncommon."[85] Olive's comments conclude with her observation on Marcia's condition, but what she fails to see is that by their impotent reaction to Marcia's pitiful appeal, the Halleck family circle sadly confirms the accuracy of Olive's insight on the uncommon character of Christianity.

Bartley Hubbard, in his quest for economic success, stumbles through a series of experiences which give evidence to his moral insensitivity and contribute to the loss of his reputation as a responsible and trustworthy person. As Bartley's fortunes decline in the wake of his personal failings, his old classmate, Ben Halleck, is witness to the disintegration of the Hubbard marriage, but he cannot alter the course of events which finally bring them to an Indiana divorce court. Although Ben is in love with Marcia, he is a traditionalist who does not believe in divorce; rather he sees divorce as a disruption of the most basic unit of civilization. As an affirmation of that tradition, he sacrifices his love for Marcia and chooses a career in the ministry. Ben's decision is curious considering his expressed doubts on the validity of Christian doctrine. Kermit Vanderbilt interprets Ben's vocational choice as follows:

> He has drifted back to the orthodoxy
> of his boyhood, a return in its way
> almost as hopeless as the Squire's
> infantilism [a reference to Squire
> Gaylord's increasing senility after
> Marcia's divorce]. At the close of
> the novel, the crippled Ben remains
> both voyager and voyeur, luxuriating

in the futile 'sweet shame' of his
sexual desire for Marcia as he
departs for the unlikely sanctuary
of a Down East church in the
backwoods.[86]

Ben's decision for the ministry appears as unrelated to
a religious commitment as Claire de Cintre's entering a
Carmelite nunnery in James' *The American*. Both choices
are essentially melodramatic plot devices which display
a sacrificing sentimentality more than an active
religious vision.

In discussing the image of religion in *A Modern
Instance*, other themes in this important novel have been
put aside, but almost all of the other social themes are
intimately connected to the religious theme. While
writing this novel, Howells was at a crucial stage in
his own development; he was becoming increasingly
restless with the status quo. George C. Carrington has
described *A Modern Instance* as an agnostic's book which

> . . . attacks the spokesmen who
> righteously and rightly condemn
> Bartley Hubbard, the standards by
> which they condemn him, and the
> belief (in these characters and in
> the reader) that these standards
> operate in real life. The public
> condemnation of moral errors is thus
> itself partially condemned--
> partially, not wholly. This is an
> agnostic's book, not an atheist's; a
> moral atheist could not write satire
> that presents an edge no matter how
> one looks at it. It is significant
> that the last words of the book are
> 'I don't know.'[87]

Several years later Howells came under the consciousness-expanding influence of Tolstoi, and the detached agnostic vision described by Carrington gave way to the literature of economic reform--*The Minister's Charge, April Hopes, A Hazard of New Fortunes, Annie Kilburn, A Traveler from Altruria, et al.* In these novels, Howells set aside the detached sensibility of *A Modern Instance* in favor of a social vision shaped by his newly acquired Christian Socialist beliefs. Although he continued to describe the chaotic state of institutional religions, he frequently used ministers as the spokesmen for reform. The matter of New England remained central to his imaginative vision, but it was now put to new uses.

Edwin H. Cady noted that Howells' maturing vision perceived the use of New England materials as

> . . . only the medium he worked in,
> the stuff through which he expressed
> his perception of themes which
> transcended the parochial. With his
> social 'audacity' begun and at
> length fully achieved he had in *The
> Minister's Charge, April Hopes,* and
> *Annie Kilburn* successively reworked
> and, at least for the present,
> exhausted his New England ores.[88]

In both *The Minister's Charge* and *Annie Kilburn,* Howells once again examined the state of religion in typical New England settings (i.e., Boston and the towns of Willoughby Pastures and Hatboro), but now his description of the decadent churches was little more than prefatory to his major subject--the need for the church to assume responsibility for social reform and thereby renew its relevance.

In *The Minister's Charge,* Howells considers the difficulties involved in a life of total Christian commitment. The Reverend Mr. David Sewell, while spending a summer in the rural setting of Willoughby Pastures, meets a young poet named Lemuel Barker to whom he gives some avuncular encouragement. Sewell is not prepared for Barker's later appearance on his doorstep in Boston. The perfunctory support offered to Barker has been misinterpreted as an offer of active patronage. Howells describes Sewell as a brilliant speaker who is rightly admired for the sweet persuasiveness of his sermons, but as a minister he is not anxious to involve himself in the problems of others. In the environs of Boston, the uninitiated Barker is bewildered and easily victimized in a series of misadventures. Much to his annoyance, Reverend Sewell finds himself being solicited to care for the country-bumpkin Barker.

Through the minister's attitudes and character, Howell illustrates the difficulties of "making the word become flesh." It is much easier to sermonize on platonic conceptions of "how the world should be" than to participate actively in relieving the suffering of a single human being. Sewell is grateful when, at one point in the novel, he thinks that Lem Barker has gone out of his life, and he looks forward to returning to the more simple business of preaching Christian principles. The portrait of Sewell is a judgement against the ineffectuality of a ministry which has isolated itself in the formalities of worship. Sewell is a decent man whose better instincts have been diverted into sermon-writing and sermonizing. Howells makes full use of the irony involved in Sewell's reluctance to act upon his own exhortations:

> Sewell had a great many things
> besides Barker to think of. But
> when Sunday came, and he rose in his
> pulpit, he could not help casting a

glance of guilty fear toward Miss
Vane's pew [where Lem usually sat]
and drawing a long breath of relief
not to see Lemuel in it. We are so
made that in the reaction the
minister was able to throw himself
into the matter of his discourse
with uncommon fervor.[89]

Although Howells is presenting a comic rendering of
Sewell's Sunday-morning Christianity in the above
passage, it becomes impossible for Sewell to disengage
himself from the insistent demands of Lemuel Barker.

As the novel unfolds, Sewell is forced by
circumstances to examine many aspects of life to which
he had previously given little thought. He observes for
the first time that the existence of a servant class
might be inconsistent with the democratic ideal. He
expresses dissatisfaction with the conventions of
betrothal which ensnare young people into marriage
against their own desires. But most important is an
increasing social awareness, which leads him to
articulate the ethical concept of complicity.

It is in the education, the ethical
evolution, of the Reverend David
Sewell that Howells contemplates
both the implications of the Boston
in which Lem has had his shocking
adventures and the fundamental
uselessness of the well-meaning
efforts which Sewell, his
parishioners, and people like them
have put forth to cope with it.
Sewell, often humiliated, learns
much from his charge—and profits in
the way of several fine sermon
inspirations. Properly enough, the

last [i.e., the sermon on complicity
based on the Pauline text:
"Remember them that are in bonds as
bound with them"], the one on which
the novel essentially closes, is the
best--and represents the best of
Howells' own ethical thought to
date.[90]

Between the minister and his charge, there gradually
develops an intellectual and moral interdependence which
makes real the doctrine of complicity.

Bromfield Corey, another character who had
appeared earlier in *The Rise of Silas Lapham*, makes the
following observation about Barker and his relationship
to Sewell:

. . . it's the youth of my sires
that I find so strange in Barker.
Only, theoretically, there's no
Puritanism. He's a thorough
believer in Sewell. I suspect that
he could formulate Sewell's theology
a great deal better than Sewell
could.[91]

Both the minister and his charge deal with the world
primarily in moral terms which is an explicit espousal
of their common Puritan heritage; however, the shared
moral vision seems to exist outside of doctrinal
definitions.

The evolution of the Reverend Mr. Sewell is
completed in his final sermon. He has been forced by
Barker, by society, and by the injustices of his time,
to speak out against unrelieved human suffering, so
frequently caused by those who attend the best churches
on Sunday. Sewell addresses his congregation in a

manner reminiscent of Mr. Hopkins in *The Minister's Wooing*, and like Hopkins he is motivated by a desire to sharpen their moral perceptions:

> If a community was corrupt, if an age was immoral, it was not because of the vicious, but the virtuous who fancied themselves indifferent spectators. It was not the tyrant who oppressed, it was the wickedness that had made him possible. The gospel--Christ-God, so far as men had imagined him,--was but a lesson, a type, a witness in everlasting of the spiritual unity of man. As we grew in grace, in humanity, in civilization, our recognition of this truth would be transfigured from a duty to a privilege, a joy, a heavenly rapture.[92]

Sewell achieves personal redemption by assuming personal and social responsibility and by realizing that each human voice which calls for help is also calling every man to his own redemption. He concludes the "complicity" sermon with these remarks:

> Happy is he in whose ears their cry for help was a perpetual voice, for that man, whatever his creed, knew God and could never forget him. In his responsibility for his weaker brethren he was Godlike, for God was but the impersonation of loving responsibility, of infinite and never-ceasing care for us all.[93]

By the end of the novel, Sewell's vision of the ministry has been transformed into a socially-oriented Christian activism. Clara M. Kirk interprets Sewell as a failure in his efforts to aid Lem Barker, but this curious interpretation can only be maintained if one ignores the expanding religious consciousness which has transformed the innocent Barker and the detached Sewell into engaged Christians.[94]

Two years later in writing *Annie Kilburn*, Howells examined the many changes taking place in the small New England towns of the late nineteenth century.[95] The female protagonist, Annie, returns to her hometown of Hatboro, Massachusetts, after eight years in Europe, most of them in Rome. She has been called home by the death of her father, and she now must preside over the Kilburn family fortune. Like many a Jamesian protagonist, the years spent abroad had ill prepared her for the changed world of Hatboro. In her first drive through town upon her return,

> . . . she could see all the changes,
> and she noticed the new town-hall,
> with which she could find no fault;
> the Baptist and Methodist churches
> were the same as of old; the
> Unitarian church seemed to have
> shrunk as if the architecture had
> sympathized with its dwindling body
> of worshippers.[96]

As a Unitarian herself, Annie speculates that the declining influence of her church is a factor in the cultural and intellectual deterioration which she perceives in newly industrialized Hatboro.

> Hatboro had suffered one kind of
> deterioration which Annie could not
> help noticing. She remembered a
> distinctly intellectual life, which
> might still exist in its elements,

> but which certainly no longer had as
> definite expression . . . . The
> decay of the Unitarians as a sect
> perhaps had something to do with the
> literary lapse of the place: their
> highly intellectualized belief had
> favoured taste in a direction where
> the more ritualistic and emotional
> religions did not promote it: and
> it was certain that they were no
> longer the leading people.[97]

What Annie Kilburn perceives as the intellectual
character peculiar to Unitarianism is precisely the
factor which makes this sect unsuitable to the religious
needs of the working population in a manufacturing
community.

Although Unitarianism with its intellectual
tradition is no longer a prominent factor in the life of
Hatboro, the Reverend Mr. Peck, the local Unitarian
minister, refuses to accommodate his faith to the
materialistic world view of his congregation. Peck's
Unitarian ministry focuses on the need for social reform
in order to achieve social justice, and as he addresses
himself to the need for fundamental changes in the
social fabric, he soon discovers that the defenders of
the status quo are the leading members of his own
church. Peck comes to identify himself more and more
with the working people who toil in the Hatboro mills,
and as a result, he is subjected to increasing criticism
from his congregation. When questioned about the
propriety of his devoting so much time to the
millworkers and actually imitating their life-style, he
answers:

> I fancied that I had authority to
> set myself apart from my fellow-
> workmen, to be a teacher and guide,

to the true life. But it was a
great error. The true life was the
life of work, and no one ever had
authority to turn from it. Christ
himself came as a laboring man.[98]

In this passage Peck functions as a spokesman for the
Tolstoian vision, with its "distinctively religious,
distinctively Christian appeal—the challenge of one who
believed that Christ meant exactly what he said, even in
his 'hard sayings,' and who had himself set out to
follow him."[99] In assuming an activist Christian
Socialism, Peck is assigned the task of propagating
those ideas and values central to Howells himself.

Mr. Peck is on a collision course with the power
structure of his own church, whose leading member is the
influential merchant Gerrish. Peck's reform-oriented
sermons have a jarring effect on the congregation, who
are not accustomed to criticism of the many economic and
social assumptions of their daily lives. He informs
them that

. . . in the truly Christian state,
there shall be no more asking and no
more giving, no more gratitude and
no more merit, no more charity, but
only and evermore justice; all shall
share alike, and want and luxury and
killing toil and heartless indolence
shall cease together.[100]

Peck speculates that if justice is not quickly achieved,
then the ruling class will have to deal with an angry
working class and that such a confrontation will have
countless innocent victims. Although this sermon
appears to be a conventional nineteenth-century warning
against the dangers of class exploitation, there is
nothing Marxian or revolutionary in Peck's prescription

80

for society's ills which is a vague call for applying Christian principles of justice to an industrialized society; the reactionary Mr. Gerrish is so enraged by such appeals issuing from the pulpit he supports that he leads his family out of church in the midst of the sermon.

Gerrish initiates a campaign to have Peck removed as minister of the Hatboro Unitarian Church. When the membership gathers to hear the case against Peck, Gerrish presents the familiar arguments against church involvement in social issues and asserts his wish that religion be more supernatural, emphasizing rewards rather than social duties. He speaks for the conservative element of the church membership when he says:

> We are tired . . . of having what I may call a one-sided gospel preached in this church and from this pulpit. We enter our protest against the neglect of very essential elements of Christianity--not to say the essential--the representation of Christ as-a-a spirit as well as a life.[101]

What Gerrish means by Christ's spirit is never made clear, but he does express a desire for more sermons on the crucifixion, resurrection, and "the precious promises of the gospel." Howells is being deliberately ironic in his portrayal of what the bourgeois merchant seeks from his church. Gerrish, like the slave-trader Simeon Brown in *The Minister's Wooing*, sees the church as a convenient appendix to his life which he is willing to support as long as it provides comfort. Confronted with the hardened attitudes of Gerrish and his sympathizers, Mr. Peck realizes that his ministry is ineffectual, and there is no likelihood that he will change the congregation's values through mere sermonizing. He decides to resign and devote himself to teaching the workers.

Annie Kilburn is one of Peck's few influential supporters within the Unitarian congregation, and she desires to participate in achieving the reforms which he has convinced her are so necessary. But the major difficulty with Peck's vision is that he has no program. Howells, for all his concern with reform, has difficulties being totally sympathetic with the character of his reformer. Edwin H. Cady observed that Howells, in his portrait of Peck, recorded

> . . . his reservations about the problem of the reformer, the deficiencies of programmatic Socialism, indeed, about Tolstoi. Devastating in prophetic judgment, Peck vacillates confusedly about positive remedies for the ills he condemns. Worse yet, he is cold and passive in human relations; the price for his intellectual clarity and high abstract moral perception has been isolation from ordinary human warmth. He is lost in speculation . . . . It is Peck's sense of failure, his own hunger for re-identification with the working poor from whom he sprang, that makes him resign his pulpit.[102]

After resigning, Peck discusses with Annie Kilburn his plans for the future, but there is a certain vagueness in his plans. He will teach, and perhaps even preach. "And if it should be necessary that I should work in the mills in order to render this, then I will do so; but at present I have another way in view--a social way that shall bring me into immediate relations with people.[103] Peck never elaborates on the "social way," and Annie Kilburn never discovers the particulars of his plans, because he is struck and killed by a train on his way to formally resign from the Hatboro Unitarian ministry.

Peck's sudden death relieves Howells of the necessity of determining what might happen to the increasingly alienated and radicalized ex-minister. Annie Kilburn has been made aware of social injustice, but she is also pathetically conscious of her inability to really change things. At the end of the novel, she takes on the singular responsibility of raising Peck's daughter, Idella. She performs a private act of charity, but is it enough? The inconclusiveness of *Annie Kilburn* was a source of frustration for Howells as well as his readers because it reflected his own confusions about the implementation of Christian ethics in a capitalist society. He expressed his dissatisfaction with this novel in a letter to E. E. Hale and concluded that:

> The most that I can do is perhaps to set a few people thinking; for as yet I haven't got to doing anything myself. But at present it seems to me that our competitive civilization is a state of warfare and a game of chance, in which each man fights and bets against fearful odds.[104]

By Howells' own admission, the novel suffers from an ideological indecisiveness, but its achievement is nevertheless significant. With *Annie Kilburn*, Howells offered another shading to the dilemma facing the old faiths of New England. Peck's confusion on how his religious virtues might benefit the disenfranchised in an industrial society was never satisfactorily resolved, but the notion that religion had a role to play in humanizing this new economic system was an important concept which foreshadows the emergence of Social Gospel theology.

* *

The recurring theme in the novels examined in this chapter is that the New England culture seemed to have played itself out. "The impulse that had characterized it seemed to be exhausted, and its mood was sad, relaxed and reminiscent . . . . If the old race was not actually dying, if the old culture was not extinguished, there were many who felt that it was merely a question of time."[105] An important aspect of the general decline was the continuing decline of religious orthodoxy, and, although the novelists might differ in treating its significance, they all agreed on its reality. Some of the novelists created sympathetic portraits of orthodox ministers: Longfellow's Pendexter in *Kavanagh*, Holmes' Honeywood in *Elsie Venner*, Stowe's Hopkins in *The Minister's Wooing*, and Deland's Ward in *John Ward, Preacher*. Each of these fictional ministers is portrayed with compassion by novelists who have ambivalent feelings about the passing of the world which they embody—the Puritan culture. Pendexter retreats into the woods in the face of his congregation's religious indifference; Hopkins, a dignified stoic who fought against slavery, prepares to spend his last years in sorrow and loneliness; Ward is victimized by the ideological intolerance of his Presbyterian congregation. Only Mr. Honeywood adjusts to the times, and he does this by setting aside doctrine for the sake of human considerations.

84

Each of these ministers has a quixotic strain which gives him dignity and stature; but, curiously enough, their religious ideology is a constant threat to their humanity. Their penchant for moral abstractions can isolate them from their fellow man (e.g., the most dramatic example in this chapter is John Ward casting out his wife). Through such adherence to doctrinal principles, the moral idealism of the ministry becomes both fascinating and frightening. The minister fascinates because he embodies the Puritan vision, and he frightens novelist and reader alike because of his capacity to harm himself and others in the name of his ideological commitment.

Not all tradition-oriented ministers are treated kindly by the novelists. Henry Adams' Hazard uses religious doctrine as a means of achieving power over people, and he is prepared to subdue all realities by fitting them into his orthodox formula. Father Frontford in *The Puritans* is similar in temperament to Hazard, but he is considerably less successful in disguising his authoritarian instincts. Both men use the closed system of their religious thought to establish a dominance over reality in general, and in particular a dominance over people. Neither Henry Adams nor Arlo Bates expresses sentiments of regret over the passing of the Puritan ideology because they both perceived it as antithetical to human development.

Unitarianism is the most important nineteenth century liberal sect arising from the general dissatisfaction with the traditional faith in New England, but most of the novelists in this chapter show a less-then-enthusiastic attitude toward it. Longfellow's portrait of Kavanagh is the exception. The gentle, kind, and tolerant Kavanagh represents what Longfellow hoped would be Unitarianism's success in filling the spiritual vacuum caused by the decline of orthodoxy. In *Elsie Venner*, Holmes satirized

Unitarianism as a soft faith which is unsatisfactory even for its minister, the Reverend Mr. Fairweather, who eventually drifts toward Roman Catholicism. The quest for a more authoritarian structure with religious pomp and ceremony provides the stimulus for Phillip Ashe in *The Puritans* to repudiate the liberal doctrines of Mr. Strathmore and, like Mr. Fairweather, embrace Catholicism. The Reverend Mr. Peck in *Annie Kilburn* is another refugee from Unitarianism, but he is not seeking the authoritarianism of Rome; he is moving toward a revolutionary application of Christian principles to all the institutions of society. Peck attempts to extend moral culpability beyond that of the individual, although his rebellion against conventional Unitarian thought is more an extension of basic Unitarian principles than a rejection of them. By the end of the nineteenth century, the novelists generally perceived the Unitarian faith as inadequate to the volatile social climate of an urban-industrial world.

There is no single literary treatment or common theme which can neatly summarize the decline of religious fervor in the New England region. Although the novelists describe the collapse of both the liberal and traditional churches, they also describe the continuing search for moral perfection on the part of their protagonists. In their rejection of existing religious forms, the novelists themselves reaffirm their Protestant sensibilities, which almost of necessity must reject what they see about them. In the secular context of novel-writing, they frequently endorse the intrinsic values of the Puritan culture. As we have seen, the Puritan culture survives in spite of disintegrating religious institutions. The concept of divine election evolved into a supercilious class and caste consciousness, and the concept of stewardship developed into the justification for the acquisition of great fortunes. But more important than the bastardization of Puritan doctrines was the continuance of the essential moral preoccupations of the Puritan sensibility, for the concept of justification survived as a moral imperative to do good for its own sake.

In *The Last Puritan* (1936), a novel which falls outside the scope of this study, George Santayana created the character of Oliver Alden, a twentieth-century secularized Puritan whose Puritanism is described as a

> . . . hatred of all shams, scorn of all mummeries, a bitter merciless pleasure in the hard facts. And that passion for reality was beautiful in him . . . . He was a millionaire, and yet scrupulously simple and silently heroic.[106]

As Alden's character is revealed, we recognize him not so much as a last Puritan but as an archetypal American; the Puritan's need to impose a moral order on the world has been absorbed for better or for worse into the national character, and as Percy H. Boynton noted in his analysis of Santayana's novel: "Puritanism . . . is a natural reaction against nature; in order to escape chaos it is ready both to impose, and to submit to, the sternest regimen. It abjures happiness and seeks peace even under the crunching of a moral juggernaut. It discards the fleshly life; it rejects the life of refinement."[107]

Oliver Alden is as hard and stoic as the Reverend Mr. Hopkins in *The Minister's Wooing*, and he is quintessentially moral in all his dealings. Even his response to the taste of champagne gives an insight into his character.

> No; he didn't like champagne. He disliked it; it made him positively feel (like Pindar) that the best of

things was water. All sensation in Oliver was, as it were, retarded; it hardly became conscious until it became moral. It spoke for the stomach, not for the palate. What he asked of things was that they should produce a happy unconsciousness of all instrumentalities, and set the mind free for its own flights.[108]

For Alden, sustenance is a means to allow the mind to function, and the proper mind functions primarily by ordering the universe into a moral scheme. The old sectarian belief is dead, but the Puritan temperament lingers in the splendid isolation of its moral preoccupations. Oliver Alden is not the last, but simply another Puritan.

The novelists presented in this chapter observed that the New England faith died a natural death from the multiple causes of enlightenment, prosperity, and formalism, but for better or worse, the moral spirit of Puritanism lived on. Perhaps the explanation for such longevity can be found in Pitrim A. Sorokin's theory on the duration of cultural systems, in which he states that the staying-power of any system is finally determined by

> . . . the greatness of the system itself. The more universal, the more essential to the survival and creativeness of humanity, the meanings, values, and norms of the systems are, the longer its span of life is likely to be. Conversely, petty systems, whose value is purely temporary, limited to their creator or to a small group, and

representing something unnecessary for either biological survival or a full mental, moral, and sociocultural development--such systems are very short-lived.[109]

Any attempt to apply Sorokin's principles to New England Puritanism must deal with what is essential to that culture. The novelists considered in this study recorded the dissolution of one aspect of the New England Puritan culture (i.e., the Church's pivotal role in the community), but what is more difficult to measure is the continuing impact of that Puritan culture on the mores and institutions of the United States.

Henry Steele Commager observed in *The American Mind* that the decline of the theological implications of Puritanism throughout the eighteenth and nineteenth centuries did not affect the moral and political aspects of Puritanism. In analyzing the lasting effects of the Puritan culture, Commager gives an historical summary of what is implicit in the writings of the New England novelists:

> Two centuries of reaction could not dissolve the Puritan inheritance of respect for the individual and for the dignity of man, of recognition of the ultimate authority of reason, of allegiance to principles rather than to persons, to the doctrines of government by compact and by consent, and to spiritual and moral democracy. These things, along with Puritanism's deepseated moral purpose, its ceaseless search for salvation, its passion for righteousness and for justice, and its subordination of material to

spiritual ends, entered into the
current of secular thought and
retained their vitality long after
the theological and metaphysical
argument which sustained them had
been forgotten.[110]

In the very act of critically analyzing the condition of
traditional religion in the New England region, the
novelists surveyed in this chapter were committing their
artistic vision and talent to that same "deep-seated
moral purpose" described by Commager. In so doing, they
were contributing with historical inevitability to a
secular moral sensibility which would fill the void of
lost religious belief.

CHAPTER II

FRONTIER RELIGION AND THE NOVELIST

As the pale of civilization pushed westward from seventeenth century Massachusetts to the late nineteenth-century Far West, certain social patterns tended to repeat themselves in the evolution of frontier settlements. During the post Civil War period, a group of American novelists, generally identified as regional realists or local colorists, chose to use their own personal experiences in transitional midwestern communities as the matter of their fiction. Inevitably, the unique and important role of religion became a central concern for these writers as they explored the conditions of settlement in the American West. Louis B. Wright, the distinguished historian of the American frontier, has written convincingly of the role played by organized religion in facilitating settlement:

> Of all the agencies utilized by man
> in maintaining traditional civiliza-
> tion on the successive frontiers in
> America, it should now be abundantly
> clear that none was more effective
> than organized religion.[1]

The novels considered in this chapter confirm Wright's assessment regarding the importance of religion in the settlement of various regions: the Ohio Valley in Eggleston's *The Circuit Rider* and Howells' *The*

91

Leatherwood God; Indiana in Eggleston's *The End of the World* and *The Hoosier School-Master*; the Illinois settlement in Kirkland's *Zury*; the peculiar character of the South during Reconstruction (when it had been reduced to a frontier economy) in Tourgee's *Bricks Without Straw* and Dixon's *The Clansman*; and the settling of California by Americans in the 1840's as rendered in Jackson's *Ramona*.

The basic thematic element in frontier fiction is the drama of converting the wilderness into a reasonable facsimile of the civilization back East. For the seventeenth-century Puritan, back-East was England, but by the nineteenth century, back-East had become the original colonial settlement east of the Appalachian Mountains. Settlers who were isolated from their roots were usually forced to create a temporary culture to satisfy their psychological and social needs until they could establish the social institutions which characterize a permanent society. By and large, all frontier cultures were temporary and transitional, whether the settlement was in seventeenth-century New England, eighteenth-century western Pennsylvania, early nineteenth-century Ohio, or the plains states of mid-nineteenth century America.

To mollify the transitional (and perhaps frightening) life of such isolated communities, the building of a church was both a symbol of hope and a sign of permanence. Church building can be interpreted as a defense against the perilous encroachments of the nearby wilderness. The process is a constant in the frontier experience as has been noted by historian Peter N. Carroll:

> The process of transforming the
> wilderness into a garden required
> both the importation of religious
> institutions and the extension of

the area of the gospel by erecting churches in new plantations. Frontier expansion and church settlement went hand in hand in New England as each inland town provided for the spiritual solace of the saints in the wilderness.[2]

A strong dependence on religious beliefs was usually most intense in the early years while the frontier settlement was most vulnerable to hostile forces. During these early years, the settler conceived of himself as a potential victim of unpredictable natural forces, hostile Indians, disease, and the terrifying unknown which lingered in the precincts of the nearby forests and beyond the western horizon.[3]

The evolution of a frontier region into a conventional community embracing traditional values took place in identifiable stages.[4] Using the regional novel as a primary source, one may trace out the following recurring pattern in the evolution of frontier religion: (1) Settler-Bible Phase, (2) Settler-Bible and Circuit Rider Phase, (3) Church Building and Minister Phase, and (4) Institutionalism and Revivalism. During the Settler-Bible phase, religious expression was by necessity one of the functions of the pioneer himself. John Westlock, for example, in *The Story of a Country Town*, functions as minister to his family in the Kansas-Missouri Territory in the early stages of its settlement. He relinquishes his preaching role when the town can afford a full-time minister. Ishmael Bush in *The Prairie* is a more primitive settler; like the biblical Ishmael, he is in exile from civilization and follows the laws of Abraham. He acts as a partriarch, providing political, economic, military, judicial, and spiritual leadership for his family. When Bush judges his brother-in-law, Abiram White, guilty of murder, he is also issuing his death penalty. His sense of law and justice is derived from his reading of the Bible, and his moral improvisations are born of the necessities of frontier isolation. As long as the Bush family resides on the edges of civilization, Ishmael Bush will retain control over the religious character of his family, but even Ishmael derives his inspiration and authority from the Bible.

The second phase in the development of the frontier faith was the transferral of religious functions from the pioneer-settler to an intinerant preacher, who, in the West, was frequently a Methodist circuit rider. This transferral of the religious office to a trained specialist was an inevitable step in the process of frontier settlement, as Harvey Wish noted in *Society and Thought in Modern America*:

> Among the stabilizing influences upon the frontier was the church . . . . The Methodist circuit rider and the itinerant preacher tried to overcome the handicap that distance put upon religion on the frontier; this had to be solely a labor of love, for there was little compensation in salary.[5]

Wish goes on to comment on the steady rise in church attendance with the erection of a church building. The circuit rider acted as emissary for both the Eastern institutional churches, like Methodism, and the general cultural values implicit in all established institutions. These preachers played an important part in changing the quality of life on the frontier. Dixon Wecter has observed that they

> . . . helped break the shell of frontier loneliness, as the grim homilectics of Cotton Mather and

Jonathan Edwards gave way to the warmth of backwoods exhorters like Lorenzo Dow and Peter Cartwright . . . . Emotional oratory from the pulpit, and reading matter like missionary tracts, henceforth became a powerful element in frontier culture, shaping its imagination and daily idioms. From the preacher, also, much backwoods education stemmed.[6]

This second phase of frontier religion received its best fictional treatment in the novels of Edward Eggleston, who portrayed the circuit rider as the central figure in the success of Methodism on the frontier.[7]

The establishment of a church within a region represented not only the third phase of frontier religion, but also the turning point in the development of an ill-defined region into a community. The frontier church was more than simply a place of worship; it took upon itself many of the diverse roles which had earlier been assumed by the settler.

A random turning of the pages of any of the old record books of the early frontier churches will soon convince one that the church was a large factor in maintaining law and order in these raw communities. Discipline was meted out to members for drinking, fighting, harmful gossip, lying, stealing, immoral relations between the sexes, gambling and horse racing. Even business dealings and intimate family affairs, such as the relationship between parents and children, were considered matters for church discipline.[8]

It was a dramatic event in the life of a settlement when the church was built because the building itself was also a symbol of civilization, and its presence in an otherwise bleak landscape gave assurance of order and progress. Although the church might continue to be used by itinerant preachers, the ultimate goal of an emerging community with a completed church was to have a permanent minister.

The time and money needed for the construction of a church were good indices of a community's affluence and its capacity to support a resident ministry. With the appointment of a minister, the religion entered into an institutional phase. The most penetrating fictional account of this critical transfer of religious authority is found in Ed Howe's *The Story of a Country Town*. For older members of the community with a nostalgia for the "old-time religion," this movement toward institutional religious expression proved to be less than satisfactory. Of the writers covered in this chapter, Eggleston most frequently lamented the passing of the heroic circuit rider and the golden age of frontier fundamentalism. He also conveys a barely concealed contempt, as we shall see, for the "genteel and respectable" Methodism which came to flourish in the quiet midwestern communities of the nineteenth century.

In the fourth phase of frontier religion, an institutional church displaces the informal character of the frontier sect. The most vital frontier sects, such as the Methodists and Baptists, had difficulty with the transition from sect to church. The evangelistic movement with its annual meetings fused into the church calendar; this codified revivalism may be interpreted as a compromise between the subdued and conventional styles of worship in established churches and the longing for the intense emotional style of "old-time religion." Revival meetings were an extremely popular form of religious expression throughout the nineteenth century. Perry Miller has offered one explanation for their enormous success during this period:

> We miss entirely the dynamics of the great revivals of the early nineteenth century if we suppose them missions to the heathen: they got their demonic power because they were addressed to those already more or less within the churches, because they operated in a society where a general consent to the principles of Protestant Christianity was taken for granted. They were not so much aimed at subjugating a wilderness as at reinvigorating the force of what was already professed.[9]

Institutionalism and revivalism, the last two phases of frontier religion, represent the social pattern typical of the Protestant sects which participated in the development of the West. The subsequent use of revivalism by the various churches would never break through to the "golden past" of the earlier sustained religious consciousness, the need for which had passed with the anxieties of frontier life. As F. I. Moats had rightly argued, "A new generation needed new ministrations. The circuit-rider exhorter could not meet the needs of a settled progressive society . . . . The old system had its place for a time on the new frontier but it had done its work . . . . The future success of the denomination depended on its ability to adapt itself to changing conditions."[10] The problems faced by fundamentalist Methodism in adjusting to the pressures of a more sophisticated society were immense. Harold Frederic in *The Damnation of Theron Ware* depicts the dilemma of a narrowly formed Methodism when confronted with the intellectual challenges of nineteenth-century modernism. Three alternatives were available to the fundamentalist believer: (1) an orthodox withdrawal back into a strict religious fundamentalism, (2) a complete rejection of religious orthodoxy because the Bible no longer made sense when subjected to scientific and historical cross-examination, or (3) a pragmatic synthesis based upon the need for faith. In some respects, the alternatives presented by Harold Frederic almost a century ago still describe the dilemmas facing the religious temperament confronting the challenges of modernism.

Edward Eggleston and Heroic Methodism

Edward Eggleston was a circuit-rider for Methodism prior to devoting his energies to his literary career. The experience of his ministry and his appreciation of Methodism's contribution to the settlement of the Midwestern states prepared him, more fully than any other American writer, to deal sympathetically with the circuit-rider in several of his novels: *The Hoosier School-Master, The Circuit Rider,* and *The End of the World.* In later years, Eggleston would also win respect for his histories of America: *The Beginners of a Nation* (1896) and *The Transit of Civilization* (1901). His evolution from novelist to historian is an important fact in the understanding of Eggleston's fiction, for the historical sense was evident even in the early novels. William Randel, in his excellent study of Eggleston, notes that:

> . . . he was aware that the recording of episodes of frontier

experience was of potential value as history . . . . In his desire for accuracy, moreover, he had acquired the historian's essential habit of consulting the most reliable contemporary records.[11]

Eggleston credited Taine's *Philosophy of Art in the Netherlands* as having encouraged him to attempt the realistic portrayals of commonplace materials.[12] In a century when the American experience was still considered culturally suspect, Taine's thesis on the proper matter of art gave a valuable European imprimatur to Eggleston's creative life.

Eggleston's treatment of Methodism was not apologetic but rather that of a sympathetic commentator on the historical drama of the circuit rider's ministry. In his "Preface" to *The Circuit Rider*, he describes the tension caused by the conflict between his loyalty to Methodism and his commitment to the tenets of realism:

It is not possible to write of this heroic race of men without enthusiasm. But nothing has been further from my mind than the glorifying of a sect . . . . There are those, indeed, whose sectarian pride will be offended that I have frankly shown the rude as well as the heroic side of Methodism. I beg they will remember the solemn obligations of a novelist to tell the truth . . . . No man is worthy to be called a novelist who does not endeavor with his whole soul to produce the higher form of history

> by writing truly of men as they are
> . . . . Much as I have laughed at
> every sort of grotesquerie, I could
> not treat the early religious life
> of the West otherwise than with the
> most cordial sympathy.[13]

This commitment to a realistic rendering of his subject demanded of Eggleston that he show its human imperfections, and by setting aside questions of doctrine and dogma as secondary to his realistic aesthetic, he separated himself from the conventional and popular religious novels of his time, such as H. W. Hilliard's *DeVane: Story of Plebians and Patricians*, whose purpose was to defend and justify Methodism as the true faith.

The Ohio Territory in the period 1814-1824 is the setting for Eggleston's *The Circuit Rider: A Tale of the Heroic Age* (1874). Brother Magruder, a Methodist circuit rider, enters a small Ohio community plagued by the avarice of its leading citizens. Magruder is antagonistic to the worldly values of the town's most successful entrepreneur, Captain Lumsden, who recognizes the minister's role as a potential threat to his own powerful position in the town. Soon after Magruder's arrival, Lumsden expresses his distrust of Methodism to Morton Goodwin, a rough but essentially decent young man: "These circuit riders are worse than third day fever 'n' ager. They go against dancing and artificials and singing songs and reading novels and all other amusements. They give people the jerks wherever they go. The devil's in 'em."[14] The naive Goodwin, although drawn into Lumsden's plan to wreck Brother Magruder's mission work, has already been moved toward conversion as a result of having heard a Methodist circuit rider during his early adolescence. This early exposure to the gospel of Methodism has left an indelible impression on Goodwin's soul which is waiting for an opportunity to be fully realized.

The ideological conflict between the worldly forces of Captain Lumsden and the heavenly forces of Brother Magruder is established at the very beginning of the novel. While Magruder conducts religious services, Lumsden competes with him by sponsoring a dance for the townspeople. Eggleston uses the character of Brady, the local teacher, as a commentator to describe the conflict. Brady's sympathy is clearly on the side of Brother Magruder, and in a stage-Irish dialect, he explains why Methodism is the only hope for this community:

> I'm no Methodist . . . . Me father
> was a Catholic and me mother a
> Presbyterian, and they compromised
> on me by making me a mimber of the
> Episcopalian Church and throyin' to
> edicate me for orders, and intoirely
> spoiling me for iverything else but
> a school taycher in these heathen
> backwoods. But it does same to me
> that the Mithodists air the only
> payple than can do any good among
> sich pagans as we air.[15]

This need of an errant people for a strict religion is a recurring theme in Eggleston's Methodist novels, in which Methodism is depicted as the socializing agent perfectly suited to such demands. *The primitive forms and manners of the circuit riders are thus justifiable in terms of their congregations and the essential needs of the frontier condition.*[16] Brady places the Methodists in the historical framework of a developing America by likening them to the seventeenth-century Puritans of the Bay Colony.

Now the Mithodists are a narry sort
of payple. But if you want to make
a strame strong you have to make it
narry. I've read a good dale of
history, and in me own estimation
the ould Anglish Puritans and the
Mithodists air both torrents,
because they're both shet up by
narry banks.[17]

Through Brady, Eggleston expresses his own understanding
of the vital contribution that the narrow creeds of
Puritanism and Methodism made to the civilizing process
in the early years of the frontier settlement.

In due time the forces of righteousness under the
banner of Methodism rout the worldly Captain Lumsden.
Two previously unregenerate members of the community,
Morton Goodwin and young Kike, become circuit riders
themselves. Goodwin enjoys the same success as Brother
Magruder, but Kike drives himself beyond the limits of
his strength and dies a martyr for Methodism. In
glorifying the ministries of the circuit riders and the
incredible difficulties which they faced, Eggleston
introduces another theme: a complete dissatisfaction
with the institutional Methodism which followed the
pioneer activities of the circuit riders. At one point
in the novel, Eggleston leaves the narrative tale to
deliver a caustic message to his contemporaries:

Dear, Genteel, and cultivated
Methodist reader . . . . Had you,
fastidious Methodist friend, who
listen to organs and choirs and
refined preachers, as you sit in
your cushioned pew -- had you lived
in Ohio sixty years ago, would you
have belonged to the Methodists,

> think you? Not at all, your nerves
> would have been wracked by their
> shoutings, your musical and poetical
> taste outraged by their ditties,
> your grammatical knowledge shocked
> beyond recovery by their English
> . . . . Methodism was to the West
> all that Puritanism was to New
> England. Both of them are sublime
> when considered historically;
> neither of them were very agreeable
> to live with, maybe.[18]

The tone of this digression underscores the pervasive
tensions between Eggleston the old circuit rider and
Eggleston the novelist. The ambiguous "maybe" with
which he concludes his remarks suggests that Eggleston
saw Methodism as a positive historical force when he
considered it in intellectual terms, but that he had not
adapted himself to the inevitable progression of the
itinerant sect into an institutional church. His
distaste for the comforts and more sophisticated forms
of the established Methodist churches indicate that he
was, in spite of himself, a victim of nostalgia for the
"golden age" of frontier faith.

Flat Creek, Indiana, is the setting for
Eggleston's most popular novel, *The Hoosier School
Master* (1871). The novel is based upon his brother
George's experience as a school teacher at the age of
sixteen, in upper Switzerland County, Indiana.[19]
Fifteen years after its original publication, George
Eggleston verified the novel's successful recreation of
his experiences when he observed that the novel's secret
is that

> . . . it is a genuine, honest and
> successful attempt to reflect a
> phase of the actual life of the real

103

American people as they are (or were) and not as a novelist would like to have them. It is realistic fiction, dealing with common people and not with 'society' apes and watering place women.[20]

The people in Flat Creek may not be "society apes," but they are not too terribly advanced on the evolutionary scale. Flat Creek is politically, intellectually and economically a backwater. An innocent youth, Shocky Thomson, describes the town's atmosphere in a warning to the new school-master, Ralph Hartsook:

> Better get away from Flat Creek.
> You see God forgets everybody down
> here. 'Cause most everybody forgets
> God, 'cept Mr. Bosaw [an intolerant
> and ineffective preacher], and I
> 'low God don't no ways keer to be
> remembered by sich as him.
> Leastways I wouldn't if I was God,
> you know. I wonder what becomes of
> folks when God forgets 'em?[21]

Shocky, whose function as a commentator is similar to that of Brady in *The Circuit Rider*, is painfully aware of the cruelties of life in Flat Creek because both his mother and his sister have been victimized by the town's coarse and rude citizens. The townspeople are backsliding Methodists. Nancy Sawyer, the heroine, is described as "a Methodist and likewise a Christian."[22] The need for this distinction becomes apparent when we encounter Mrs. Means, who is a Methodist but not a Christian, and in whose household Shocky's sister is an indentured servant.

Eggleston's characterization of Mrs. Means owes more to Dickensian portraiture than to his own expressed commitment to realism suggesting that the artist may not always be able to harness the imagination into an assumed aesthetic theory.[23] As a result, the reader is given a memorably grotesque comic figure.

The central drama of *The Hoosier School Master* unfolds with the protagonist Ralph Hartsook facing an apparently hopeless fight against ignorance and hostility in his attempt to educate the townspeople. He, fortunately, finds an ally in Bud Means, the toughest youth in Flat Creek, and together they begin to achieve some results. The alliance is terminated when hostile townspeople accuse Hartsook of committing a robbery, a false accusation for which there appears no defense except the slender hope that the guilty party would come forward and confess. At this point in the novel, Eggleston introduces Brother Soden, an itinerant circuit rider in the revivalistic tradition. Flat Creek is Methodist, but backsliding Methodist, and Brother Soden delivers a "hell-fire and brimstone" sermon in order to terrorize the town's evil and malicious citizens. The sermon is so successful that the actual thief, Walter Johnson, makes a public confession in which he also names his conspirators and thereby exonerates Ralph Hartsook.

Having portrayed the salutory effects of revivalistic oratory, Eggleston interrupts the narrative to make absolutely clear his intentions regarding this story.

> There are many mean-spirited men
> like Walter Johnson, whose feeble
> consciences need all the support
> they can get from fear of perdition,
> and who are incapable of any other
> conception of it [religion] than a
> coarse and materialistic one. Let
> us set it down to the credit of

Brother Soden, with his stiff stock,
his thunderous face, and his awful
walk, that his influence over Walter
was on the side of truth.[24]

As a result of Brother Soden's sermon, the community of
Flat Creek is once again both Methodist and Christian.
The development of literacy and the cultivation of
civilized forms can now proceed under the direction of
Ralph Hartsook. Eggleston emphasizes that the
civilizing of the West was dependent upon religious
instruction and admonitions to restrain rude, coarse,
and sometimes violent frontier folk so that they would
eventually accept the moderating influence of education.
Both Brady in *The Circuit Rider* and Hartsook in *The
Hoosier School Master* are teachers who knew little
success until the evangelistic circuit rider arrives to
subdue the lawless spirit of the frontier community.
Eggleston's analysis of the important role of religion
in settling the West is supported by modern historians
such as Louis B. Wright, who has observed that ". . .
churches and schools were closely linked throughout the
period of [nineteenth-century] expansion, and in
addition to serving as guardians of morals and religion,
the churches acted as a centrifugal force in society."[25]

Eggleston also recognized that there were inherent
dangers in revivalistic oratory. If men could be so
emotionally aroused by oratory that they would radically
change the course of their lives, couldn't they also be
aroused by charismatic preachers bearing a false
message? After all, the success enjoyed by Brother
Magruder and Brother Soden was largely based on the
naivete of their followers. The easy manipulation of a
rural settlement by a religious fanatic is the very
theme of Eggleston's *The End of the World* (1873).[26]
This novel, set in Clark Township in the Ohio Valley of
1843, is an indictment of the Millerite sect whose
followers believed that the world would end in the

summer of 1843. A romantic triangle is established as a
narrative framework for the novel: a poor but honest
Dutch boy, August Wehle, vies for the hand of the
beautiful and wealthy Julia Anderson. Competing with
August Wehle is Mr. Humphrey, the local singing-master,
who combines in his character the greed of Ichabod Crane
and the obtuseness of David Gamut. The resolution of
this romantic tale takes three hundred pages, and there
are no surprises in the conventional love triangle.
This novel is, however, a departure for Eggleston as
regards his treatment of Methodist circuit riders; he
portrays two of these men as rather narrow and stupid in
their dealings with their devout followers.

Brother Goshorn and Brother Hall are asked by
Cynthy Ann, a Methodist, for a religious dispensation so
that she might marry her fiance, Jonas, who is a New
Lighter.[27] The response of Goshorn and Hall to this
minor doctrinal matter becomes an occasion for Eggleston
to criticize the legalistic rigidity of the religiously
orthodox mind. The very doctrinal considerations which
weigh so heavily upon the mind of Brother Goshorn make
him appear foolish and repugnant.

> Hopes and joys were as nothing to
> him where the strictness of
> discipline was involved. The
> discipline meant more to a mind of
> his cast than the Decalogues or the
> Beatitudes. He shook his head. He
> did not know. He must consult
> Brother Hall. Now, Brother Hall was
> the young preacher traveling his
> second year, very young and very
> callow . . . . [Hall] said that it
> was a pity for a Christian to marry
> a New Light. It was clearly a sin,
> for a New Light was an Asian. And
> an Asian was just as good as an

> infidel. An Asian robbed Christ of
> His supreme deity, and since he did
> not worship the Trinity in the
> orthodox sense he must worship a
> false god. He was an idolator
> therefore, and it was a sin to be
> yoked together with such an one.[28]

Goshorn's inflexible principles and Hall's circuitous
reasoning mark them as zealots who do not achieve heroic
stature, not only because they are doctrinal legalists
but because they are ministering to a more settled
community. The previously described ministries of
Brother Magruder and Brother Soden possessed religious
and cultural significance because of their beneficent
impact upon communities where the Devil himself reigned
prior to their coming. The failings assigned to the
later ministries of Goshorn and Hall are intertwined
with the historical events which diminished their roles.
Having realized the missionary task of early Methodism,
the new generation, as described by Eggleston, was
reduced to bickering over doctrinal matters.

The only religious experiences given sympathetic
treatment in *The End of the World* are those which are
natural and primary such as the revelation that comes to
August Wehle while he is walking through a forest:

> Through the trees, on which the buds
> were just bursting, August looked
> out on the golden roadway made by
> the moonbeams on the river. And
> into the tumult of his feelings
> there came the sweet benediction of
> Nature. And what is Nature but the
> voice of God?[29]

The pantheistic undertones of this passage, and August's
sensitive response to natural beauty, reveal not only a

shift in Eggleston's concept of religion but also a radical departure in his very vision of man's capacity to respond to anything spiritual other than strong, letter-of-the-law moralizing.

Another dimension of Eggleston's expanding notions of the religious spirit is later illustrated in Julia Anderson's break with conventional Methodism. Eggleston interrupts the narrative to deliver a brief homily to any reader who might be so callous as not to appreciate the meaning of Julia's decision:

> The True God, who is a Father, and who is not Supreme Selfishness, doing all for his glory, as men falsely declare; the True God--who does all things for the good of others--loved her, I doubt not, for refusing to worship the Conventional Deity thus presented to her mind.[30]

In acknowledging both the God of Nature and the narrowness of conventional sectarianism, Eggleston is apparently moving toward the broader streams of nineteenth-century American religious thought.[31] The rejection of sectarian values is consistent with the response of many artists of his time, but is it consistent with the characters of Eggleston's other novels? If Julia Anderson and August Wehle are good, decent people who gravitate toward the virtuous life without the threats and intimidations of frontier evangels, then what does this say about the need for the stern Methodism described in *The Circuit Rider* and *The Hoosier School-Master*? The possible contradiction may be explained as being consistent with Eggleston's vision of Methodism as a socially useful institution for civilizing frontier settlements, but useless to sensitive characters such as Julia and August.

Julia Anderson, eventually, resolves her religious dilemma by repudiating Methodist orthodoxy as defined by Goshorn and Hall, and choosing a more personal religious experience based on her reading of the Bible. Eggleston uses a passage from the New Testament to describe Julia's state of mind and give scriptural support for her religious transformation:

> 'Come unto me all ye that labor and are heavy laden,' she read and stopped . . . . 'And I will give you rest.' And so she drank in the passage clause by clause . . . . She prayed for August, for now the two loves, the love for August and the love for Christ seemed not in any way inconsistent . . . . The presence of God was not a terror but a benediction. She had found rest for her soul, and He gave His beloved sleep.[32]

Julia's return to the Bible seems to complete the cycle of religion on the frontier because in rejecting the coarse Methodism of Goshorn and Hall, she relied on her own religious conscience, thus keeping within the Protestant tradition. Toward the end of the novel, Eggleston explains why he chose to give such an unflattering portrait of Methodist circuit riders:

> Some people think a minister of the gospel should be exempt from criticism, ridicule, and military duty. But the manly minister takes his lot with the rest. Nothing could be more pernicious than making the foibles of a minister sacred . . . and why should not I, who have been a callow circuit-preacher

> myself in my day, laugh at my
> Brother Hall, for the good of his
> kind?[33]

That Eggleston felt the need for such a justification is
the most interesting aspect of this passage. He has
portrayed Hall and Goshorn as hapless fools, but he does
not wish to give offense to any of his orthodox readers.
By declaring that he was once a circuit rider himself,
Eggleston attempts to have the artist's freedom of
censure while avoiding any controversial consequences.
One might also read this apologia as nothing more than
marketplace pragmatism in which Eggleston was
anticipating a critical reaction to his portrayal of
clerics.

Eggleston's strongest criticism in *The End of the
World*, however, is reserved for the Millerites, a
strange sect which believed that Christ's second coming
would occur in 1843.[34] The religious naivete of the
townspeople is satirized in a scene where they gather to
await the momentous event:

> A large bald hill overlooking the
> Ohio River was to be the mount of
> ascension into heaven. Here
> gathered Elder Hankin's [the local
> Millerite leader] flock with that
> comfortable assurance of being the
> elect that only a narrow bigotry can
> give. And here came others of all
> denominations, consoling themselves
> that they were just as well off if
> they were Christians as if they had
> made all the fuss about the
> millenium.[35]

The end of the world appears in the comic guise of a
summer thunder shower which provides a literal cleansing

for the loyal followers of Elder Hankin. Redemption has been indefinitely postponed as they return to the drudgery of frontier life which predisposed them to accept Miller's premillenialism. In the wake of this farcial proceeding, one character observes: "It is the evil of all day-dreaming--day-dreaming about the other world included--that it unfits us for duty in this world of tangible and inevitable facts." The responses of the various citizens who went to the hill only to be disappointed by the non-event, are both tragic and comic. Implicit in all this is Eggleston's indictment of religious fanaticism as an essentially destructive force in people's lives:

> One simple-minded girl was a maniac. Some declared that the world had ended, and that this was the new earth, if people only had the faith to receive it; some still waited for the end, and with some the reaction from credulity had already set in, a reaction that carried them into the blanket atheism and boldest immorality.[36]

Eggleston thus concludes his novel with a warning against religious emotionalism that not only fails to stimulate virtue and a love of God, but destroys the humanity of its adherents. The Millerites and Methodists removed themselves from the teachings of Christ, and the only characters who survive the events of the novel are those who make their peace with God outside the narrow confines of sectarian creeds. Eggleston's message is clear: God is in nature; Christ's life-style is in the gospels; and salvation is possible for those who listen to God and not to the voices of errant prophets. With this novel, Eggleston entered the mainstream of nineteenth-century American religious thought. In later years, Eggleston would come to reject religious orthodoxy by asserting his acceptance of nineteenth-century scientific thought, and in so doing, he fused himself with the New England break from orthodoxy conducted by Ralph Waldo Emerson and others a half-century earlier. The journey from orthodoxy to religious liberalism spanning two centuries of the New England experience was thus encapsulated in the lifetime of Edward Eggleston. His spiritual journey did not conclude with this, for in later years, he would come to be a vigorous spokesman against religious orthodoxy as he championed the acceptance of nineteenth-century scientific thought.[37]

William Dean Howells and Frontier Evangelism

William Dean Howell's *The Leatherwood God* appeared in 1916; its setting was suggested by the author's childhood, although the actual incident upon which the novel was based occurred in Ohio during the 1820's, a decade before Howells was born. Time and setting are essential to the theme of the novel, for the citizens of Leatherwood Creek are living in cultural isolation far from the political, commercial, and intellectual stimulants in the mainstream of American life in the 1820's. The oppressive dullness of such a place is not hard to imagine, and as Howells describes it, religion

> . . . was their chief interest and the seriousness which they had inherited from their Presbyterian, Methodist, Lutheran, and Moravian ancestry was expressed in their orderly and diligent lives; but the general prosperity had so far relaxed the stringency of their several creeds that their

113

distinctive public rite had come to
express a mutual toleration.[38]

Religious services in such communities served not only
spiritual needs but also lessened the day-to-day sense
of isolation. As Francis P. Weisenburger has observed:
"Lonely people in a new location often seem starved for
religious expression and turned out on the hottest days
to pack a church when a visiting home missionary was
present. Denominational differences were inevitably
minimized."[39] The religious toleration among the
various frontier sects, which De Crevecoeur had earlier
described in *Letters from an American Farmer* (1782),
developed in part from a growing indifference to
doctrinal distinctions. Disputes over theological
principles seemed to dissipate on the frontier, and in
such a setting, the revivalist flourished for a very
simple reason—he brought people together.

In *The Leatherwood God*, Howells created an
evangelist named Joseph Dylks who claims to be God and
finds a receptive audience in the 1820's Ohio Territory.
This character created by Howells possesses all the
necessary attributes for a successful evangelist: the
rhetorical gift to move an audience, a supreme
confidence in the offered gospel of redemption, and the
capacity to fuse himself with the aspirations of his
followers.[40] Strangely enough, most of the townspeople
accept Dylks' claim to be God at face value, with the
exception of an agnostic justice-of-the-peace, Matthew
Braile, and the town rowdies who resent the magnetic
hold which Dylks has on the young women of Leatherwood
Creek. The detached observer, Matthew Braile, functions
as Howells' commentator within the novel. His attempts
to understand the significance of Dylks' ministry are
expressions of Howells' own concern with the meaning of
evangelism in frontier America.

114

Evangelist Dylks is eventually labelled a fraud
for failing to perform a promised miracle; his fall from
grace with his followers is linked to his own escalating
claims of being God's witness to being God-like. When
questioned by Matthew Braile as to how this came to be,
Dylks provides the following explanation:

> Nobody can understand it that hasn't
> been through it! How you are
> tempted on, step by step, all so
> easy, till you can't go back, you
> can't stop . . . . When you begin
> to give out that you're a prophet,
> an apostle, you don't have to argue,
> to persuade anybody, or convince
> anybody. They're only too glad to
> believe what you say from the first
> word; and if you tell them you're
> Christ, didn't He always say He
> would come back, and how do you know
> but it's now and you?[41]

Dylks sobs throughout his confession, and in this scene
Howells gives him a tragic dimension. No longer can
Dylks be interpreted as a charlatan feeding on the hopes
of a naive congregation, for it is the people of
Leatherwood who insist on his being a deity out of their
own needs, and it is Dylks who will eventually pay the
price for failing at this hopeless task.

Edwin H. Cady in *The Road to Realism* argues that
Dylks' success, especially with women, is based on his
sexual magnetism. He interprets Dylks' attention-
getting device of snorting as being suggestive of a
stallion, and he puts considerable emphasis on Braile's
fears that the evangelist's popularity might lead one of
the women in Leatherwood Creek to commit an
"indiscretion" with the snorting, long-haired "god."[42]
The sexual undertones of revivalism hinted at in the

genteel mode of Howells' realism were to be presented more explicitly eleven years later in Sinclair Lewis' *Elmer Gantry*. It would be a mistake, however, to equate the sexual-religious undercurrent in these two novels, for sexual magnetism as portrayed in *The Leatherwood God* is a partial but not completely adequate explanation for the phenomenal success of revivalism, and, although such magnetism may explain the success of an individual preacher, the source of evangelism's hold over the frontier settlement of Leatherwood Creek is even more elemental.

At novel's end, Braile provides another kind of psychological explanation for Dylks' early success in Leatherwood Creek seeing it as little more than a projection of the people's needs.

> You see . . . life is hard in a new country and anybody that promises salvation on easy terms has got a strong hold at the very start. People will accept anything from him. Somewhere, tucked away in us, is the longing to know whether we'll live again, and the hope that we'll be happy. I've gotten fun out of the fact in a community where I've had the reputation of an infidel for fifty years; but all along, I felt it in myself.[43]

With this summation, Howells demonstrates his understanding of the psychological principle, proffered by William James in "The Will to Believe" and Freud in *The Future of an Illusion*, that in harsh circumstances man creates his compensations. The overpowering need to believe in some form of salvation is felt even by the self-proclaimed village atheist. Dylks is a pathetic "god" whose humanity is abused by the needs of the

Leatherwood populace. This is Howells' ironic
observation on revivalism: the evangelist is victimized
by the needs of his followers, who have themselves been
victims of a harsh life. They feed upon each other
until, as in the case of Dylks, someone is destroyed.

Joseph Kirkland: Religious Humanism in the Illinois Territory

The setting for Joseph Kirkland's *Zury: The
Meanest Man in Spring County* (1887) is the Illinois
Territory of the 1850's. As a community, Spring County
is at the same transitional stage as Leatherwood Creek,
Clark Township, and Flat Creek. Throughout *Zury*, one
senses that Kirkland shared with Eggleston an ambivalent
attitude toward primitive Midwestern religious
expression. His protagonist, Zury Prouder, is committed
to the Protestant work ethic and is indifferent to
religious worship because his energy is devoted to
making money and receiving full value for every dollar
he spends. The word "meanest" refers to Zury's
frugality not to any sadistic tendencies, and he is
curiously enough admired for his skill in never getting
the short end of a bargain. Anne Sparrow, the heroine,
is a teacher from New England who learns through town
gossip of Zury's independent character even in matters
of religion. Anne is informed by Alpha, a local
resident, that:

> 'Zury dooz 'ccordin' tew his lights,
> and he's too good a friend t' the
> church t' make 'em's pertickler as
> they'd be 'th yew 'n' me. He's
> often be'n made the objeck of
> special prayers; to meetin' 'n'
> campmeetin's 'n' sech; 'n' he's ben

> led t' th' anxious seat more times
> n' ye c'd shake a stick at--but nary
> tear ner cry fer mercy could they
> ever git outer him! Not even when
> others, men, women, and childer wuz
> a-fallin' 'n' a-shoutin' all over
> the place. 'N' so it goes.'[44]

Zury is a secular figure in a sectarian society, but he tempers his indifference to religion by shrewdly recognizing its importance in the lives of his neighbors. His donations to the local churches are a sound public relations investment which keeps Zury in the good graces of the local ministers, who in turn have tremendous influence in the lives of the townspeople. He is thus relieved of the necessity of church-going, while at the same time defusing the potential critics of his religious indifference.

Anne Sparrow's teaching efforts are undermined by the town rowdies, as were Ralph Hartsook's in *The Hoosier School-Master*, and the harassment culminates in the burning of Anne's school. The community is largely indifferent to her plight because she is a stranger whose odd New England ways have set her apart from this backwoods Illinois community. Elder Masten, the local preacher, finds Anne an attractive addition to the dreary town life, so he champions her cause like the "Son of Thunder" with a sermon based on a scriptural admonition: "He that taketh the sword shall perish by the sword." In his sermon Masten analyzes the legitimate uses of violence, concluding with a condemnation of illegitimate violence such as that used against Anne Sparrow and her school. This successfully arouses the lethargic congregation into a state of moral outrage for what has taken place in their community. Masten's power to direct the congregation in their attitudes and courses of action is evident in the remarks made by one of his parishioners after the sermon:

> Why, he mought a come t' th' conclusion th't 't was abaout time fer th' perishin' t' begin! 'Twouldn' take but a whisper fr'm preacher t' wipe aout them fellers offen th' face o' th' arth-- leastways aouter th' baoundries o' Spring County![45]

Although Masten's sermon initially creates a desire for revenge against the arsonists, he is able to convert the people's anger into more worthwhile channels, and in the process, he rescues the Spring County educational system.

After saving Anne Sparrow from the most boorish elements of the community, Elder Masten begins his ill-fated courtship of her. His opening gambit is to invite Anne to join his church, but she is not particularly enthusiastic about this kind of romancing. She informs Masten that she cannot join his congregation because she is a daughter of Boston and a self-proclaimed heretic, but she does agree, in order not to offend him too greatly, simply to attend a service. On this occasion, Masten is foolish enough to make disbelief such as Anne's the subject of his sermon. Anne, a sophisticated Easterner, views the religious enthusiasm of Masten and his flock with critical detachment:

> Shouts of 'Glory' A-a-a-men! Bless His name! and other wild cries and groans . . . . Every heart in the crowded house was carried along in the torrent of the preacher's eloquence--every heart but one [Anne Sparrow], a large one under a small

> bodice, which only murmured 'goose'
> in response to him [Masten], and
> 'geese' in protest against them [the
> congregation].[46]

The evangelical style and fundamentalist interpretation of the Bible are unacceptable to Anne's cultivated religious sensibility. As with Julia Anderson in *The End of the World*, the best solution seems to be the simple avoidance of public worship.

Throughout the novel, Joseph Kirkland describes the disparity between the social and cultural benefits achieved by a primitive evangelical style with its inevitable failings as a viable mode for religious experience with a better educated society. As in the fiction of Eggleston, the symbiotic relationship between educators and ministers is presented as crucial in the civilization of a frontier community. A coarse evangelical religion is offered as a precondition for intimidating a community to tolerate and accept the effects of education. Ironically, the alliance between education and religious fundamentalism inevitably dissolved as an increasing knowledge of the world produced a more sophisticated people, who would collectively say "goose" to the evangelist and "geese" to those foolish enough to listen to his religious cant. As both Eggleston and Kirkland noted in their novels, the seedling institution of education needed the protection of religion only in its early stages.[47]

The morality of slavery is another question which confronts the people of Spring County as they find themselves engulfed by the political and ideological conflicts of the ante-bellum period. The feet-washing Baptists have no difficulty providing a religious justification for the institution of slavery, while the self-proclaimed infidel Anne Sparrow is the champion of abolition. She converts Zury to her way of thinking, and he wins a seat in the Illinois legislature with an abolitionist platform. His victory climaxes the ideological triumph of New England idealism in the Illinois Territory. The denouement of the novel is concerned with Zury's continuing initiation into the values of New England humanism, and his successful courtship of Anne Sparrow. Anne thus completes "a very mean deal" herself; the price of her hand in marriage has been Zury's full submission to her social and cultural values. The marriage completes Anne Sparrow's triumph; besides being an effective daughter of New England by transplanting Eastern culture to frontier Illinois, she has also converted the "meanest" man in Spring County into its most humane citizen.

Albion Tourgee and the Religious Impulse in Reconstructionism

The slavery issue described in Kirkland's *Zury* is primarily the ante-bellum conflict focusing upon the question of whether the Illinois Territory would align itself with the Pro-Slavery advocates. The questions of Free or Slave Territories would be forever resolved by the American Civil War; however, the ideological conflict for men's minds did not end at Appomattox. Albion Tourgee's *Bricks Without Straw* (1880) is a fictional account of the cultural impact of Northern missionary churches (especially Congregationalism) on the lives of emancipated slaves after the war. Tourgee had served as an officer in the Union Army and later as a Federal official during Reconstruction; his sympathies were clearly with the oppressed Blacks, and he had no patience with the self-serving Southern Whites who had profited from the slave economy. The frustrations he endured as a Reconstruction official inspired his first novel, *A Fool's Errand* (1879).[48]

The heroine of *Bricks Without Straw* is Mollie Ainslie, a New England Congregationalist schoolteacher who has travelled South to help in educating the emancipated Blacks so that they may fully exercise their new rights as citizens. Tourgee's attitude toward women such as Mollie Ainslie is one of unabashed admiration, as is evident in the honorific rhetoric of the following passage:

> It was the noblest spectacle that Christian civilization has ever witnessed--thousands of schools organized in the country of a vanquished foe . . . free to the poorest of her citizens [black and white], supported by charity [i.e., Northern church donations], and taught by kindly-hearted daughters of a quick-forgiving enemy . . . . Thousands of white-souled angels of peace, the tenderly-reared and highly-cultured daughters of many a northern home, came into the smitten land to do good to its poorest and weakest.[49]

The moralistic and melodramatic tenor of this passage reflects the general propagandistic intent of Tourgee's novel. In his rendering of the Reconstruction Era, Tourgee was celebrating that Northern idealism which had come to be characterized as predatory carpetbagging.

Mollie Ainslie's educational mission puts her in direct conflict with the traditional values of the Old South. Her work among the Blacks is naturally greeted with suspicion and hostility by the remains of the Southern power structure which she is trying to dismantle. Her black students become targets of reactionary wrath: the cripple Eliab Hill becomes a teacher and is hounded by local ruffians; Nimbus, a muscular and energetic Black who escaped to the North during the war returned as a Union sergeant, is resented because he is a successful farmer. Mollie finds that every sign of progress manifested by her students is resented by the Whites because it undermines the validity of their racial stereotypes. The former slaves are assumed to be too stupid to learn, but Eliab Hill is more educated than those who judge him. Blacks are assumed to be too lazy and irresponsible to support themselves, but Nimbus works harder than any of his white neighbors. As the envy of the white community develops, Eliab likens the newly-emancipated slaves to the children of Israel:

> I thought for a while that we were just standing on the banks of the Jordan--that the promised land was right over yon, and the waters piled up like a wall, so that even poor weak 'Liab might cross over. But I see plainer now. We're only just past the Red Sea, just coming into the Wilderness and if I can only get a glimpse from Horeb, wid my old eyes by and by, 'Liab'll be satisfied.[50]

The religious humanism of nineteenth-century New England is not as relevant to Eliab Hill as are the tales of the Israelites, whose quest for a homeland gives mythic meaning to the black man's quest. Biblical tales of the persecution of the Jews shaped the Christian vision of the black man in the South just as they had influenced Mollie Ainslie's white ancestors in the settlement of the Bay Colony. For both the Puritan settlers and the Southern Blacks of the Reconstruction Era, the anxieties of daily life were punishing and relentless. To be vulnerable in an alien land, as has been noted earlier, is a likely catalyst for religious expression.

Later in the novel, Tourgee elaborates on the historical similarities between the Jew and the Black.

> The helplessness of servitude left no room for hope except through the trustfulness of faith. The generation which saw slavery swept away, and they who have heard the tale of deliverance from the lips of those who had been slaves, will never cease to trace the hand of God visibly manifested in the events culminating in liberty, or to regard the future of the freed race as under the direct control of the Divine Being. For this reason the political and religious interests and emotions of this people are quite inseparable.[51]

Tourgee further extends his historical analogies by noting that

> . . . the colored race in America are the true children of the Covenanters and the Puritans. Their faith is of the same unquestioning type, which no disappointment or delay can daunt, and their view of personal duty and obligation in regard to it is not less intense than that which led men to sing psalms and utter praises on board

the stormbound 'Mayflower.' The
most English of all English
attributes has, by a strange
transmutation, become the leading
element in the character of the
Africo—American.[52]

Tourgee is perhaps guilty of his own white chauvinism in
tracing the religious faith and endurance of the Blacks
to the Puritans, and there appears to be a hint of
racial arrogance in the assertion that such faith was a
"strange mutation" of English into African. He would
have been closer to the truth if he had limited himself
to noting that both the New England Puritans and the
Southern Blacks drew their religious consolations from
the same Old Testament, and in so doing, they shared
certain similarities of style and emphasis. It is
interesting that both Eggleston and Tourgee observed
that the tribulations of the Jews, the threatened people
in a hostile land, were more meaningful to the frontier
settler and the black man than the New Testament.
Although the Christocentric religious experience is not
denied, it appears to have less relevance for a people
passing through trial and deprivation.

In *Bricks Without Straw*, Tourgee presents two
white Southerners who are sympathetic with the goals of
Reconstruction: the aristocratic Hesden Le Moyne and
the poor Jordan Jackson. Both men are decorated
veterans of the Confederate army and neither of them
feels threatened by the new freedom won by the Blacks.
In fact, Jordan Jackson sees the breakdown of the ante-
bellum economy as advantageous to his chances of making
a decent living. The villains in *Bricks Without Straw*
are those Southern Whites who never had to work in the
past, who never even fought to save the Confederacy, and
who have been the principal beneficiaries of the slave
economy. As Tourgee portrays them, the lazy, the
cowardly, and the avaricious are the principal

beneficiaries in the maintenance of the ante-bellum economy and its attendant injustices.[53]

The major characters in the novel all resolve their conflicts with the Southern power structure by abandoning any hope of changing it. Mollie leads a number of Blacks to resettle in the Kansas Territory, the freedom and vitality of which are contrasted with the sloth and rigidity of the South. Jordan Jackson, who had been persecuted by his neighbors for expressing sympathy with political egalitarianism, finds Kansas a sanctuary for his democratic sympathies. In writing to his friend Hesden Le Moyne, he describes a different American West than that found in the fiction of frontier realists.

> Everybody is good-natured and in dead earnest. Everybody that comes is welcome, and no questions asked. Kin and kin-in-law don't count worth a cuss. Nobody stops to ask where you come from, what's your politics, or whether you've got any religion . . . . The West takes right hold of everyone that comes into it and makes him a part of itself, instead of keeping him outside in the cold to all eternity, as the South does to strangers who go there.[54]

As the past traps the South into making fugitives of its most energetic children, the expanding West absorbs them. The West described by Tourgee has no cumbersome institutions to place limits on man's capacity to fulfill himself. Jordan Jackson notes that the people settling in the West are simply not interested in anything about one's past because "They don't care, if only you mean 'business.'"

If the West seems an Eden for those fleeing the
South, it is only an illusory one. Jackson's sense of
escape from the rigid class system of the old South is
given greater significance by his sense of freedom and
opportunity in Kansas, but in Tourgee's novel, the West
is more a metaphor for freedom than an actual place. By
novel's end, the significance of Tourgee's title is
apparent. The reconstruction of the South is impeded by
shoddy materials (i.e., bricks without straw), and the
proper use of human resources has been impeded by
unregenerate prejudice and ignorance. The good and the
energetic people of both races have resettled in Kansas
where their efforts will be properly rewarded, and where
Mollie Ainslie will be unimpeded in dispensing New
England wisdom and values much as Anne Sparrow had in
Zury.

Thomas Dixon and Religious Based Racism

In radical contrast to Tourgee's account of
religious humanism's failure to change the South, Thomas
Dixon's *The Clansman* (1905) was one of the most popular
of the pro-South novels, which celebrates the rise of
the Ku Klux Klan as a heroic episode in Southern life.[55]
The Klan's development is portrayed primarily as an
outgrowth of white reaction to the immoral excesses of
emancipated slaves during the period of Reconstruction.
Senator Stoneman, a crippled New England abolitionist,
is the villain of the novel; his character is based on
that of Congressman Thaddeus Stevens of Pennsylvania, a
Republican leader with strict Reconstructionist views.
In opposition to Stonemen, Dixon portrays Abraham
Lincoln as a segregationist who dismissed the
Constitution as inapplicable to Blacks. Dixon assigns
the following sentiments to his fictional Lincoln: "We
can never attain the ideal Union our fathers dreamed,

127

with millions of an alien, inferior race among us whose assimilation is neither possible nor desirable." Stoneman, "the cynic" replies with part of a biblical quotation on the unity of mankind through God, but Dixon's Lincoln is not taken in. He says: "Yes--but finish the sentence--'and fixed the bounds of their habitation.' God never meant that the Negro should leave his habitat . . . the tragedy will not be closed until the black man is restored to his home."[56] Dixon imagines that Lincoln is supporting the thesis of black inferiority on the same *religious* grounds as did the Southern characters in the novels of Joseph Kirkland and Harriet Beecher Stowe. Later, the reader learns that Stoneman's concern for black men and their civil rights is based solely on his own sexual bondage to his black mistress.

As a result of Lincoln's assassination, the South, in Dixon's narrative, loses an ally. Under the protection of the Reconstructionists, Blacks plunder and rape all that is sacred to their former masters. When the Fiery Cross finally appears, it seems a salvation to persecuted Southern Whites. The Klan strikes back using the cross as a license for nightriding terrorism. The KKK is given an explicit religious justification in Dixon's narrative when the Reverend Hugh McAlpin intones the following benediction at a Klan ceremony:

> Lord God of our Fathers, as in times past thy children, fleeing from the oppressor, found refuge beneath the earth until once more the sun of righteousness rose, so are we met to-night . . . . Have mercy on the poor, the weak, the innocent and the defenseless and deliver us from the

body of the Black Death . . . .
Forgive us our sins--they are many,
but hide not thy face from us, O
God, for thou art our refuge![57]

The conclusion of *The Clansman* reveals Dixon's intention
as a propagandist for the Klan. Their holy mission now
proceeds to its inevitable conclusion in which
"civilization has been saved, and the South redeemed
from shame. The Fiery Cross is lost among the stars."[58]
This alliance of racism and religious sectarianism under
the incongruous symbol of the cross was the antithesis
of the religious humanism Tourgee described in *Bricks
Without Straw*, yet both authors found justification for
their contradictory visions in the Bible suggesting that
the Bible has as many uses as statistics and is equally
malleable to ideological adaptations.

Ed Howe and the Failure of Religious Fundamentalism

The Kansas-Missouri Territory in the post-Civil
War Period is the setting for Ed Howe's *A Story of a
Country Town* (1883). Whereas Tourgee, in *Bricks Without
Straw*, had employed this same territory as a metaphor
for freedom, Howe as a realist was committed to a
faithful rendering of what he had experienced. He was
convinced

> . . . that the local history of his
> or any other town in America
> contained the same strange incidents
> of which Tolstoi and Daudet had made
> use to show how much alike the
> 'human story is . . . in every clime
> and every age.'[59]

Howe wished his novel to be "locally true," because he felt that the elemental nature of man was revealed in the microcosm of regional realism.

A *Story of a Country Town* begins in the years following the Civil War. The narrator, Ned Westlock, describes how his father, John, served as the community's preacher when he wasn't farming, just as Howe's own father had done when the family first settled in Harrison County, Missouri. John Westlock's religious vision is a hard one, rooted in a pessimism born of fear and nourished by nightmarish images of eternal hell-fire engulfing the damned. The negative principle which lay at the heart of such religious notions is found in William James' *The Varieties of Religious Experience*:

> In the religious consciousness . . . the negative or tragic principle is found . . . . There are Saints who have literally fed on the negative principle, on humiliation and privation, and the thought of suffering and death--their souls growing in happiness just in proportion as their outward state grew more intolerable.[60]

If one accepts James' thesis, the hard religion practiced by John Westlock during his early years in the Kansas-Missouri Territory can be regarded as not only appropriate for that time and place, but inevitable. With the passing of years and the easing of hardships on the frontier, religious pessimism such as Westlock's no longer had great adversity on which to feed. His faith is vitiated by a prosperity putting him outside mainstream American Protestantism which interpreted material fortune as a sign of God's beneficence.

The evolution of frontier piety into bourgeois moralism described in Howe's novel was a common phenomenon.

> Just as the early frontier hardships had been held to be a test of the fitness of an Elect people in their incessant warfare against sin, so success in subduing the wilderness was tantamount to entering the kingdom of Heaven and seemed to demonstrate a direct causal relationship between moral and material reward.[61]

However, John Westlock does not follow this pattern of justification, for he truly believes that life is essentially a battle against hopeless odds, and that any rewards are postponed until after death. His success undermines his belief in life as a bitter trial, and he finds himself unprepared for the joys of prosperity.[62]

As Ned Westlock recalls episodes from his childhood, he conveys the sense of bleak isolation in the early years of the town's settlement. Ned, whose sensitive nature is made morbid by his father's preaching, describes his reaction to a funeral service which the entire family was forced to attend:

> After a funeral--which we were compelled to attend so that we might become practically impressed with the shortness of life, and where a hymn commencing 'Hark, from the tomb, a doleful sound,' was sung to such a dismal measure that the very dogs howled to hear it--I used to lie awake in speechless terror for a great many nights, fearing the Devil

would call on me in my room on his way out to the grave lot to see whether the person just buried belonged to him.[63]

The effect of such morbidity on Ned is profound, for it leads to his dismissal of the entire religious viewpoint in adulthood. Just as the adult Stephen Dedalus comes to despise the violation of his innocence by the sadistic Jesuit in the retreat sermon, Ned Westlock comes to reject the violence of his father's religious vision. The rougher fundamentalist faith which Eggleston justified as necessary to the frontier has an unanticipated effect on Ned. He passes from the initial stage of childhood fear to skepticism and, ultimately, to a total rejection of religion.

With prosperity, the people of Twin Mounds can afford to institutionalize religious worship and education. A church is constructed, and the community replaces John Westlock with a properly trained minister, The Reverend Goode Shepherd, who comes to Twin Mounds with a New England seminary degree. The new minister is an embodiment of the liberal theology which prevailed in New England in the wake of the Unitarian and Transcendentalist movements. He demonstrates the extent of his cosmic optimism in conversation with Ned Westlock:

> I sent word to your father that he would oblige me by preaching a sermon on future punishment. It is one of the rules of the church that this disagreeable topic be discussed from the pulpit at least once a year. I dislike it, and am glad to shirk it. Your father is very fond of the subject, I am told. But no difference what he says about it

[hell], I will apologize next
Sunday, and deny it . . . religion
seems to make the people miserable;
I shall change it if I can. I have
been religious all my life, and it
never caused me sorrow. I don't
believe in devils much, but I
believe a great deal in angels.[64]

Shepherd's optimism seems as unbalanced a means of
engaging the world as Westlock's unbridled pessimism.
Neither man's religious convictions serve him when
confronted with a personal crisis: Westlock abandons
his strict creed to have an adulterous affair, and
Shepherd's optimism is shattered by his daughter's
unfortunate marriage and subsequent insanity.

Religious commitment in Twin Mounds declines as
the prosperity of the community continues to increase.
The people no longer use the Bible for inspirational
purposes; rather, it becomes a tool for conversational
polemics and a popular forum for disputes. One is
reminded of the theological disputes in Eggleston's *The
End of the World*, when Ned Westlock describes the new
role of religion in Twin Mounds.

They never discussed politics with
any animation, and read but little,
except in the Bible to find points
to dispute; but of religion they
never tired . . . . No two of them
ever agreed in their ideas . . . and
in many instances the men who argued
the most were those who chased deer
with hounds on Sunday, and ran horse
races, for they did not seem to
discuss the subject so much on

account of its importance as because
of its fitness as a topic to quarrel
about.[65]

By relegating religion to an occasion for cracker-barrel
debates, Howe is underscoring the trivialized status of
religion in Twin Mounds. Functioning as little more
than a curiosity or an occasion for gamesmanship, it has
come to bear no relationship to the faith which
prevailed in the early perilous years of settlement.

Beyond the diminished significance of religion,
Howe suggests that prosperity has ushered in a bourgeois
complacency which has eroded the very character of the
townspeople. As the years pass, Ned Westlock continues
to observe the townspeople with clinical detachment:

As I grew older, and began to notice
more, I thought that every man in
Twin Mounds had reason to feel
humiliated that he had not
accomplished more, but most of them
were as conceited as though there
was nothing left in the world worthy
of their attention. Their small
business affairs, their quarrels
over the Bible, and an occasional
term in the town council, or a
mention for the legislature or a
county office, satisfied them, and
they were counted as men who really
amounted to something.[66]

This annoying self-complacency, as described by Ned,
seems the inevitable by-product of prosperity in a
cultural and intellectual backwater like Twin Mounds.
The ascetic life which characterized the early years of

settlement has been put aside; the Bible which once gave meaning to life, survives as a plaything, and in such a climate Christianity lingers as a social amenity.

Howe's novel concerns itself with a midwestern settlement's passage into a permanent community. The next generation of American novelists would pick up where Howe ended--Lewis's *Main Street*, Anderson's *Winesburg, Ohio*, Tarkington's *The Magnificent Ambersons*--and in comic and tragic modes, they expressed the same discomfort with the cultural and spiritual failings of the newly-minted midwestern America. Accepting the accuracy of their fictional portrayals, established churches in these new communities evolve into extensions of their congregations' materialistic values. In *Babbitt*, Lewis describes *the* church of Zenith to be the Chatham Road Presbyterian presided over by Reverend John Jennison Drew. His church is "the largest and richest, one of the most oaken and velvety, in Zenith," but more important than physical amenities, Reverend Drew provides style and grace for an essentially bourgeois gospel:

> He presided at meetings for the denunciation of unions or the elevation of domestic service, and confided to the audience that as a poor boy he had carried newspapers . . . he wrote editorials on "The Dollars and Sense Value of Christianity," which were printed in bold type surrounded by a wiggly border. He often said that he was 'proud to be known primarily as a businessman . . . .'[67]

The corrupting impact of prosperity on religion described by Ned Westlock in Howe's novel has taken on institutional definition in Lewis's world view.

Helen Hunt Jackson:
The Annihilation of the California Missions

In the late eighteenth century, long before the westward migration swept across North America, the Franciscan mission system had established a permanent social and political community which was both unique and successful in advancing the interests of the indigenous population. Under the authority of the Spanish crown, the Franciscan Order assumed the missionary task of disseminating Roman Catholicism. If successful, their work would provide the ancillary benefit of providing a cultural buffer against the forays of Russian, English, and American interests. What happened to this most humane of all North American colonial ventures is one of the tragic tales of history.

Mexican independence in 1821 had a profound effect upon California—by 1833 the missions were secularized, and the mission property passed into private hands.[68] Although the agricultural and cattle-breeding innovations introduced by the Franciscans continued to make California the richest of all the territories, a political vacuum existed because a weak Mexican government was incapable of taking upon itself the varied administrative tasks previously handled by the Missions.

President James K. Polk led the United States into war with Mexico with the express intention of annexing all Mexican territories south to the Rio Grande in Texas, the New Mexico Province, and California. After General Winfield Scott's successful invasion of Mexico, culminating in the occupation of Mexico City, a newly-formed Mexican government sued for peace. On February 2, 1848, the treaty of Guadalupe-Hidalgo was signed with Mexico ceding California and New Mexico to the United States. The American presence in California, which had been that of a scattered minority up to this time, was destined to become the dominant voice in California life in a very short period.[69]

Helen Hunt Jackson, in her novel *Ramona* (1884), gives a vivid account of the cultural conflict which took place after the Treaty of Guadalupe-Hidalgo, when the Spanish-Catholic settlements of California were faced with the vast migration of Americans and all land claims had to be settled with the United States Government. Mrs. Jackson describes how the Indians, who had settled around the Missions as landowners or workers, soon discovered that their economic existence had been totally disrupted by U.S. policy toward the Missions, and more important, that they were not eligible to file for land ownership even on land they had owned under the two previous governments, Spanish and Mexican.

Father Salvierderra, an elderly Franciscan priest in the novel, is appalled at the suffering arising from the shift in governments; he gives whatever food or clothing he owns to the dispossessed poor. Mrs. Jackson describes Salvierderra as a symbolic refugee from another era who is

> . . . fast becoming the most tragic yet often sublime sight, a man who has survived, not only his own time, but the ideas and ideals of it. Earth holds no sharper loneliness; the bitterness of exile, the anguish of friendlessness at their utmost, are in it; and yet it is so much greater than they, that even they seem small part of it.[70]

Father Salvierderra had outlived the gentle and orderly existence of Mission life; he had outlived the

California where Indian, Mexican, and Spaniard gathered together in developing a successful agricultural economy while also producing an art and architecture reflecting the three converging cultures.

Mrs. Jackson describes the settlement of California by her countrymen with moral disapproval, showing the American soldiers of occupation as barbarians in their casual desecration of the San Luis Rey Mission.

> Aghast at the sacrilegious acts of the soldiers, who were quartered in the very church itself, and amused themselves by making targets of the eyes and noses of the saints' statues, the sacristan, stealthily, day by day and night after night, bore out of the church all that he dared to remove . . . to be given back into the hands of the Church again, whenever the Mission should be restored, of which at that time all Catholics had good hope.[71]

The impact of the United States Government is devastating to the simple religious beliefs of the Mexican and Indian Catholics, who lose faith in their God because of His inability to protect them from the Yankee invasion. When Juan Cenito, a Mexican worker, breaks his leg, his anguish is intensified because his religion is no longer a comfort to him. As Juan sees it, the saints are meaningless: "What are they for, if not to keep us from harm when we pray to them? I'll pray no more. I believe the Americans are right, who laugh at us."[72] The contempt the Yankees express toward Juan's God hastens his eventual abandonment of his Catholic religion.

Allesandro, the Indian chief, finds his people despised and mistreated by the Americans. Ramona, the half-Spanish and half-Indian heroine of the novel, listens to Allesandro's complaints about the impotence of his adopted Christian God and the Saints who are displeased.

> They do not pray for us any more. It is as my father said, they have forsaken us. These Americans will destroy us all. I do not know but they will presently begin to shoot and poison us, to get us all out of the country, as they do the rabbit and the gophers; it would not be any worse than what they have done.[73]

Later in the novel Ramona marries Allesandro and shares the hardships of being an Indian outcast under American tyranny. When Temecula, the Indian village ruled by Allesandro, is confiscated by the American government, a chain of suffering begins which affects every man, woman, and child in the village. Father Gaspara, another Franciscan, views the violence of the Yankee occupation as a nightmare of social injustice, and in a speech which reveals his outrage and frustration he curses the government which allows such suffering to occur under its jurisdiction:

> The United States Government will suffer for it . . . . It is a government of thieves and robbers! God will punish them. You will see; they will be visited with a curse, —a curse in their borders; the sons and their daughters will be desolate.[74]

These angry words do not turn the tide of history; the religious institutions over which Father Gaspara has presided are shattered; Mexican and Indian have discovered that the God of the Franciscans is no match for the unswerving faith in Manifest Destiny which sanctions the new American settlers.

The image of the American settler in *Ramona* is not completely unfavorable. Aunt Ri, a settler from Tennessee who has not lost her humanity in the arduous trek across the country, develops an empathy for the plight of the displaced Indians during her brief stay in California. Mrs. Jackson also uses Aunt Ri to comment on and evaluate the California immigrants. Her observations on the Merrill family, who are representative of the new arrivals from the Midwest, are amusing and perceptive. She sees their industry as a manifestation of their Methodism:

> They're Methodys, terrible pious. I used ter tell Dad they talked a heap about believin' in God; I don't allow but what they dew believe in God, tew, but they don't worship Him so much's they worship work; not nigh so much. Believin' 'n' worshippin' tew things.[75]

This distinction between belief and worship is not developed in the novel, but it is a distinction which separates the new American settlers from the California culture which they disrupt and finally destroy. Whereas the Spanish-Catholic culture had emphasized the aesthetic and contemplative aspects of religious worship, the American Protestants sublimate these religious impulses into the work ethic which finally manifests itself in the old Puritan concept of stewardship. These new Californians, like their New

140

England ancestors, will serve God by increasing their bounty on earth, and material success will confirm their righteousness.

Helen Hunt Jackson views the frontier as destructive of the human spirit; the pragmatic demands of survival, as seen throughout *Ramona*, are not sympathetic to a refined moral sensibility. Yet Mrs. Jackson was able to perceive a fundamental decency in many of the American settlers, such as Young Merrill.

> Underneath the exterior crust of the most hardened and ruffianly nature often remains . . . a realm full of the devout customs, doctrines, religious influences, which the boy knew, and the man remembers . . . . He was not many years removed from the sound of a preaching of the straitest New England Calvinism. The wild frontier life had drawn him in and under, as in a whirlpool; but he was a New Englander at heart.[76]

Although this description of Young Merrill is sympathetic and understanding toward the environmental forces which often distorted the humanity of settlers in the West, this very sympathy tends to weaken Mrs. Jackson's indictment of the American plunder of California. In fact, this ambivalence regarding the character of the American settlers is what rescues *Ramona* from being more than a propaganda novel against American expansionist policies during the nineteenth century. The explanation for Mrs. Jackson's ambivalence might rest on the tensions between her aesthetic sensibility, which is shocked by the wanton destruction of the Mission culture, and her own national, religious, and racial identity which impelled her to describe the Americans as decent folk and "New Englanders at heart."

The polarity of feeling is never resolved and the conclusion of the novel is sentimental and unsatisfactory. Ramona's death is removed from the context of the historical forces which contributed to her becoming a refugee in her own land; her death is sentimentalized as a sacrifice made in the name of love, the beautiful death-inducing love found throughout American fiction in the nineteenth century. The racism so central to the earlier events in the novel is apparently resolved for Mrs. Jackson when an aristocratic woman adopts the child of Ramona and Allesandro, but the cultural conflicts early in the novel dissolve into expressions of pity, with neither a conclusion nor a consistent point of view.

Harold Frederic:
Methodism meets Modernism

The decline of religious belief is a familiar consequence when a simple faith is exposed to an intellectually sophisticated critique. As Kirkland, Eggleston, and Howe observed in their fiction, a primitive fundamentalism was a necessary prerequisite to control the frontier settler and make him receptive to the refinements of a secular education. The evolution of sect-like frontier Methodism into an institutional church was disturbing to a former circuit rider like Eggleston because the tenets of Methodism did not, to his mind, wear well in a bourgeois and respectable setting. The final novel to be examined in this chapter, *The Damnation of Theron Ware*, is not a frontier novel, but it does examine the impact of nineteenth-century modernism upon the simple tenets of Methodism. Harold Frederic's *The Damnation of Theron Ware* (1896), set in the small town of Octavius in the northern part of New York state, describes the ideological confrontation between late nineteenth-century secular thought and Methodism, and the inability of that simple faith to provide a rational defense against such a challenge. In effect, Frederic gives an explicit analysis of a theme suggested in the frontier fiction of Kirkland, Eggleston, and Howe.

Theron Ware is a simple, conscientious, and poorly-educated Methodist minister whose effective preaching gives promise of an excellent career in the Church, but in spite of his preaching skills he received a rather unattractive appointment to the Methodist Church of Octavius, New York. The leading trustee of the congregation, Loren Pierce, informs Theron that the Octavius Methodists are simple folk who take their religion plain and straight. Pierce seems to be an echo from another age of Methodism as he tells Theron what is expected of his ministry. "What we want to hear is the plain, old fashioned Word of God, without any palaver of 'hems' and 'ha's.'" He elaborates on his notion of God's word:

> What we want here, sir, is straight-
> out, flatfooted hell,--the burnin'
> lake o'fire an'brimstone. Pour it
> into 'em, hot an' strong. We can't
> have too much of it. Work in them
> awful deathbeds of Voltaire and Tom
> Paine, with the Devil right there in
> the room, reachin' for 'em, an' they
> yellin' for fright; that's what
> fills the anxious seat an' brings in
> souls hand over fists.[77]

This combination of shrewdness and simplemindedness is offensive to Theron Ware, whose religious sensibility has advanced beyond the sadistic pleasures of terrifying people, but there is little difference between Pierce and Ware in their shared ignorance of men like Voltaire

143

and Paine. The Reverend Mr. Theron Ware is made attractive by his sense of decency and his commitment to traditional virtues, whereas Loren Pierce is the embodiment of the worse aspects of religious fundamentalism.

The three most sophisticated citizens of Octavius --Father Forbes, Dr. Ledsmar, and Miss Celia Madden-- are fascinated by Ware's naivete and find his rustic innocence a refreshing experience. Because they like him, they welcome him into their lives, not anticipating the effect that their intellectual and cultural milieu will have upon him. Father Forbes is a well-educated Roman Catholic priest whose faith has become so intellectualized by his theological studies that he can speak of the "Christ myth" to the astonishment of Theron Ware. Forbes' theological speculations inadvertently contribute to the dissolution of Ware's simple virtue by stripping away the credibility of the Methodist beliefs which give support to his spiritual life. At one point, Forbes delivers a peroration, based on New Biblical criticism, that the story of Abraham must not be taken as the literal truth; Ware is theologically incapable of defending the Bible except in fundamentalist terms, and he chooses not to do so, afraid perhaps of appearing foolish in the eyes of Father Forbes. Dr. Ledsmar is an agnostic scientist and close friend of Forbes, and although he is charmed by Ware's disarming innocence, he inadvertently contributes to the minister's loss of faith by introducing him to the scientific contradictions and inaccuracies found in the Bible. Celia Madden, a friend to both Father Forbes and Dr. Ledsmar, is probably the most important factor in Theron Ware's education. Intellectually, Celia is the embodiment of Pre-Raphaelite aesthetics, but even more importantly, she advocates greater sexual freedom using the life of George Sand as her reference point. This is enough to make Celia exotic and seductive to Theron, and he mistakes her intellectual theorizing for a romantic overture. In any event, the narrow fundamentalist faith that sustained frontier settlers is not enough to protect Theron Ware from the triple-headed assault of Modern Biblical Criticism, Modern Scientific Thought, and Modern Cultural and Sexual Attitudes.

Theron Ware's exposure to the world of ideas destroys not only his faith but also the homely virtues which arose from his belief. He cannot absorb and integrate Forbes' theology, Ledsmar's skepticism, and Celia's cultural theorizing into his own character and beliefs; he loses his simplicity and his naivete in his attempts to deal with the new ideas which his friends have thrust upon him. Celia described Theron's initial impact on Forbes, Ledsmar, and herself:

> You impressed us as an innocent, simple, genuine character, full of mother's milk . . . . Your honesty of nature, your sincerity in that absurd religion of yours, your general *naivete* of mental and spiritual get-up, all pleased us a great deal.[78]

Implicit in Celia's patronizing language is her analysis of Theron Ware as a bumpkin whose real simplicity she and her two friends almost cannot believe. Theron ceases to amuse when he begins to ape them. His dismissal of Methodist values and his pathetic attempts at sophistication destroy his value as an object of amusement. As Celia notes:

> What you took to be an improvement was degeneration. When you thought that you were impressing us most by your smart sayings and doings [e.g., slighting his wife as too ignorant, and ridiculing the simple faith of

145

> his congregation in order to win the
> approval of his new friends], you
> were reminding us most of the fable
> about the donkey trying to play lap-
> dog. And it wasn't an honest,
> straightforward donkey at that.[79]

Theron Ware has lost his innocence; he discovers that the price for acquiring secular wisdom is the loss of faith. His fall from Adamic innocence has also caused his alienation from the very characters responsible for his downfall. He is Frederic's symbol of fundamentalist Protestantism at the end of the nineteenth century, representing, in the traumatic upheaval of his own life, the inevitable consequence of a purely emotional approach to religious expression. The fundamentalist Methodism described by Frederic had failed to deal with the major intellectual currents of the nineteenth century, and this failure produces the symbolic trauma in Theron Ware; he discovers too late that he cannot assimilate new ideas into his simple and rigid faith. Having rejected the Methodist heritage, and in turn having been rejected by his sophisticated mentors, Ware enters a nightmare of spiritual and ideological alienation. He wanders about New York City in a half-deranged state of mind. This is the same Theron Ware who once believed that his abandonment of Methodism was a first step toward a new and more glorious identity. He had envisioned himself "a Poet,-- a child of light, a lover of beauty and sweet sounds, a recognizable brother to Renan and Chopin--and Celia."[80] The illusions and self-delusions have been shattered and Ware discovers that he is damned not to the hell-fires about which he once preached, but to an apparent isolation from all communities of men.

The nursemaid for Ware's sickness is, ironically, Sister Soulsby, a traveling evangelist whose theatrical background enables her to manipulate her audience/congregation into an emotional fervor at annual revival meetings. She uses the evangelical forms of religious expression with a detachment that would have been impossible for a personally involved preacher such as Dylks in *The Leatherwood God.* Sister Soulsby is indeed an ironic vehicle for salvation. Throughout the novel, Frederic describes her artfulness in developing religious emotions as bordering on the cynical, due to her clever methods of crowd manipulation. She is, however, portrayed as humanistic in her handling of Ware's spiritual crisis. On the one hand she gives the simple folk in rural communities like Octavius a sturdy emotional ladder to climb, while on the other hand she provides compassion and personal guidance for the more complex problems of Theron Ware. She recommends a westward journey for Ware, a fresh start on life for both him and his wife. Even though Sister Soulsby recognizes that religion can no longer be a vehicle for Ware's personal salvation, nor the ministry his livelihood, she feels that his excellence as a speaker can serve as the foundation of a new career out West, possibly as a politician. Soulsby, the skeptic-believer, gives the right advice to the anguished minister, and in so doing, she fulfills her own need to relieve suffering in others.

Sister Soulsby is a religious pragmatist whose commitment is based not so much on dogma as on the effect of her actions. As Theron Ware represents the decline of religious fundamentalism, Soulsby represents the rise of a new humanitarian thrust in American Protestantism at the end of the nineteenth century. Henry Steele Commager describes this shift in the functions of American churches as having an historical inevitability:

> The church was, on the whole, the
> most convenient and probably the
> most effective organization for

giving expression to the American
passion for humanitarianism, and it
rarely interposed any awkward
dogmatic prerequisites. Doing good
was interpreted broadly: it might
mean saving men from drunkenness,
rescuing fallen women, sending
flowers to the local hospital.[81]

By the end of the nineteenth century, the humane act was
for many the sole justification for the continued
existence of religious institutions. Sister Soulsby is
in the mainstream of this newly-emerging religious
sensibility with its emphasis on action rather than
dogma.

The Methodism which had helped to sustain and
civilize the settlers on the frontier had exhausted
itself and outlived its social usefulness. By the end
of the century, the frontier had become part of
America's past, although Octavius, New York is still a
reasonable facsimile of the rural Midwestern towns that
Eggleston, Kirkland, and Howe portrayed in their novels.
In *The Damnation of Theron Ware*, the religious
ossification personified in the character and speech of
Loren Pierce is as significant a factor in Methodism's
decline as is Ware's total break with its fundamentalist
precepts. With the passage of time, the dogma and style
of the frontier sect seemed increasingly irrelevant and
absurd. Theron Ware is one of the casualties of the
confrontation with modernism, a prophetic symbol of the
failure of fundmentalism in the twentieth century.[82]

* *

The novelists examined in this chapter--Eggleston,
Kirkland, Tourgee, Howe, Howells, Jackson, and

Frederic--described the impact of frontier religious sectarianism on their fictional characters and their evolving frontier settlements. With the exception of Howells and Jackson, these novelists were writing from first-hand experience with frontier religion, and they focused on the importance of religious sects in forming and sustaining the frontier character, as well as on the historical inevitability that sectarian belief would enter the limbo of religious formalism once the frontier was settled. Although the faith of the frontier settler was described by the regional realist with sympathy and understanding, the formalization of that faith into a conventional church was distrusted. As seen in *The Damnation of Theron Ware*, fundamentalist religion was portrayed as unsuitable for more sophisticated levels of religious consciousness.

The generally sympathetic treatment accorded religious sects by the regional novelists was fairly unusual for American novels written during the period 1860-1920. The understanding and empathy shown toward the frontier settlers, and their dependence on religion, may be colored and perhaps even distorted by the regional writers' nostalgia for an age and culture that were vanishing from the American scene. For these novelists were writing amid the turmoil of a rapidly changing nation that was transforming itself into a new urban-industrial society. In their perception of the importance of religion in settling the West, the novelists anticipated the twentieth-century historian's analysis: "Civilization included education, cultivation, and good manners, and the churches labored persistently on the side of the angels of cultural light. Their success was far greater than cynics have been willing to admit. The churches always fought to re-establish traditional civilization and their conservatism usually prevailed."[83] As the frontier passed into the shadows of a new civilization, the American regional writer paid proper tribute to the

crucial role of religious sects in facilitating
settlement. Their fictional worlds, derived from first-
hand experience, continue to provide valuable primary
evidence for all interested in the social and cultural
dynamics of the American West in the nineteenth century.

CHAPTER III

THE NEW RELIGIONS: NATIVE-BORN AND IMMIGRANT

In the decade prior to the Civil War, the increasing number of immigrants from Ireland and Germany signaled a shift occurring in the composition of the American people which would have profound implications on the cultural and institutional character of American life. After the war, the trend to a more pluralistic population accelerated with the flow of immigrants arriving from such non-traditional sources as the Scandinavian countries, the Mediterranean basin, and Eastern Europe. Not only did these new Americans diversify the ethnic composition of America, they also imported their religious cultural heritages: Lutheranism, Roman Catholicism, Judaism, and a number of pietistic Protestant sects. The least affluent of these new immigrants tended to settle in their ports of debarkation and enter the urban-industrial economy as unskilled workers. Besides being the poorest and most visible of the new immigrants, they were also religiously identifiable as Catholics and Jews. In *New England: Indian Summer*, Van Wyck Brooks provides the following description of how Boston was transformed by these new Americans:

> The religious tradition [of New
> England] . . . seemed exhausted.
> There was little to withstand the
> Catholic power, except the dubious

faith of Christian Science, and
within a few years the most
prominent objects in Boston were the
Catholic cathedral, the dome of the
Synagogue and the dome of Mrs.
Eddy's Mother Church. The
prevailing religion was comfort,
with accessories, which varied from
mind-cure and easy-going optimism to
cults that gave aesthetic
satisfaction . . . . The faith-
healer had won the day . . . . The
miracles of mind-cure were naturally
numerous . . . . A modish high-
Anglicanism led the other cults,
together with drawing-room faiths
from Arabia and Persia.[1]

The new religions filled the vacuum left by the decline
of the old orthodoxy. That these new religions were
important factors in American life is obvious, and those
novelists, committed to a realistic aesthetic, were
compelled to recognize and deal with the social
consequences of both the American-made and immigrant
religions.

The increasing presence of Catholics and Jews is
easily explained by the facts of immigration, but the
rise of new cults is a more difficult phenomenon to
comprehend. Clifton E. Olmstead interprets the rise of
American-born sects and cults as an extension of
religious freedom:

A basic contributory force was the
voluntary principle, which admitted
no state church and encouraged the
fullest freedom of religious
expression. Equally important
factors were the heterogeneity of

American society, the competitive impulse in religion, and the spirit of individualism. There were also social and economic considerations. For the poor, crowded into vermin-possessed tenements and forced to lead what seemed an inconsequential existence, some of the cults offered refuge and release. They also provided a haven for those with unfulfilled emotional needs and gave them a sense of belonging and a resuscitated hope for the future.[2]

Granted that one could choose a faith without incurring the wrath of state or institutional church, Olmstead's thesis does not explain why one would choose a single generation cult over the established churches. Using Olmstead's insight, one might further speculate that the freedom to choose a belief transferred authority from a clerical hierarchy to the newly-empowered religious *consumer*. The proliferation of Made-In-America religions, cults, and sects down to the present day might then be interpreted as flowing from consumer demands for specific spiritual needs.

With the exception of the Reincarnationist Elizabeth Stuart Phelps and the Jewish writer Abraham Cahan, the novelists covered in this chapter examined the New American religions, both immigrant and native-born, from a perspective shaped by traditional Protestantism. The moral perfectionism implicit in this perspective had little patience with or understanding of such amoral phenomena as seances and faith healing. The absence of an intellectual component in any number of emotion-based cults further contributed to the generally unsympathetic treatment rendered by these novelists. All the major religious movements and many insignificant ones were scrutinized by the novelists of the time.

Although Henry James had little sympathy with the post-Civil War craze for mediums and seances, in writing *The Bostonians*, he was more concerned with their psychological implications; Edward Eggleston, the old Methodist circuit rider, was less tolerant when examining the Christian Science phenomenon in *The Faith Doctor*; William Dean Howells' criticism of the Shaker movement was characteristically tempered with compassion in both *Undiscovered Country* and *The Day of Their Wedding*; and Helen Martin provides an insightful diagnosis of sectarian isolationism in her Amish novels.

The impact of Judaism and Roman Catholicism on American life was much more extensive and permanent than that of the more transitory cults and minor sects. Catholicism was portrayed in countless novels as a Janus-faced presence; for some, it posed a threat to the democratic principles of the still young republic, while for others, it promised spiritual sustenance for the nation's exhausted religiosity (e.g., *The Marble Faun, A Connecticut Yankee in King Arthur's Court, A Mortal Antipathy, The Puritans,* and *The Damnation of Theron Ware*). The unique tensions experienced by the Jew in America were given the first full expression in Sidney Luska's *The Yoke of the Thorah* and by Abraham Cahan in *The Rise of David Levinsky*. Protestant novelists concerned with the influx of Jews and Catholics were impelled to examine the historical biases against both groups, and what is striking in their fictional portraits of Jews and Catholics is the consistent and conscious effort to be fair. This is not to say that Protestant novelists such as Howells and Twain did not share some of the American nativists' prejudices toward these newcomers who were disrupting American life with their foreign ways, but in general, the serious American novelists reserved their harshest criticism for the new sects and cults.

154

One of the most popular novels in the nineteenth century was Elizabeth Stuart Phelps' *The Gates Ajar* (1868). In the opinion of Howard Mumford Jones, this novel was a pivotal work in American thought because it

> . . . marked a gentling, a softening, a feminization of Protestant Christianity, which was to have its greatest Boston triumph in the rise of the Christian Science church, the founder of which is known as Mother Eddy, and one of the tenets of which is that God is simultaneously Mother-Father . . . . This humanization of Protestant creeds, this blurring of intellectual issues, this eschatological optimism is a salient fact in postwar Boston.[3]

The Gates Ajar is historically significant because it addressed itself to the many thousands of grieving survivors of the Civil War dead. Traditional Puritan concepts of the afterlife provided little emotional relief for the mourning survivors as already noted in the discussion of *The Minister's Wooing* and *John Ward, Preacher*. Orthodox belief was more likely to intensify grief rather than alleviate it. The failings of traditional creeds contributed as much as any other factor to the enormous success of *The Gates Ajar*. Fred Lewis Pattee perceived the novel as intimately woven into the evolving spirit of New England, this new spirit

. . . that had been awakened by the war called for reality and concrete statement everywhere, and it found in the book, which made of heaven another earth--a glorified New England perhaps--with occupation and joys and friendships unchanged, a revelation with which it was in full accord. It brought comfort, for in every line of it was the intensity of conviction, of actual experience. It quivered with sympathy, it breathed reality from every page, and it seemed to break down the barriers until the two worlds were so near together that one might hold his breath to listen.[4]

The novel, which tells of Mary Cabot's inconsolable grief after the death of her brother Roy in the Civil War, is based upon Elizabeth Phelps' own experience of loss during the war--"it was she who had tried to square the teachings ingrained into her Puritan intellect with the desolation of her woman's heart."[5] Like her creator, Mary Cabot finds no comfort in a Puritan faith whose rational pieties torment rather than console her, and when she informs the deacon of her church that she will not resign herself to the will of God, her break with orthodoxy begins. With the repudiation of orthodox belief, Mary experiences deep depression and anxieties until she discovers the doctrines of Spiritual Materialism.

Spiritual Materialism, or the Creed of the Reincarnationist, is a religion to which Mary is introduced by her Aunt Winifred Forceythe. This new religion had developed in the rural West, and Winifred, accompanied by her symbolically named daughter Faith, is in effect bringing regeneration to the spiritually exhausted East. Faith's effect on Mary Cabot is similar to Phoebe's effect on Hepzibah in *The House of Seven Gables*, in that she functions as a restorative agent to Mary during her sorrow and confusion. In repudiating her traditional faith, Mary understandably experiences some misgivings, but young Faith's ingenuous dismissal of orthodox forms and ceremonies gives needed support to Mary's decision. She tells Mary that she thinks "it's splendid to go to church most of the time . . . all but the sermon. That isn't splendid. I don't like the great big prayers 'n' things."[6] Mary is enchanted by Faith's simple goodness which is the antithesis of her intellectually and morally grounded Presbyterianism, and she comes to realize more fully the wisdom of Faith's distaste for "gre-at big prayers 'n' things." In several respects Aunt Winifred's new faith recalls that old New England heresy of Antinomianism, but the major doctrine of Spiritual Materialism is not salvation through faith--it is physical reincarnation. As the novel develops, Aunt Winifred tells Mary how these beliefs helped her to adjust to the sorrow of her husband's death. For her, the resurrection of Christ foretells the resurrection of all men; the fact that Christ's resurrection took a material form prefigures the corporal reincarnation which awaits all men after death.

The novelty of Winifred's beliefs rests on the emphasis which is placed on corporal reincarnation, and this is precisely the doctrine from which so many readers drew comfort when they read *The Gates Ajar* Phelps' conceptions of death and heaven were not abstracted visions, but the keen anticipation of reunion with loved ones. Aunt Winifred gives a vague but pleasant picture of the heavenly rewards which await men after death: "All that Art, the handmaids of the Lord, can do for us, I have no doubt will be done. Eternity will never become monotonous. Variety without end, charms unnumbered within charms." Anticipating possible objections to the doctrinal legitimacy of her vision, Winifred develops the following thought for consolation:

> Two things that He [Christ] has taught us give me beautiful assurance that none of these dreams with which I help myself can be beyond his intention to fulfill. One is, that eye hath not seen it, nor ear heard it, nor the heart conceived it,--this lavishness of reward which He is keeping for us. Another is, that 'I shall be satisfied when I awake.'[7]

These two passages are perfectly appropriate for allowing Mrs. Phelps' imagination and the imaginations of her readers, to define heaven for themselves. The psychological benefits rendered by *The Gates Ajar* are self-evident, particularly the notion that the heavenly experience would be a reunion with departed loved ones, and it was precisely this notion in the novel that the guardians of orthodoxy found so objectionable. They felt that it was a soft doctrine catering to flabby souls.

After a summer with Aunt Winifred and Faith, Mary Cabot is no longer melancholic. She is now a Reincarnationist, for whom death is not the grim reaper but rather an instrument of joyful reunion with her beloved brother Roy. The final testament to the viability and reliability of Aunt Winifred's new faith comes at the conclusion of the novel when she discovers that she has breast cancer and is about to die. During her illness, Winifred draws comfort from her Reincarnationist beliefs, and she only regrets that she must leave Mary and Faith in order to be joined in heaven with her loves ones; quite predictably, she consoles herself with the thought that they will soon all be together again. In welcoming death, Winifred dramatically demonstrates the basic theme of the novel-- the gap between the quick and the dead is neither as vast nor as frightening as men have been led to believe.

The Gates Ajar gave solace to a wide reading audience by transforming death into a desirable state, and by filling a spiritual and emotional vacuum in the lives of many people who found no comfort in traditional religion. Phelps did not repudiate the traditional beliefs--she reworked them into a new formula. Commenting on the synthesizing process in the novel, Helen Sootin Smith observed that *The Gates Ajar*:

> . . . affords a case study in the general assimilation of new forms. Behind it lies an essentially Protestant and provincial culture; ahead lies a secular, international world of letters. In origins it belongs to a New England genteel tradition that a democratic and materialistic society has largely outgrown. Elizabeth Phelps translates the old ideas into new terms using . . . any literary form that will appeal to her audience. *The Gates Ajar* embodies sacred allegory, sentimental romance, Platonic dialogue, sermon, realistic story of New England life, and confessional diary. A similar absorption of diverse elements distinguishes the book's philosophic content, in which Calvinism joins romanticism, Scottish Common Sense philosophy, evolution, idealism, and materialism.[8]

Whether or not the novel is quite the ideological smorgasbord suggested by Helen Smith is not as important as the fact that its success illustrated an increasing inadequacy on the part of orthodox religion to satisfy the psycho-spiritual needs of the people.

Elizabeth Stuart Phelps had grown up in the rigidly orthodox Calvinist community of Andover, Massachusetts, and she came to reject those abstract religious doctrines which failed to provide her with either enlightenment or solace. By celebrating a new religion in her fiction, she catered successfully to delicate sensibilities such as her own, which found cold comfort in the Ramusian syllogisms of Edward A. Park, the leading orthodox Professor of Theology at Andover from 1847 to 1881. Elizabeth Phelps did not object so much to Christianity as to what the established New England clergy had made of the Christian tradition, whose "failure lies in its clergy's reluctance to adapt doctrine to the complex hearts of men and women."[9] Adaptation of doctrine was the leveling response to the various challenges which faced traditional creeds in the nineteenth century, but Phelps went far beyond the previously examined New England authors. While Harriet Beecher Stowe had also objected to doctrinal coldness, her response was more restrained; she wrote a sentimental portrait of an old-fashioned minister and, in her private life, she quietly converted to the gentler doctrines of Episcopalianism. Both Phelps and Stowe were alike in their objection to the tyranny of a Puritanism that refused to recognize man's fragility and his need for comfort rather than condemnation. Howard Mumford Jones characterizes this wave of rebellion as "the feminization of Protestant Christianity," and what he apparently means by this, is the humanization of Protestant Christianity through the subordination of doctrinal abstractions in favor of human values.

One approach to understanding the phenomenal success of *The Gates Ajar* is to accept the thesis that religious beliefs evolve from the *needs* of the people, and that the belief in corporal reincarnation was a much needed antidote for the epidemic-like suffering of millions who had lost loved ones in four years of Civil War. Merle Curti, in *The Growth of American Thought*, noting the great popularity of *The Gates Ajar*, observed that Phelps

> . . . tapped a vast reservoir of need; people still mourning for sons and husbands lost on the battlefields craved reassurance that life is really eternal, that heaven really is just within reach. The subsequent psychic novels of Mrs. Phelps elaborated with much detail the actualities of the Other World and of daily life within the golden portals.[10]

She wrote three sequels to *The Gates Ajar: Beyond the Gates* (1883), in which the heroine dreams that she dies and goes to heaven; *The Gates Between* (1887), which tells of the death of an agnostic doctor and his adventures in the other world; and *Within the Gates* (1901), which is a dramatized account of the adventures of the agnostic doctor. As Arthur Hobson Quinn has noted, perhaps too harshly, Mrs. Phelps should have stopped with her initial success because when she attempted to detail her theological beliefs in later fiction, she was entering the realms of madness.[11] The accuracy and fairness of Quinn's judgment should be tempered by acknowledging the appetites which Phelps was apparently satisfying. For a reading audience with modest religious allegiances, her fiction provided immediate gratification for the gnawing questions of mortality and immortality without insisting upon any

161

doctrinal pre-conditions. By the standards of William James, Phelps was an extraordinary success in promulgating the comforting beliefs of Reincarnationism. As with much popular culture, the extraordinary success of *Gates Ajar* is a barometer of mass needs as well as tastes, and although its literary merits fail the test of time, *Gates Ajar* remains a seminal work for social historians.

Henry James: The Occult in New England

In writing *The Bostonians* (1885), Henry James was consciously reflecting the influence of the French naturalists by attempting to give a faithful rendering of life in Boston.   It is indeed ironic, as Oscar Cargill pointed out, that James' efforts "to establish the environment that produced Olive Chancellor" is the critically most neglected point about *The Bostonians.* "Olive is as much a product of post-Civil War Boston as Gervaise and her husband in *L'Assomoir* are a product of the Paris of their day."[12]   In the broadness of its conception and the diversity of its social themes, *The Bostonians* is an atypical James novel, and this uniqueness is no doubt partly responsible for the failure of many Jamesian critics to give it a serious examination.   After lamenting that James did not write *The Bostonians* in the same economical style as *The Europeans*, Leon Edel reaches the following conclusion:

> What he created instead [of the great American novel] was a series of vignettes; and certain pages valuably critical of American institutions--the invasion of privacy by the press, the meddlesome character of Boston reformers, the

general tawdriness and banality of
certain aspects of the American life
of the time on which he had dwelt in
his other tales.[13]

Although the major *social* theme in this novel is the
suffragette movement, the all-encompassing motif is the
increasing spiritual and cultural desperation of New
England life, as manifested in the pursuit of the occult
and in the rise of charlatans and opportunists who
paraded themselves as traditional New England reformers.
As Louise Bogan has observed, the background for the
novel's action is the

> . . . tepid atmosphere of post-
> Abolition idealism. It is an
> atmosphere still peopled by cranks,
> faddists, cultists, evangelists,
> revolutionaries, and dogmatists so
> usual in America in the forties and
> fifties--the intellectual and
> emotional debris of the breakdown of
> faith, the beginning of the
> 'scientific view,' of the general
> ethos of still crude industrial and
> moral revolutions. James knew these
> visionaries, of all shades of
> sincerity and sanity, well; his
> father's New York home had been a
> sort of clearing-house for them.[14]

The critical phrase employed by Bogan is once again "the
breakdown of faith," and it is the absence of a unifying
belief that produces a fragmented cultural setting which
lacks the intellectual norms necessary for value
judgments. Such a setting is fertile ground for the
subjective certitudes of spiritualism and religious
cults framed around charismatic leaders. What James

163

describes as incidental to post-Civil War Boston would evolve into a national epidemic a century later.

The conflict in this novel centers on Verena Tarrant, who has been raised by her parents to be a spiritual medium. Olive Chancellor, a prominent figure in Boston feminist circles, wants to enlist Verena's special talents as a medium in the cause of the suffragettes. The intensity of Olive's pursuit appears to have sexual implications in the possessive imagery which she employs speaking to the innocent Verena. "It isn't your father, and it isn't your mother; I don't think of them, and it's not them I want. It's only you--just as you are."[15] There is an ambiquity in Olive's attitude toward Verena, but her overt interest in the girl is to utilize her spiritism as a device for attracting attention to the political ambitions of the nineteenth-century feminists. Vying with Olive for Verena's affection is a Southern lawyer named Basil Ransom, whose desires are the more conventional ones of the time--marriage and a stable home life. In the figure of Basil Ransom, Henry James

> . . . created with remarkable prescience a type of intellectual who has only in the last few decades come to the fore in the English-speaking world . . . a type exemplified in writers like T.S. Eliot or the school of Southern agrarians, whose criticism of modern civilization is rooted in traditional principles. Thus James anticipated . . . one of the major tendencies in the twentieth-century thinking.[16]

The Ransom perspective develops into an adversarial one for a variety of reasons. Besides the above-mentioned regional factor, Ransom is set apart from the prevailing values of Boston: he is an objective rationalist amidst subjective intuitionists; he is an agrarian physiocrat in an urban culture; and he is a man of action in a community dominated by women. Although an alien, he refuses to be coerced, and his eventual confrontation with Olive Chancellor is a symbolic encounter between traditional and modern values.

Olive is the "new woman" attempting to overcome the traditionally male-dominated world; just as Elizabeth Phelps created a new religious identity to replace an inadequate orthodoxy, Olive wants to resolve the confusion of the times by working out a synthesis between spiritualism and feminism which will have a *quasi*-religious character of its own. Her efforts are destined to fail because she had not come to grips with her own problems. Louise Bogan notes that

> . . . Olive is yet sterilized by an aridity of spirit, baffled by genteel prejudices, and warped by a nervous constitution. Set against James's portrait of a woman reformer of an earlier period—the warm-hearted, eccentric, but touching Miss Birdseye—Olive Chancellor is a rather terrifying resultant of Puritanism gone to seed, a female organism driven by a masculine will, without the saving graces of masculine intelligence or femininess [sic] tenderness and insight.[17]

Olive's desperation manifests itself in her desire to possess Verena without apparently recognizing or understanding her emotional and sexual motivations. Through the spiritualist exercises with Verena, Olive converts her half-articulated desire for physical possession into an ideological convention which is agreeable to the decayed remnants of her Puritan sensibility, but Olive's suppressed feelings are not easily contained as when she implores Verena: "Promise me not to marry."[18]

As the innocent Verena is gradually being absorbed into feministic spiritualism with its sublimated lesbianism, Basil Ransom enters the narrative as an adversary to Olive and a champion of traditionalism. Ransom is a Southerner whose sense of practicality is in constant conflict with the New England prediliction for abstraction. In his opposition to Olive's plans for Verena, he is not so much an anti-feminist as a heterosexual male who is strongly attracted to Verena, wishes to marry her, and views spiritualist activities with the jaundiced disbelief of one trained in the rational dialectics of law. In Basil's judgment, Verena has been the victim of a faulty upbringing because her parents trained her to be a spiritual medium for their own financial advancement; he also perceives that Olive wants to use Verena, although he never quite understands the intensity of Olive's feelings. In his description of Basil Ransom, James is establishing an ideological antagonist to Olive Chancellor. Basil

> . . . was by natural disposition a good deal of a stoic, and that, as the result of a considerable intellectual experience, he was, in social and political matters, a reactionary. I suppose he was very conceited, for he was much addicted to judging his age. He thought it [i.e., the age, particularly as represented by Olive Chancellor] talkative, querulous, hysterical, maudlin, full of false ideas, of unhealthy germs, of extravagant,

dissipated habits, for which a great
reckoning was in store.[19]

At one point in the novel, Verena lectures Basil on the
oppression of women and the need for reform, and his
rebuttal is to challenge the concept that suffering is
an exclusive experience of female in society. As Basil
states it:

> The suffering of women is the
> suffering of all humanity. Do you
> think that any movement is going to
> stop that--or all the lectures from
> now to doomsday? We are born to
> suffer--and to bear it, like decent
> people.[20]

When Basil criticizes the faddishness of reformers,
Verena's authority, derived from her role as a medium,
collapses because she has only been trained to make
speeches, not to think. The undeveloped character of
Verena is a critical factor for explaining the intense
competition to possess her. She is a catalytic agent
because she is so vacuous (anticipating Ralph Ellison's
protagonist in *Invisible Man*). Her parents wish to make
money from "her medium" talents; Olive wishes to mold
her into the fulfillment of her psycho-sexual needs; and
Ransom wishes to possess her in a traditional marriage.
Her pliability offers no resistance to the various needs
deposited upon her, and in this respect, she is the
classic Jamesian reverberator.

Basil pleads with Verena to abandon her career and
accept his proposal of marriage. The climactic scene
occurs when he refuses to allow Olive to use Verena for
spiritualist exercises before an audience. He assumes a
proprietorship over Verena, ostensibly to prevent her
exploitation:

> . . . not for worlds, not for
> millions, shall you give yourself to
> that roaring crowd. Don't ask me to
> care for them, or for anyone! What
> do they care for you but to gape and
> grin and babble? You are mine, you
> are not theirs.[21]

When Basil asserts his command over Verena, the fragile
world Olive Chancellor created out of her half-realized
dreams and confused longings collapses. The boldest
claimant takes final possession of the hapless Verena
with "You are mine, you are not theirs."

   The Bostonians may be read as James' reaction to
faddish religious movements in post-Civil War New
England. To offset this theme, James included in his
novel the character of Miss Birdseye, a representative
of an earlier generation of moral idealists who
addressed themselves to the injustices of slavery; even
the former Confederate Army officer, Basil Ransom,
admires Miss Birdseye and the selflessly humanitarian
character of her life. What Miss Birdseye and her
generation represent has been distorted by Olive
Chancellor and her generation, the new generation having
lost the moral perspective and sense of charity while
retaining an inflated sense of righteousness. In this
novel, James

> . . . shows us perfectionists blind
> to their own imperfections, liberals
> neutralized by their liberality,
> radicals bound by unyielding dogma
> to callousness and sadism; as well
> as the 'moist emotional' yearners
> and the hysterics of both sexes,
> unconsciously seeking a ritual and a
> master that they consciously
> reject.[22]

In the vacuum of values underscored by Miss Birdseye's death, there is nothing left but improvisational ritual making, and it is all evanescent. In rescuing Verena from becoming a sideshow medium, Basil symbolizes hope for the stabilization of those traditional values for which he has been a spokesman throughout the novel. The denouement almost suggests that James has written an ideological allegory relating the confusions born of modernism in nineteenth-century Boston. Miss Birdseye, the representative of traditional New England morality, is dead; Olive Chancellor, the confused representative of a generation which is repudiating the past and improvising the present, is defeated and cast aside; Basil Ransom, who stands for traditional values, is victorious in his confrontation with the uncertain reformers of this transitional age. The prize for the ideological battle is Verena Tarrent, an innocent representative of the new generation. Oscar Cargill accurately described *The Bostonians* as a novel in which the "environment of ideas is as substantial as Zola's environment of things."[23]

It is interesting to note that when James attempted to deal with larger social themes, as in *The Bostonians*, he described the breakdown of the New England culture from the same perspective as his friend, William Dean Howells. Although James and Howells shared the same concern over the breakdown of values, James resolved his drama in the victory of Basil Ransom, a conservative-reactionary, whereas Howells (as we shall see in Chapter IV) drifted toward a more socially-responsive Christianity. *The Bostonians* does indeed contain "an environment of ideas," and they are transmitted through the essentially conservative sensibility of Henry James who had little sympathy with the rising popularity of spiritism and the occult, but as a novel of ideas, the victory of the reactionary Ransom seems an inadequate resolution to the intellectual and cultural problems introduced.

The Christian Science sect under the direction of Mrs. Mary Baker Eddy of Concord was the most successful native-born religious movement in post-Civil War America. As noted by Sidney Ahlstrom in *A Religious History of the American People*, it grew out of the same "great religious disquietude that was spreading through New England . . . . Her dissatisfaction with evangelical revivalism and orthodox dogmatism was shared by the Universalists, Spiritualists, Transcendentalists, and Swedenborgians as well as mesmerists, faith healers, and health seekers with whom her life was entwined."[24] The central premise of Christian Science was denial of the physical world, which resulted in the reduction of sin, poverty, sickness, and death to no more than illusions or errors created by the mind. Only a troubled mind not in harmony with the Eternal Mind could produce illusionary sicknesses; once the troubled mind was properly directed, the bad illusions would disappear. There was little new thought in Mrs. Eddy's doctrines:

> Christian Science taught what philosophers and theologians had asserted for two thousand years: that sin, pain, disease, and death have no reality, and that, through grace and faith, the mind can triumph over these and find its way to health, happiness and salvation. Where philosophers from St. Augustine to Josiah Royce had propounded this doctrine as a metaphysical theory, Mrs. Eddy advanced it as a scientific fact.[25]

Mrs. Eddy extended the old truism of "mind over matter" into a complete religious system which she recorded in her book *Science and Health* (1875).

In 1902, Mark Twain wrote a series of articles on Christian Science for the *North American Review*, contrasting its great success with the limited appeal of other "isms" such as Utopianism, Nationalism, Swedenborgianism, and Spiritualism. It was Twain's opinion that the success of Christian Science rested on the universality of its appeal:

> And who are attracted by Christian Science? There is no limit; its field is horizonless; its appeal is as universal as is the appeal of Christianity itself. It appeals to the rich, the poor, the high, the low, the cultured, the ignorant, the gifted, the stupid, the modest, the vain, the wise, the silly, the soldier, the civilian, the hero, the coward, the idler, the worker, the godly, the godless, the freeman, the slave, the adult, the child; *they who are ailing in body or mind, they who have friends that are ailing in body or mind.* To mass it in a phrase, its clientage is the Human Race. Will it march? I think so.[26]

The appeal is so universal because, as Twain tells us, its great offer is *"to rid the Race of Pain and Disease."* Twain was not himself an enthusiast of Christian Science. In his final installment for the *North American Review*, he grimly prophesies a day when Christian Science will rule the earth and ultimately bring about a Black Night "never again to lift."[27] Eleven years prior to Twain's dire prophecy, Edward

Eggleston had written his last novel, *The Faith Doctor* (1891), which is a scathing indictment of the faith healing craze in general, and Christian Science in particular.

By 1891, Eggleston's views on religion had undergone a drastic change from his earlier Methodist commitment. He had discarded his Western identity and had become a militant agnostic with little patience for traditional religions and no patience whatsoever for the charlatanism which had become so fashionable in the Northeastern cities.[28] Although Eggleston still retained a certain nostalgic fondness for Methodism as a socially useful religion, he had no use for the cultists and spiritualists whom he now saw flourishing without helping anyone but themselves as they exploited the spiritual emptiness in the lives of so many nineteenth-century urbanites. Eggleston gave explicit expression of his feelings in his "preface" to *The Faith Doctor*:

> In one age men cure diseases by potable gold and strengthen their faith by a belief in witches, in another they substituted animal magnetism and adventism [e.g., evangelism as portrayed in *The Leatherwood God*]. Within the memory of those of us who are not old, the religious fervor of millenianism [e.g., the Millerites in *The End of the World*] and the imitation science of curative rappings and clairvoyant medical treatment [e.g., *The Gates Ajar* and *The Bostonians*]. Now spiritism in all its forms is passing into decay, only to leave the field free to mind-doctors and faith-healers. There is nothing for it but to wait for the middle ages

to pass; when modern times arrive,
there will be more criticism and
less credulity, let us hope.[29]

Eggleston's criticism, limited to the religious fads of
his time, might be characterized as politic considering
the average nineteenth-century reader's attitude toward
religion, but his displeasure with such fads is probably
as much a part of his own lingering orthodox sentiments
as anything else. He had once preached salvation
through the good life and although he was now an
agnostic, Eggleston's vestigial Methodism was offended
by the amoral character of the religious faddist.

Merle Curti tells us that the appeal of Christian
Science could partly be explained

> . . . by the American love for
> novelty in religions and in part by
> the repressed but nonetheless
> authentic yearnings for mysticism in
> the American as in all forms of
> civilization. It took hold mainly,
> but by no means exclusively, in
> cities where, in common belief, the
> pace, the stress, the strain of life
> produced more nervous disorders than
> in the country. It appealed among
> others, to the restless and the
> aspiring. It also appealed to the
> comfortable and the prosperous.
> This was possibly true because it
> provided a psychological
> compensation for their actual
> overemphasis on material values in
> daily living: it was people like
> that, in any case, that Edward
> Eggleston satirized in his novel,
> *The Faith Doctor*.[30]

Eggleston used New York City, the most frenetic and populous of all American cities, as the setting for *The Faith Doctor*. As Curti noted, the failure of urban institutions to meet the needs of the people contributed to the huge success of Christian Science. One character in the novel complains of the impersonality so common to the urban churches:

> Ministers . . . they are just after money nowadays. W'y, I joined the Baptist church . . . when I came to New York, and the minister never come a-nigh us. We are not fine enough, I suppose. Ministers don't believe the plain Bible . . . . I say take the plain Bible, that a plain man like me can understand . . . the Bible says in one place that if a man's sick the elders are to pray over him and anoint him with oil . . . . But did you ever know any elder to do that?[31]

Eggleston understood that the attraction of the new urban sects, such as Christian Science, was bound to the mission of trying to fill a spiritual and psychological emptiness in the lives of first-generation immigrants to the city. The poverty and low social status of this new urban class gave them a marginal relationship to the established city churches. It was almost inevitable that they would seek a more congenial setting for religious worship, and in so doing, they anticipated the store-front churches which served the Southern Blacks who migrated to Northern cities after World War II.

Eggleston is less tolerant when he describes the religious pursuits of comfortable, middle-class New Yorkers. He is repelled by the slovenly character of

174

the overindulged *nouveau riche* and appalled with the
cynicism which contrives to invent a religion compatible
with their life-style. In *The Faith Doctor*, Mrs.
Frankland is the embodiment of such opportunism.
Eggleston informs us that when

> . . . Mrs. Frankland became aware
> that there was unbelief, latent, and
> developed, among her hearers, the
> prow of her oratory veered around,
> and faith became now, as
> consecration had been before, the
> polestar toward which this clever
> woman aimed . . . . Solemnly
> insisting on a renunciation of all
> possibility of merit as a condition
> precedent to faith, she proceeded to
> exalt belief into the most
> meritorious of acts. This sort of
> paradox is common to all popular
> religious teachers.[32]

Mrs. Frankland's success as a teacher is based on the
undemanding character of her beliefs. For her and for
her followers, a simple expression of belief is
redemptive, a pleasant doctrine which proves to be both
popular and profitable. Mrs. Frankland's theology, if
that be an accurate term for her faith, is the *reductio
ad absurdum* of that seventeenth-century heresy
Antinomianism which led to Anne Hutchinson's expulsion
from the Bay Colony. Eggleston's disdain for a religion
which promises salvation without "a covenant of works"
is understandable in the context of his earlier
affiliation with a morally rigorous Methodism.

Philleda Callender, the young heroine of the
novel, comes under Mrs. Frankland's influence and is so
inspired by her teachings that she wants to devote her
life to relieving the sufferings of the poor. Unlike

her cynical mentor, Philleda does not limit her ministry to the wealthy. She goes to work among the sick and the needy on the Lower East Side of New York, and in the course of her missionary work she apparently cures, through the power of her faith, a crippled child. As the news of her supposed healing powers spreads through the community, Philleda finds herself being absorbed into the faith healing sub-culture. Mrs. Frankland uses her increasingly for curing the nervous disorders of her followers, and Philleda's fiance, Charles Millard, becomes more and more disenchanted with the older woman's manipulations.

The tensions between Millard and Mrs. Frankland are in some respects reminiscent of those between Basil Ransom and Olive Chancellor in *The Bostonians*. Millard perceives Mrs. Frankland as his adversary in a contest for Philleda. He characterizes her as a woman who loves to talk and

> . . . to have people crowd around her and tell her how much good she is doing. She denies herself nothing; she feeds her vanity on the flattery she gets, and then thinks herself a saint besides. She exhorts people to a self-sacrifice she wouldn't practice for the world.[33]

Philleda is not only unwilling to accept this analysis of her mentor, she breaks her engagement to Millard as proof of her loyalty, and in this respect, there is more to Philleda than Verena Tarrant.

With her success as a faith healer, Philleda comes to the attention of the local Christian Science representative, Eleanor Arabella Bowyer, who immediately begins recruiting her for Christian Science. Miss

Bowyer describes her religion as "the science of sciences. It's as much above the rude method of primitive faith-cure practiced by the apostles as the heavens are above the earth." She goes on to deliver a jargon-filled lecture on the theoretical complexities of Christian Science:

> We understand from knowing the philosophy of miracles the reason why we do not always succeed. We can not always secure the impressible condition by producing the quiescence of the large brain. But if we understand the theory of hypnotism we shall be able to put the cerebrum at rest and secure the passive impressible state of the cerebellum; that is, an introverted condition of the mind. This securing of interior perception is the basis of all success.[34]

The naive Philleda is mystified, intimidated, and impressed by Miss Bowyer's pseudo-scientific explanations, and she decides to accept the doctrinal postures of Christian Science. In fact, the success of Christian Science can be understood through this scene, in which the pseudo-scientific language is woven into a religious dogma, thereby giving the illusion that Christian Science had harnessed scientific knowledge in order to serve religious goals. As it develops in the novel, the purpose of Eleanor Bowyer's recruitment of Philleda is more a business deal than a religious conversion, because Philleda's earlier faith healing success had made encroachments into Eleanor's territory. Eleanor tells Philleda:

Some of our Christian Science people
are all enthusiasm, but I am trained
to business, and I carry on my
practice on business principles.
There is no reason why a doctor who
treats diseases on the mortal plane
of medication should be paid for his
time, and you and I not be. Is
there?[35]

It turns out that not only is Eleanor Bowyer interested
in eliminating Philleda as competition, but she also
wishes to use her as a contact for the affluent uptown
society to which Philleda belongs.

The transparent vulgarity of Eleanor's design to
make money out of her faith cures is so appalling to
Philleda that she rejects Christian Science and
immediately begins to reexamine her own activities on
the Lower East Side. Her growing awareness of the
inherent dangers of faith cures reaches a climax when
she is called upon to cure a boy with a sore throat, and
she finds that the boy has diphtheria. When Philleda
asks the boy's father, a devout Christian Scientist, to
call in a medical doctor, he refuses and instead calls
on Miss Bowyer to treat his son's illness. Eleanor
Bowyer treats the "belief in the sore throat" by using
magnets to bring the child into harmony with the
magnetic forces of the earth. Watching the boy die,
while Eleanor plays with magnets, cures Philleda of any
further allegiance to the tenets of faith healing.

In *The Faith Doctor*, Eggleston acknowledges that
there is some merit to the success of the faith healers.
As one character in the novel observes, their success
rests on their ability to activate the human will to
desire good health and "that's the way that the
mesmerists and magnetizers, and the new faith-cure
people work their cures largely. They enlist the will,

178

and they do some good. They often help chronic invalids whom the doctors have failed to benefit."[36] In spite of the legitimate success in activating dormant wills, Eggleston clearly disapproved of Christian Science because he felt that it misused human potentialities such as the will, and that by denying the reality of sickness and death, it created evils which offset the good it accomplished. *The Faith Doctor* contains perhaps the strongest attack on a religious sect in all American literature. In recalling Eggleston's kinder descriptions of Methodists, Baptists, Roman Catholics, and Episcopalians in his early Midwestern fiction, it seems clear that his impatience was not with sectarian peculiarities, but with what he viewed as the dubious motives of many in the faith cure business. The tone of the novel is moralistic, and Eggleston's lack of detachment in describing what he perceived as religious charlantanism suggests that, even as an avowed agnostic, his Protestant sensibility was still very much intact.

William Dean Howells: Spiritualism and the Shakers

The Undiscovered Country (1880) opens with Howells examining seances, mesmerism, and mediums as they flourished in post-Civil War Boston.[37] In a conversation between two minor characters in the novel, Mr. Phillips and Mr. Eccles, Howells dramatizes the desperate temper of an age that pursues religion through the expedient of spiritualism. When Phillips observes to Eccles that one should approach a seance with the same piety as a church service, his use of religious terminology is not accidental—the seance is in fact his substitute for an abandoned orthodoxy. Eccles enthusiastically supports Phillips' theories on seances, and he attempts to give a rationale for the fashionable

spiritualism of his day by distinguishing it from
traditional religious observances. He declares that

> . . . a seance is not exactly a
> religious service. No, it partakes
> rather of a dual nature. It will
> doubtless be elevated in character,
> as the retro-and inter-acting
> influences improve. But at present
> it is a sort of informal reception
> at which friends from both worlds
> meet and commingle in social
> intercourse; in short, a kind of bi-
> mundane--bi-mundane--[38]

Eccles' attempt to present an illusion of rationality is
reminiscent of Miss Bowyer's cumbersome discourses on
Christian Science in *The Faith Doctor*. Howells, like
Eggleston, was perhaps as much offended by the assault
on language as by the dogma professed.

Dr. Boynton, the central character in the novel,
has sacrificed his medical career, and is in the process
of sacrificing the health of his daughter Egeria, in
his attempt to make contact with the spirit of his dead
wife. He has trained Egeria to be a medium (the plot
motif and father-daughter spiritism contains the basic
outline employed six years later by Henry James in *The
Bostonians*). Boynton is so committed to the
legitimizing of his search into the mysteries of
immortality that he is in a constant state of self-
deception. When Ford, the skeptical journalist, attends
a seance and points out that the rapping noises did not
originate with a spirit, Boynton ingeniously replies
that it is sometimes necessary to show the spirits how
to communicate. Later in the novel Egeria, under the
increasing influence of her admirer, Ford, begins to
complain about the deceptions practiced during the
seances, but her father is still able to justify them:

> The only *perfectly* ascertained fact
> of spiritistic science is the rap.
> This, with the innumerable exposures
> and explanations which expose and
> explain all other phenomena, remains
> a mystery . . . . We *must* advance
> beyond it . . . as an investigator I
> take my stand boldly upon the
> necessity of first doing ourselves
> what we wish the spirits to do. A
> feeble sense of right and wrong may
> call it deceit; a vulgar nihilism
> may call it trickery; but the
> results will justify us,--[39]

Boynton is an essentially good man who has been driven
to spiritism by his inability to adjust to his wife's
death; as an agnostic who has abandoned the
Congregational faith of his childhood, he is searching
for something with which to fill an emotional and
spiritual void. Since he is committed to the truth of
spiritism, Boynton masks his self-deception under the
high-sounding name of "solicitationism," that is, the
use of noises to solicit responses from the real
spirits. Once again, Howells is demonstrating that the
cultist abuses language to disguise the shoddiness of
the doctrine.

In the process of writing *The Undiscovered
Country*, Howells wrote to his father that his new novel

> . . . was no 'mere love-story' but
> 'serious work' that treats of
> serious matters . . . . The
> spiritualism which Howells had
> encountered in youth . . . was being
> revived . . . in the seventies as a
> desperate substitute for theological
> faith.[40]

Besides being a careful study of spiritualism, *The Undiscovered Country* contains Howells' first fictional treatment of the Shakers. As George N. Bennett has noted, this novel was "the result of an extended gestation, and that during the maturing process Howells came to think of Shakerism and spiritualism as related manifestations of the central problem of belief."[41] When Dr. Boynton becomes acquainted with the Shaker faith he is immediately interested in its spiritualistic aspects, but he soon discovers that the Shakers are extremely suspicious of the motives behind the popularization of spiritualism. One of the Shakers tells Boynton: "As soon as the money element touched it, it began to degenerate, and now it's a trade, like any other. They are tempted all the while to eke it out with imposture."[42] This cynical evaluation does not take into account men such as Boynton whose motivation is not money but a need to alleviate the anguish caused by the loss of belief.

The desperate character of Boynton's search is demonstrated by his spontaneous acceptance of Shakerism after brief exposure to it. He is convinced that the Shaker environment is the ideal one in which to make contact with the spirit world. His enthusiasm for the Shakers is related to their apparent success in spiritism rather than the earthly aspects of their communal life, and in his enthusiasm Boynton conveys his ignorance of basic Shaker doctrine:

> I understand now how you can make the only just claim to the development of these phenomena. In your community alone is the unselfish, the self-devoted, basis to be found, without which we can rear no superstructure to the stars.

I have wasted my life! . . . wasted
my life! Does your community live
near here?[43]

As Dr. Boynton sees it, the ambiance of the Shaker community is another kind of medium through which he might make contact with the spirit world. Since Egeria is sick and temporarily unable to function as his medium, he decides to continue his experiments by joining the Shaker community at Yardley, Massachusetts.

Boynton soon discovers that the Shaker attitude toward the spirit world is quite different from his. Soon after arriving at Yardley, he engages the Shaker elder Brother Joseph in a discussion of the supernatural events described in a book by Elder Evans. Both Boynton and Brother Joseph accept the truth of the events reported in the book, but they differ considerably in their attitudes toward the supernatural. As Brother Joseph notes, Shakers "do not follow up such experiences. They serve their purpose, and that is enough. We try to live the angelic life. That will bring what is good to us, and we need not go to it." Boynton has difficulty understanding such passivity in the face of supernatural phenomena, and he replies to Brother Joseph: "These intimations are given expressly to pursue. That is what miracles are for."[44] Boynton's preoccupation with spiritualism is foreign to the primary values of Shaker communal life, and to answer his objections to the Shakers' indifference to the supernatural, Brother Joseph cites Christ's resurrection as a single sign which is all that was necessary: "Once is enough in miracles."

When he cannot persuade the Shaker community to support his attempts to communicate with the spirit world, Dr. Boynton's enthusiasm for the Shakers proves

short-lived. The intensity of his disaffection is
revealed in a speech to Egeria, in which he tells her
they are leaving the community:

> They think that my utilization of
> their conditions will undermine
> their whole system. And so it will.
> Their system is unnaturally and
> ridiculously mistaken; next after
> their spiritualism, their communism
> is the only thing about them that is
> fit to survive. Their angelic life,
> as they call it, is an absurd
> delusion, the dream of a sick
> woman.[45]

Whether it be dream or delusion, Howells has discredited
Boynton's capacity to be a judge in such matters. Not
only is he frustrated in his attempts to use the
community for seances, but he soon discovers that in the
process of Egeria's recuperation under the care of the
Shaker sisters, she has been "despiritualized" and is no
longer a fit subject for Boynton's exercises in
mesmerism.

Before leaving Yardley, Boynton explains to the
community why he is seeking a means to contact the
spirit world, and his motivation is reminiscent of
Emerson in "The Divinity School Address." He is seeking
an antidote to the disease of skepticism because it is
an age

> . . . honey-combed with skepticism.
> Priests in the pulpit and before the
> altar proclaim a creed . . . but
> neither priest nor people believe.
> As yet, this devastating doubt has
> not made itself felt in morals; for

those who doubt were bred in the
morality of those who believed.[46]

In such an age, Boynton feels that spiritualism is the
only answer and that the great danger of disbelief is
its long-range effect on the moral tone of the
community. In expressing the notion that religion is
the custodian of morality, Howells raises the spectre of
social chaos following the decline of religious belief.
Boynton's last attempt to use the Shakers is his
suggestion that they abandon their retreat from the
world to form a new religion, "a Shakerism which shall
be devoted to the development of spiritualistic
science." His plea is both wrong-headed and
unsuccessful.

Upon leaving the Yardley community, Boynton's
health falters and as his condition deteriorates, his
fanatical attitudes gradually fade to reveal a long
dormant critical faculty. In a long conversation with
Ford, he acknowledges that "the spiritualist's quest for
tangible proof of immortality is both materialistic and
amoral--a counterfeit of the religious ardor of the
ages."[47] In his speculation on man's morality, he
summarizes his state of mind by referring back to the
Christian tradition which he had abandoned so long ago.

> Then that is the only hope,--that
> only story of a credulous and
> fabulous time, resting upon hearsay
> and the witness of the ignorant, the
> pedantic wisdom of the learned, the
> interest of a church lustful for
> power; and that allegory of the
> highest serving the lowest, the best
> suffering for the worst,--that is
> still the world's only hope![48]

As Boynton's health continues to fail, he recalls
Hamlet's observation on death as "The undiscovered
country from whose bourn no traveler returns." The
mystery of what, if anything, awaits man after death is
not resolved for Dr. Boynton. He tells Ford: "We are
better with no proof. Yes; yes! The undiscovered
country--what a weight of doom is in the words--and
hope!"[49]

Throughout the novel, Boynton has given meaning to
his life by his experiments in spiritism, while the
Shakers find meaning in a unique style of living as
service to God. In their distinctly different ways,
Boynton and the Shakers pursue the same goal--attempting
to define life by coming to terms with the notion of
immortality. At the end of the novel,

> Egeria is rescued from the darkness
> of her father's obsession and her
> life brought into the clear light of
> rationality. Not only are Ford's
> social roughnesses [sic] smoothed,
> but his scientific scepticism is
> leavened by a return of faith and an
> infusion of humility.[50]

The cycle of belief is completed when Egeria is not only
released from the world of spiritism, but is baptized an
Episcopalian and marries Ford in the Episcopal church.
The novel concludes on the following note: "If Boynton
had found the undiscovered country, he has sent no
message back to them, and they do not question his
silence. They wait, and we must all wait."[51]

Although the focus of *The Undiscovered Country* is
on the spiritualist movement, Howells also examines the
Shakers for the first time in this novel. His
fascination with this sect was based, as he tells us in
Three Villages, on his recognition of the Shakers as

186

"simple, sincere, and fervently persuaded of the truth of their doctrine, striving for the realization of a heavenly ideal upon earth." Shakers figure prominently in three subsequent novels by Howells: *A Parting and a Meeting* (1896), *The Day of Their Wedding* (1896), and *The Vacation of the Kelwyns* (1920). Edward Wagenknecht has summarized Howells' attitude toward the Shakers in the following way:

> With their asceticism he had no sympathy, and he was too sophisticated and aesthetic to be a Shaker himself, but they attracted him on the side of their simplicity and their spiritually-minded Communism, which was quite free of violence and materialism.[52]

Although the cloistered communal life was not adaptable to the larger world, many principles implicit in Shaker values were later incorporated into Howells' political convictions.

The peculiar innocence of the Shakers and their inability to survive normal, everyday life is the theme of *The Day of Their Wedding*. The two protagonists, Lorenzo Weaver and Althea Brown, are in love and wish to be married. Since this is a violation of the Shaker doctrine of celibacy, they flee the community for Saratoga, New York, where they hope to be married. The relevance of this decision is, as Althea observes, larger than the simple act of leaving the Shaker community: "We are going to give up the angelic life."[53] Althea and Lorenzo's simplicity and sincerity are set against the vulgar materialism of the Saratoga resort area. Their response to the materialism and inhumanity of the outside world mirror the relationship between Mr. Homos and Boston society in *A Traveler from Altruria* which was written in the same year. They are

Christians traveling through the strange and hostile environs of industrial America, and they maintain a running commentary on the differences between the "angelic life" and what they see about them, much as Homos measures the state of America by the ideal standards of his mythical homeland Altruria.

Although Howells greatly admired the communal system of the Shakers, and its success in relieving the faithful from the anxieties of survival which haunted the lives of so many Americans of the time, he was not above satirizing the eccentric and sometimes righteous character of their doctrines. During one scene in *The Day of Their Wedding*, the minister who is to marry the young Shakers attempts to reassure Althea that marriage is a right and proper undertaking for a young woman, only to have Althea rebuke him with a defense of the Shaker belief in celibacy:

> The voice of Althea broke in upon him, still tremulous but clear, and gaining firmness to the close: 'And Jesus answering unto them, the children of this world marry and are given in marriage; but they which shall be accounted worthy to obtain that world and the resurrection from the dead neither marry nor are given in marriage; neither can they die any more; for they are equal unto the angels; and are the children of God, being the children of the resurrection.[54]

This "unbridely" outbreak bewilders the presiding minister whose attempts to be supportive only aggravate Althea's anxieties over her break with Shakerism. After going through with the marriage ceremony, she decides that, having once known the heavenly order of Shaker

communal life, she cannot accept the outside world.
Althea's feelings toward nineteenth-century America are
similar to those of Mr. Homos--they have both known a
better world and cannot adjust to the harshness and
vulgarity of this society.   In telling Lorenzo of her
decision, Althea expresses the strength of her
commitment to the Shaker life:

> I have thought it all out at last.
> I don't blame the earthly order;
> it's the best thing there is in the
> world-outside. But we have known
> the heavenly order, and if--even
> if--we were to be happy together
> . . . *it's too strong for me now*,
> and it would be too strong for as
> long as I lived. I have got to go
> back.[55]

At the railroad station, she gives Lorenzo one dutiful
kiss before they both board the train that will bring
them back to the Shaker community and life-long
celibacy.   In the absurdity of their behavior, Howells
is depicting his own misgivings with certain aspects of
sects such as the Shakers, and although he shared their
dissatisfaction with the earthly order, he cannot
sympathize with the price demanded for membership in
their community.   In his Shaker novels, Howells explores
the temptation to retreat from the discordant temper of
his times.   Indeed the agrarian-communal world of the
Shakers was much closer to his personal experiences
growing up in the Ohio Territory than what he daily
encountered on the streets of New York in the 1890's,
but unlike his Shaker characters Althea and Lorenzo,
Howells chose to work for social change rather than
personal withdrawal "and that . . . made all the
difference."

Helen Reimensnyder Martin: Chronicles of Amish Isolationism

The process of assimilating immigrant cultures, including religion, into the existing framework of native American institutions has been mythically described with a "melting pot" metaphor, but Will Herberg in *Protestant-Catholic-Jew* more accurately describes this phenomenon as being more a "transmutation pot" in which the imported culture is "transformed and assimilated to an idealized 'Anglo-Saxon' model."[56] To avoid losing one's historical identity, the only survival formula is to remain isolated from the dominant native culture, and there are identifiable minority sects which have successfully preserved their traditional beliefs at the price of isolating themselves. One such group is the Mennonites, more familiarly known as either the Amish or the Pennsylvania Dutch, who settled in the rural precincts of Lancaster, Pennsylvania. The Amish have been the subject of many sympathetic fictional portrayals, but the most incisive examination of this unique people may be found in the novels of Helen Reimensnyder Martin whose perspective was shaped growing up on the fringe of the Amish sub-culture in Lancaster.

Martin does not sentimentalize the Amish, and her judgment could be unashamedly harsh as is evident in the following caustic assessment:

> There really does seem to be a bovine dullness about the Pennsylvania Dutch equalled only (in my experience of the human family) by the rural inhabitants of some remote localities in England. It is their heavy, unceasing toil, the deadening sameness of their daily

routine, the narrowness of their creeds, the absence
among them of all lightness and frivolity, that makes
them so dull."[57] For all their alleged dullness, they
did provide Helen Martin with the subject matter for
many fictional treatments, including: *Tillie the
Mennonite Maid: A Story of the Pennsylvania Dutch*
(1904), *Sabina: A Story of the the Amish* (1905), *The
Revolt of Anne Royle* (1908), *Martha of the Mennonite
Country* (1915), and *Yoked with a Lamb* (1930). It is her
second novel in this cycle, *Sabina*, which contains her
most thorough treatment of the social implications of
the Mennonite faith. *Sabina* depicts the cruel
narrowness of Amish doctrines while extending a grudging
admiration for some aspects of Amish life. Martin's
ambivalent feelings toward the Amish are reminiscent of
Howells' attitudes toward the Shakers. Both sects are
unworldly, and as Martin observes:

> The followers of the Amish faith do
> not 'live in the world,' their
> religion, by its unique customs, and
> the peculiar garb it imposes,
> setting them apart from the rest of
> humanity, prohibiting 'a life of
> vanity,' and rigidly enforcing a
> plain and frugal manner of life and
> conversation.[58]

The peculiar clothing which the Amish wear is symbolic
of the barriers which they build between themselves and
the outside world, and this convention of social
isolation is the central theme of *Sabina*. The
cultivated ignorance toward the outside world reinforces
the desired isolation of the Amish community and,
according to one Amish character in *Sabina*, this is a
conscious process:

The reason we marry our cousins so
much is that we like to stick close
to each other and form Amish
settlements, still. We try to make
farmers of all our sons and give 'em
farms near us when they get married,
so they don't move away. To keep
'em satisfied to be farmers, we
darsent leave 'em get too much
educated, so we just send 'em to the
district school a while, and that
has to do 'em.[59]

The farmer's analysis of the logic behind Amish customs
is correct—exposure through education and contact with
other value systems does represent a real threat to the
Amish way of life. The successful transmission of
traditional cultures—from the Amish farmers of
Pennsylvania to the Hasidic Jew of present-day
Williamsburg—demands isolation from the dominant
coercive culture.

When Sabina Wilt, the central character in the
novel, leaves her Amish home in New Holland,
Pennsylvania, to pursue her worldly education, she
experiences culture shock in her contact with mainstream
America. Not only does she find values and attitudes
substantively different than those of her Amish
upbringing, but she finds that even her speech, manners,
and clothing set her apart from the other girls in the
school. To survive in this world, Sabina begins
adjusting to her environment, and in so doing, her
assimilation begins.

Helen Martin develops a parallel situation in the
novel through the character of Augustus Acker, a young
artist who has come to New Holland to learn about the
Amish and eventually use them as subjects for his work.
The sickly Augustus boards with the Wilt family, and in

the course of the narrative, he also undergoes a reverse transformation—his ill health gradually improves under the influence of the robust Amish life style. Both Sabina Wilt and Acker benefit from exposure to new attitudes and values; Sabina grows intellectually and socially while Augustus profits physically as well as artistically. Although Helen Martin is most critical of Amish isolationism, she also indicts the smugness of the outside world. She is particularly harsh on a Lutheran minister's jingoistic sermon in which "he foretold that the millenium was coming to the United States, whose boundaries would, before long, include both North and South America. 'This great land of ours will stand when Gabriel comes! Other nations are passing away, but our great nation will stay!'"[60] It is ironic that a Lutheran minister serving a first generation German immigrant church has so quickly assumed the political prejudices associated with the presidency of Theodore Roosevelt. This alliance between an immigrant denomination and national politics was not unique to Lutheranism, but rather it surfaces as a commonplace in American immigration history. This passage also provides a partial justification for the cultural and religious withdrawal of the Amish.

When Sabina Wilt returns to New Holland, her conversations with Augustus reveal another weakness of the Amish; as a child of the culture, she continues to be unresponsive to artistic expressions. The Pennsylvania Dutch are shown as incapable of even enjoying the beauty of their elaborate hex signs, since any aesthetic merit the signs possess is incidental to their religious function—warding off evil spirits. When Augustus asks Sabina if she would like to attempt a painting, she answers with the old certainty of her narrow upbringing:

193

> I couldn't waste my time. What good
> to a body is a picture of a thing?
> When you've got the trees and sky
> all around you, what's the use of
> wastin' time makin' pictures of 'em.
> It ain't worth while.[61]

Sabina's speech explains in part the dreariness of Amish
life, for it contains a rationalization for the
avoidance of all creative activity; art is nothing more
than the inadequate mirror of nature's glories. Sabina
speaks for the Amish culture when she reduces the
aesthetic faculty to a simple contemplation of nature,
and in such a view, the aesthetic faculty becomes an
adjunct to the religious sensibility. Unconsciously,
Sabina is echoing that Puritan aesthetic principle
articulated in the "Preface" to the first book published
in North America, *The Bay Psalm Book* (1640): "God's
altar need not our pollishings." While Sabina's
functional aesthetic has the historical imprimatur of
the New England founding fathers, she is nevertheless
expressing an anachronistic principle for twentieth
century America.

Toward the end of *Sabina*, Helen Martin gives an
indication of the occasionally bitter feelings which
surfaced between the Amish and their Pennsylvania
neighbors. Sabina's brother Aaron plans to marry a town
girl, Elephena Schwenkfelders, who has been raised a
Lutheran. Elephena's mother is opposed to her daughter's
marrying an Amish boy, because in her view, the Amish
are both dirty and stingy. Augustus Acker attempts to
mediate the conflict, and he chastises Mrs.
Schwenkfelders for her intolerance: "Is that the spirit
taught in the Lutheran Church? The Amish teach
something very different. They seem to believe in
charity and forgiveness toward those who despitefully
use them." Mrs. Schwenkfelders is not dissuaded,
informing Augustus that "as fur them Amish, if one of

them marries outside the church they get put off of meeting and disinherited by their pop."[62] Augustus abandons the role of mediator without bothering to answer Mrs. Schwenkfelders, whose intolerance is identical to that which Amish parents would feel. In many respects, Mrs. Schwenkfelder's intemperate outburst is the inevitable consequence of the suspicions engendered when a sect isolates itself from the assimilating norm.

As already noted, Helen Martin did not sentimentalize the Pennsylvania Dutch.[63] Reflecting upon some of the angry responses her stories of the Pennsylvania Dutch had earned her, Mrs. Martin observed that the members of the Amish communities did not make objections because they didn't read her stories or anyone's stories for that matter. The resentment came from

> . . . those who had sufficient brains and forcefulness to have worked themselves free of the stultifying conditions of their farm life into a broader, fuller existence; and some of these people, full of a loving sentiment for the home of their youth, for the quaint customs of their forebearers, and even for the religion which they have discarded, are wounded by my perfectly accurate pictures; the more accurate they are, the more they are hurt.[64]

The accusations against Helen Martin's portrayal of the Pennsylvania Dutch usually ignore the fact that she was an unabashed admirer of their moral character and fortitude. If they were dullards, she saw them as decent dullards who strove to lead the good life. As

Augustus Acker discovers in *Sabina,* the Amish life
provides a retreat into a more primitive tribal
consciousness, and acceptance of this communal identity
has many physical and emotional benefits. Helen Martin,
like William Dean Howells, could sympathize with the
naivete of the communal sects, while also recognizing
that such a life was not a realistic option for modern
man.

Sidney Luska: Protestant Perspective on Jewish Assimilation

The Jewish experience in America has been analyzed
in hundreds of twentieth-century novels. Abraham Cahan
charts the spiritual cost of Americanization for a
Russian-Jewish immigrant in *The Rise of David Levinsky*
(1917); Michael Gold describes the brutalization of the
Jew in the American ghetto in *Jews Without Money* (1930);
Saul Bellow analyzes the various stages of Jewish
alienation from *The Victim* (1947) to *Mr. Sammler's
Planet* (1970); Bernard Malamud, in *The Assistant* (1957),
portrays the misfortunes of an atheistic Jewish
shopkeeper who still is faithful to the Law; and more
recently, Joseph Heller has provided a comic treatment
of Jewish assimilation in *Good as Gold* (1979). Although
these Jewish novelists are distinctive in their separate
styles and treatments, they are all fundamentally
traditionalists who lament, in their own way, the
dissolution of the Jewish heritage through assimilation.
As Nathan Glazer has observed, the great threat to
Judaism in America has not been the pogrom but the
process of assimilation, since

> . . . it is inconceivable that
> Judaism could survive the
> disappearance of the Jewish people,

except as a subject for scholarly study. And so the assimilation of Jews--that is, the disappearance of Jews as an identifiable and distinct people--is a real threat to the Jewish religion.[65]

This theory is based on Glazer's assessment of Judaism not so much as a body of religious doctrine but as an enormous body of cultural values and practices. Traditionally, the Jew maintained his cultural identity in the European ghetto where Jewishness gave meaning to his isolation in a hostile society. For the Jew who attempts to preserve his Jewishness in a heterogeneous urban setting, there develops the great tensions which provide the basic motif for Jewish-American fiction.

The rich tradition of Jewish-American fiction begins, ironically, with a novel written by a white-Anglo-Saxon Protestant named Henry Harland who used the pseudonym of Sidney Luska and claimed to be a Jew. The novel, *The Yoke of the Thorah* (1887), has been neglected by literary historians, who tend to discount all of the novels Harland wrote under the name of Luska.[66] Harland is usually remembered as the editor of *Yellow Book* (1894-1897) and for his romance, *The Cardinal's Snuff-Box* (1900). His years as an interpreter of the German-Jewish immigrant experience are either ignored or subjected to the sort of criticism found in *American Authors 1600-1900*:

Sidney Luska's novels are hardly worth appraisal; they have a rough power and crude promise, but are primarily pot-boilers full of dated sensationalism. Henry Harland's fiction in his own name, the later

197

> work at least, is delicate and
> witty--if decadent--the work of a
> slighter, less subtle, and simpler
> James.[67]

Donald A. Roberts provides another unflattering evaluation of Luska's failings with his

> . . . sense of melodramatic plot,
> moderate skill in verisimilitude,
> and a consistent if not brilliant
> power of characterization. The
> style, florid in spots, is in
> general commonplace and reveals no
> trace of his later manner.[68]

Putting aside matters of style and execution, Luska's novels, especially *The Yoke of the Thorah*, command our attention because they attempt to understand the dilemmas facing a Jew in America. Leslie Fiedler in his monograph *The Jew in the American Novel* (1959), made the first serious attempt at understanding *The Yoke of the Thorah* and though he only deals perfunctorily with the novel, he did appreciate what Luska was attempting--an examination of the dual problems of identity and assimilation for the Jew in America. Fiedler suggests that a Protestant posing as a Jew had the ideal credentials to write such a novel: "The very concept of such a novel involves an attempt to blend two traditions, to contribute to the eventual grafting of whatever still lives in Judaism on to an ever-developing Americanism."[69]

Henry Harland, by assuming the Luska identity, acquired the freedom to candidly discuss the intense pressures facing the Jew in his adjustment to American life. Oppression in Europe had forced the Jew into the ghetto, and as long as there was an easily identifiable enemy, there was no problem reenforcing the idea of

Jewish identity--Christians reminded the Jew of his Jewishness every day of his life. *The Yoke of the Thorah* examines what happens to the American Jew who is not forced to remain in the ghetto. Luska carefully analyzes the tensions experienced by a man who is torn between loyalty to his heritage and a desire to realize his full potential as an American. Although the crisis of the Jew in America is similar to that of all immigrant groups whose religious and racial identity differed from that of the Protestant majority, the Jewish history of religious persecution intensified feelings of disloyalty for those Jews who drifted toward assimilation and the American mainstream.

The protagonist of the novel is Elias Bacharach, a second-generation Jew, who is a skilled portrait painter. Although he continues to live with his religiously orthodox uncle, The Reverend Dr. Felix Gedaza, Rabbi to the Congregation Gates of Pearl, Elias' profession brings him into daily contact with many Gentiles whose life style is attractive to him. In the course of his work, Elias meets a wealthy Protestant businessman, Matthew Redwood, who commissions him to do some family portraits. Redwood, who functions as a representative of the American culture, is defined by the three paintings which hang in his house: the Last Supper, the Signing of the Declaration of Independence, and the Landing of the Pilgrims. He is a Christian, a democrat, and a man whose racial identity is bound up with the English settlement of America; he is the embodiment of the American identity which is absorbing Elias Bacharach. Redwood also has a beautiful daughter Christine whose name has symbolic connotations to the novel's theme. Although Elias has been raised to believe that no Jewish man may marry a Christian without violating the Law, he nevertheless falls in love with Christine.[70]

When Elias announces his plans to marry Christine, Uncle Felix assumes the responsibility for preventing such a marriage from ever taking place. To legitimize his opposition, he reads Elias a sermon that his great-grandfather, Rabbi Abraham Bacharach, had delivered when a young man in his congregation married a French-Catholic girl. The sermon's tone is caught in the following passage:

> For the blood of Israel mixed with
> the blood of a strange people, is
> like sweet wine mixed with aloes.
> His sons shall be weak of mind and
> body. His daughters shall be ugly
> to look upon. To him and to his
> Lord our God will show no mercy,
> even unto the brink of the grave.
> They shall be as if touched with the
> leprosy, shunned and despised of all
> men. To the Goy they will continue
> to be Jews; but to the Jew they will
> become Goym.[71]

In this passage, the implication of the novel's title is made clear--"Thorah" literally means the body of Jewish literature and tradition as a whole, containing the laws, teachings, and divine knowledge of the religion. Uncle Felix's inflexibility on the subject of mixed marriages is based on a historical sensitivity to the consequences of such marriages. Rabbi Abraham Bacharach's sermon against such marriages is drawn from the wisdom of the race, but it cannot take into account the possibility of a social fabric substantially different from the European one. It is Elias' sense of the possible that inspires him to ignore his uncle's protestations, although he himself is unaware of how strongly he is emotionally yoked to the tradition from which he has made an intellectual break.

The conflict of assimilation is so carefully structured into the narrative of *The Yoke of the Thorah* that the novel borders on allegory. Elias, the alien Jew in a Christian culture, will enter the American mainstream if he marries Christine Redwood; of necessity, he will leave Uncle Felix and his preoccupation with Jewish identity. Luska punctuates many key moments in the narrative with the tolling of the bells of St. George's Church on Stuyvesant Square to remind Elias and the reader of the omnipresent Christian culture. In his attempts to break the bonds of his Jewish heritage, Elias has little to sustain him beyond his love for Christine. Luska makes the following observation on the powers of love:

> What has become of his Judaism? his race-pride? his superstition? Love, apparently, had swept them clean away. Not a vestige of them remained. At a touch, it seemed, love had converted Elias Bacharach from the most reactionary sort of orthodoxy, to a rationalism, the bare contemplation of which, a few days ago, would have appalled him.[72]

There is little of the rational in Elias' evolution and perhaps with a sense of irony, Luska concludes the passage: "The man had got the better of the Jew." Elias' apparent rejection of the intellectual tradition which shaped him strikes the reader as abrupt and emotionally impossible, and this is precisely Sidney Luska's intention. Uncle Felix is always reminding Elias that he simply cannot reject his Jewishness because he *is* that Jewishness, and a rejection of his Jewish heritage is a rejection of self. As Uncle Felix perceives it, Elias is committing an act of self-hatred in the name of his love for Christine.

The tensions which beset Elias are greater than he initially realized, and he eventually collapses under the stress and falls into a coma. When he begins to recover, the omnipresent and relentless Uncle Felix renders a religious diagnosis of the illness:

> . . . the Lord has been your guide
> from the beginning. You were
> becoming indifferent . . . to your
> religion. You had not zeal enough.
> You dwelt in a Christian community;
> and the Christian atmosphere was
> infecting you, was corrupting you
> . . . . The Lord saw it. He wished
> to call you back . . . . He allowed
> you to harden yourself to the
> thought of committing the extreme
> sin—to the thought of marrying her.
> Then at the last moment, He
> manifested Himself. He rescued you
> from your danger.[73]

Felix's campaign is successful; Elias weakened by sickness, surrenders himself to tradition in his feeble utterance, "I shall always be a good Jew after this."

Having made his decision to be a "good Jew," Elias has misgivings about the abruptness of his decision and its possible ill effects on Christine. He decides to see her in order to explain his change of heart, but Uncle Felix fears that if the couple meet again his work will be destroyed. He spews up all the bitterness of centuries of persecution:

> . . . the Lord will not allow you to
> feel for her. You have suffered
> enough. Her turn has come now. If
> you have no sympathy for her, it is
> because she is entitled to none.

202

> The Lord desires that she shall
> receive none. She is a Christian, a
> Goy, despised and abominated by the
> Lord. She has served her purpose.
> Now she must serve her punishment.[74]

Felix's ranting seems to convey the impression that Judaism is narrow and destructive—Christine is viewed not as a person but as a symbol of the enemy. The passage seems to have an anti-Semitic bias of its own, but Luska balances Uncle Felix's intemperance toward Christians with the revelation of Matthew Redwood's latent anti-Semitism. Redwood berates Elias for the callous manner in which his engagement to Christine was terminated: "But, but God . . . if it does kill her, I--I'd rather have it, by God! than have her married to you, now that I know what you are, you damn, miserable, white-livered Jew!"[75] Felix Gedaza and Matthew Redwood are the traditional voices of Jewish and Christian prejudices, playing off each other's hatred and renewing it in the process. By reaffirming the distrusts and hatreds, they renew in the lives of Elias and Christine all that is destructive in the historical relationship of Jews and Christians.

Elias, recovered from his illness, is introduced to "a nice Jewish girl" named Tillie, and their romance is nurtured and supported by Felix and other members of the Jewish community. They marry and Elias completely recovers his health. He begins to read widely and to develop new interests that are independent of Jewish community life, and it becomes apparent to him in this process of self-education that he made a terrible mistake in allowing Felix to interfere in his life. He looks back on the break-up with Christine and the marriage to Tillie as acts performed in a half-sleep. He regards Felix's religious interpretation of his illness as a "blasphemous lie," and he speculates further:

My superstition was the dragon,
whose breath poisoned our joy,
withered our world, burned out our
hearts. The dragon was killed at
last, but too late--after its
ravages had been accomplished, after
it had done its worst.[76]

Elias is the victim of an alienation much larger than
the cultural alienation of an Uncle Felix. He can no
longer draw comfort from the faith of the ghetto, and
his love for Christine can never be realized. He
wanders through New York City seeking glimpses of her,
floating toward total ennui. The novel concludes with
Elias' death in the deserted precincts of Central Park,
with the distant church bell ringing. Although the
Thorah yoked him, it could not sustain him. Elias
Bacharach is the first Jewish protagonist in American
literature to face the hydra of assimilation and be
destroyed.

Abraham Cahan: The Tragedy of Assimilation

In writing *The Rise of David Levinsky* (1917),
Abraham Cahan gave an excellent analysis of the
conflicts experienced by the Jewish immigrant to
American, and Cahan, unlike Luska, was writing from the
viewpoint of the Jew. Cahan's characters are not yoked
to tradition--they long to pass for Americans--and the
old ways of the European ghetto are abandoned in one
generation because, as Cahan observes, the immigrant has
made an act of faith in America. In *American Judaism*,
Nathan Glazer notes that the case of David Levinsky
illustrates:

. . . the crucial point that Judaism
in eastern Europe, as in Germany,
tended to ignore everything that
might be considered theology. Only
the practices of Judaism were
taught. One was brought up to
observe the commandments, and, for
this reason, as soon as one came in
touch with a kind of thought which
questioned fundamentals, one was at
a loss. In other words, it may be
said that Jews lost their faith so
easily because they had no faith to
lose: that is, they had no
doctrine, no collection of dogmas to
which they could cling and with
which they could resist argument.
All they had, surrounding them like
an armor, was a complete set of
practices, each presumably as holy
as the next.[77]

As a rabbinical student in Russia, David Levinsky's
Jewish identity was accentuated for him by his isolation
from Russian life. In America he faces the choice of
whether to remain in the ghetto or take his chances in
the dominant business culture. By Glazer's standards,
assimilation will be facilitated by the fact that he is
unencumbered by dogmatic beliefs.

At the beginning of the novel, David Levinsky
informs Reb Sender that he is planning to leave Russia
and emigrate to America. Reb's immediate response is
one of concern for David's Jewishness, and through the
character Sender, Cahan states the major theme of the
novel: "To America! Lord of the World! But one
becomes a Gentile there."[78] In contrast to Reb Sender,
David's sweetheart, Matilda, expresses great enthusiasm
for his emigration. That he might lose his religion

seems to Matilda a step in the right direction: "A penny for your piety . . . . When you are in America you'll dress like a Gentile and even shave. Then you won't look so ridiculous. Good clothes would make another man of you."[79] This scene is prophetic, for "good clothes" do change David into another man. Matilda and Reb Sender represent opposing tensions in David's personality throughout the narrative, and it is David's inability to reconcile the forces of tradition with his insatiable drive for success that provides the central drama of the novel.

David's initial response to America is the cliche of disappointments when he discovers that the streets are not paved with gold. Threatened by his new surroundings, he retreats into his religion for comfort and security, but he soon learns that his religious erudition is not marketable and is useless to his quest for financial success. He also perceives that his adherence to religious law will have to be modified if he is to compete with the Gentiles who do not spend their weekdays in prayer and worship. When his efforts seem unavailing, he seeks relief in his religion:

> I spent many an evening at the
> Antomir Synagogue, reading Talmud
> passionately . . . . It was the
> only pleasure I had in those days
> . . . . My former self was
> addressing me across the sea in this
> strange, uninviting, big town where
> I was compelled to peddle shoe-black
> or oil-cloth and to compete with a
> yelling idiot.[80]

David's initial reliance on his religion is part of the historical pattern observed earlier in this study; whether a frontier is rural or urban, the first generation in a new and hostile environment finds security in religious belief. What is so unusual with David Levinsky's experience is the speed of his assimilation into the mainstream of American life. He either had to adjust to the tempo of a highly competitive society or be forced to relinquish his dream of success. In opting for success, David deludes himself into thinking that he is putting aside his Jewishness only temporarily and that sometime in the future, when his position is secure, he will return to the faith of his fathers.

The long-range effect of the Americanization of the Jewish immigrant is a weakening, if not total disintegration, of his affiliation with the traditions of Judaism. At one point in the novel, David speculates that the fault lies in the uncompromising character of orthodox Judaism:

> It does not attempt to adapt itself to modern conditions as the Christian Church is continually doing. If you are a Jew of the type to which I belonged when I came to New York and you attempt to bend your religion to the spirit of your new surroundings, it breaks. It falls to pieces. The very clothes I wore and the very food I ate had a fatal effect on my religious habits. A whole book could be written on the influence of a starched collar and a necktie on a man who was brought up as I was.[81]

His link with the laws of orthodox Judaism breaks down in the course of his assimilation, but even as he is drawn into the worship of Mammon, David Levinsky never loses the moral sensibility formed while a rabbinical student. Although he becomes a frequenter of prostitutes, he views their deceits as mocking reflections of his own deceit.

> Many of these women would simulate love, but they failed to deceive me. I knew that they lied and shammed to me just as I did to my customers, and their insincerities were only another source of repugnance to me.[82]

His resentment of the prostitutes is a rejection of his new, capitalist self; his early Talmudic training provides him with a perspective on the personal debasement springing from his own pursuit of profits. His mind is no longer an instrument for learning—he has leased it for profit in much the same way that the prostitutes lease their bodies. What he has yet to learn is that such pursuits will permanently alter his humanity.

A chance meeting with a fellow immigrant gives David the opportunity for a business venture in the garment district, and he foolishly believes that this business will release him from financial cares and permit him to study at the City College of New York. He hopes that a college education will fill the cultural void in his life:

> My old religion had gradually fallen to pieces . . . if there was something that appealed to the better man in me, to what was purest in my thoughts and most sacred in my emotions, that something was the red, church-like structure on the southeast corner of Lexington Avenue and Twenty-third Street [City

> College of New York]. It was the
> synagogue of my life . . . the
> building really appealed to me as a
> temple, as a house of Sanctity, as
> we call the ancient Temple of
> Jerusalem.[83]

David's commitment to the "religion" of education
proves to be as transitory as his commitment to Judaism,
and he abandons it for the same reason that he abandoned
his orthodoxy—it distracts him from the business of
business. With the almost total sublimation of the
religious and emotional aspects of his personality,
David evolves into an archetypal businessman of the
period. Cahan is being ironic when he has David, the
former student of the Talmud, express his desire to pass
for an American:

> I was forever watching and striving
> to imitate the dress and ways of the
> well-bred American merchants with
> whom I was, or trying to be, thrown.
> All this, I felt, was an essential
> element in achieving business
> success; but the ambition to act and
> look like a gentleman grew in me
> quite apart from these motives.[84]

Levinsky's concern with appearance is symptomatic of his
assault on his own historical identity. He is
reconstructing himself into the mirror image of the
dominant culture. His urgency in achieving this
assimilation is the antithesis of the isolating
stratagem of Orthodox Judaism.

Not only does David drift away from the values of
religious and humanistic traditions, but he comes to
violate both traditions. In his reading of *Social
Studies, Origin of Species,* and *Descent of Man,* he

develops an intellectual rationalization for his own behavior. From these books he extrapolates a "survival thesis" to legitimize his own ruthless business tactics. David observes that:

> Apart from the purely intellectual intoxication they gave me, they flattered my vanity as one of the 'fittest.' It was as though all the wonders of learning, acumen, ingenuity, and assiduity displayed in these works had been intended, among other purposes, to establish my title as one of the victors of Existence. A workingman, and everyone else who was poor, was an object of contempt to me—a misfit, a weakling, a failure, one of the ruck.[85]

His contempt for his fellow man extends to his personal life; he abuses Max, his friend and benefactor, by having an affair with Max's wife. After achieving financial success, David feels even more acutely the need for the accessories and manners of success.[86] He is constantly repressing any remnants of his Jewishness, as when he admonishes himself: "Speak in a calm low voice, as these Americans do. And for goodness' sake don't gesticulate!" In suppressing the volatile style which is natural to him, David seeks anonymity so that he will not be spotted as a foreigner in the cool chambers of the Protestant business culture.

With the passage of time, David Levinsky becomes the sole owner of a lucrative garment business. Success has mellowed his aggressive instincts, and he now has the leisure to reflect on life. He recognizes that he cannot return to the orthodox *Weltanschauung* of his childhood in the Russian village of Antomir because

"Spencer's Unknowable had irrevocably replaced my God. Yet religion now appealed to me as an indispensable instrument in the great orchestra of things." David's subsequent analysis of religion recalls Mr. Dudley in *Esther*:

> I felt that most [wealthy people] looked upon churches or synagogues as they did upon police courts; that they valued them primarily as safeguards of law and order and correctness, and this has become my attitude.[87]

But David now seeks a substitute for his truncated spiritual and emotional life. He wants to revive those human affections which he had so successfully sublimated in his pursuit of money, and as he tells us, "dreams of family life became my religion. Self-sacrificing devotion to one's family was the only kind of altruism and idealism I did not flout."[88] In making this single affirmation, he is preparing himself for bitter disappointment because the one person he wants to marry, Anna Tevkin, rejects his proposal and crushes his hopes of recapturing his lost humanity.

By the novel's conclusion, David Levinsky has become painfully aware of the full price he has paid for success. The people whom he meets out of his own impoverished past see him only as a potential benefactor, and the irony of his situation is that the wealth which he so assiduously pursued now prevents him from having normal human relationships. His reflections in the closing paragraph capture the tragic dimension of his rise:

> I can never forget the days of my misery. I cannot escape from my old self. My past and present do not

211

> comport well, David, the poor lad
> swinging over a Talmud volume at the
> Preacher's Synagogue, seems to have
> more in common with my inner
> identity than David Levinsky, the
> well-known cloak manufacturer.[89]

This awareness of what he has done to himself is the price David Levinsky will have to pay for the remainder of his lonely life.

These two novels of Jewish experience, *The Yoke of the Thorah* and *The Rise of David Levinsky*, deal exclusively with the cultural shock confronting Jews entering a predominantly Protestant American society. Luska's Elias Bacharach is destroyed because he does not fulfill his instinctive drive for assimilation and accommodation; Cahan's David Levinsky is destroyed by his rapid assimilation into the materialistic values of the American business culture. Luska, as a member of the dominant class, writes of the cultural conflict from the perspective of his own background, and in spite of his Jewish persona, it is Henry Harland who makes Uncle Felix the instrument of his nephew's destruction. The voice of orthodoxy is a slightly mad one in *The Yoke of the Thorah*, and Elias Bacharach is in the end victimized by his allegiance to the taboos of that orthodoxy. In contrast, Abraham Cahan writes from the perspective of a Jew viewing the same cultural encounter, but he focuses on the process of assimilation. Cahan asks the pertinent question: what is the price of becoming an American? In *The Rise of David Levinsky* the price is David's identity as a Jew, and Abraham Cahan clearly thinks this price is too high.

There was no Abraham Cahan to render an informed and sympathetic portrait of the tensions experienced by the Catholic immigrant in Protestant America. Although there were American Catholics writing fiction, the bulk of their work was apologetic in character and absurdly sentimental in tone. The first American Catholic novel, *Father Rowland* (1824), was representative of the Catholic novels which followed in that it was a rebuttal of an earlier anti-Catholic novel titled *Father Clement*. After this inauspicious beginning, there came a series of equally undistinguished works--Boyce's *Shandy McGuire*, Bryant's *Pauline Seward*, Sadlier's *Bessie Conway*, Miles' *The Governess*, and Sarah Bronson's *At Anchor*. In their *Survey of Catholic Literature*, Brown and McDermott underscore the poor quality of these novels and comment: "these novelists have a place in American Catholic literature only for historical reasons. Their novels and short stories lack almost all the marks of good fiction save proper intention."[90] Considering the cultural and economic background of the Catholic immigrants entering America in the second half of the nineteenth century, there is nothing surprising in their failure to produce a significant literature. In addition to social and economic factors, there were other reasons for this failure. When Catholics like Boyce, Sadlier, and Bronson wrote religious fiction there was a total lack of objectivity and critical distance. The critic John Pick has listed the following deficiencies:

> First, a failure to deal with Catholic life on anything but the most superficial level. Second, the failure sufficiently to realize that the novel is an art form and that it cannot be overloaded with an

obtrusive thesis; the result is that
the product is a polemic not a
novel. Third, an emasculation, a
false prudence, and a Puritanism
which has even been called
Jansenistic. All three defects are
regrettable, though understandable
in terms of the cultural history of
Catholicism long on the defensive in
America.[91]

The above limitations assigned to nineteenth-century
Catholic writers could apply to most fiction being
written in America, but there were no first-rate
Catholic writers to offset the unfortunate failings
itemized by Pick.

The literary image of Catholicism in nineteenth-
century American fiction was largely based on portraits
drawn by Protestant novelists, including a number of
hysterical Nativists. Describing the literary aspects
of the Anti-Catholic Crusade, Merle Curti wrote:

Alarmed, the theologian Lyman
Beecher turned out a *Plea for the
West* in 1835. Pointing to Catholic
activity on the frontier, Beecher
called for Protestant effort.
Catholicism, he said, was
undemocratic, un-American, monar-
chial, aristocratic. Catholicism
was led by alien priests, Beecher
continued; its head was the Pope of
Rome, and it put allegiance to the
Holy See above loyalty to country.
Even stronger views were expressed
in that same year in *The Imminent
Dangers to the Free Institutions of
the United States Through Foreign*

Immigration, by Samuel F.B. Morse,
who later invented the telegraph.
Morse insisted that Jesuits were
plotting to undermine American
liberties, and that immigration, the
source of Catholic strength, must be
checked. Rebecca Reed's *Six Months
in a Convent*, also published in
1835, purported to 'tell the truth'
about conditions inside the Ursuline
convent school which a Boston mob
had burned the year before. More
sensational volumes followed. Even
when the most notorious, Maria
Monk's *Awful Disclosures*, was proved
a dishonest hoax, the credulous
continued to insist on the truth of
the indictments.[92]

Twenty years after Reed's *Six Months in a Convent*, Helen
Dhu (pseud. for Helen Black) wrote an anti-Catholic,
anti-Jesuit diatribe in the form of a novel titled
Stanhope Burleigh (1855). The bigoted tone of the novel
is anticipated in the Preface, where Dhu asserts that:

> Nothing is more certain than that
> *Jesuitism must be foiled, and
> suppressed in this country, or the
> Institutions of the country must go
> down.* They cannot both continue to
> exist in their strength and vigor.
> One or the other must give way.
> There is an eternal hostility in
> their very nature, between the
> principles of Washington and the
> principles of Loyola--between the

spirit of the Generals of the
Company of Jesus, and the spirit of
the Fathers of our Republic.[93]

Throughout *Stanhope Burleigh*, Jesuitism functions as a
metaphor for Roman Catholicism, and both are seen as
incompatible with American institutions.

Having cited some of the more notorious anti-
Catholic literary works, it should be noted that serious
Protestant novelists of the period did not share the
anti-Catholic fears expressed in Nativist literature,
even though one can find unflattering portraits of
Catholic individuals in Brown's *Wieland* and Cooper's *The
Prairie*. In a different vein, Arlo Bates concluded *The
Puritans* with the observation that New England tradition
was in perfect harmony with Roman Catholicism, and that
for the troubled Protestant conscience at the end of
the nineteenth century, there were only two logical
alternatives: abandon religion entirely and adopt a
secular morality, or surrender to the authority of the
Roman Church. The notion that Puritan backgrounds make
an excellent preparation for Roman Catholicism is a
questionable thesis, but there is little doubt that the
moral preoccupations of Puritanism shared certain
similarities with the doctrinal rigidity of the
immigrant Catholic church presided over by an Irish
Catholic hierarchy.

A major difference between the Puritan and
Catholic sensibilities can be traced to the antithetical
attitudes regarding the function of the senses in
religious experience. Catholicism has traditionally
incorporated art and ritual for inspirational purposes,
while the intellectually-oriented Puritan temperament
was suspicious of the seductive powers of the merely
decorative. This culture conflict provides a
subordinate motif for James' *The American* (1877) and
Hawthorne's *The Marble Faun* (1860). In the climax of

216

The American, the aristocratic, Catholic, and tradition-bound Bellegarde family reject the democratic, individualistic Christopher Newman as a future in-law, and Madame de Cintre, the object of Newman's suit, resolves her situation by quietly retiring to a convent. Newman has great difficulty comprehending such behavior; his Protestant temperament simply cannot understand this willing submission of one's entire personality to an external authority. When he goes to the Carmelite convent to listen to the singing of the nuns in hope of seeing Madame de Cintre, he takes personal offense at the ceremony he witnesses: "The priests long, dismal intonings acted upon his nerves and deepened his wrath; there was something defiant in his unintelligible drawl; it seemed meant for Newman himself."[94] Newman's perception of the Latin ceremony as a personal rebuff is symbolically accurate. What he is witnessing *is* "unintelligible" to him, as a good deal of his encounter with European culture has been; he is now paying the price for his ignorance. To punctuate Newman's ineffectuality the traditional Latin service proceeds without taking notice of his presence.

> Suddenly there arose from the depths of the chapel, from behind the inexorable grating, a sound which drew his attention from the altar--the sound of a strange, lugubrious chant uttered by women's voices. It began softly, but it presently grew louder, and as it increased it became more of a wail and a dirge. It was the chant of the Carmelite nuns, their only human utterance. It was their dirge over their buried affections and over the vanity of earthly desires.[95]

In this passage James reveals his own rejection of the Catholic culture by his characterization of the nuns' singing as a "dirge over their buried affections." It seemed like a dirge to Newman not only because the disembodied voices ignore his presence, but because the music transcends the very age in which he lives. He senses his impotence for the first time.

> The chant kept on, mechanical and monotonous, with dismal repetitious and despairing cadences. It was hideous and horrible . . . . He rose and abruptly made his way out. On the threshold he paused, listened again to the dreary strain, and then hastily descended into the court.[96]

Withdrawal into the contemplative life is, for Newman, an incomprehensible course of action. Early in his life in the Western Territories of the United States, he had sublimated his entire personality into the Protestant work ethic and was so successful in this transference of all his energies that he could not imagine an alternative behavior. Although Newman is clearly the moral superior of the Bellegardes, he never understands how European traditions in general, and the Roman Church in particular, have contributed to his defeat; his reaction to Madame de Cintre's decision to become a nun results not in illumination but rather a bewildered withdrawal.

Rome is the setting for *The Marble Faun*; Hawthorne admired the fusion of pagan and Christian traditions in the Roman life style, but as a New Englander he was cautious about the dangers lurking in sensual experience. As Henry James observed:

> The plastic sense was not strong in
> Hawthorne; there can be no better
> proof of it than his curious
> aversion to the representation of
> the nude in sculpture. This
> aversion was deepseated; he
> constantly returns to it, exclaiming
> upon the incongruity of modern
> artists making naked figures . . .
> his jealousy of undressed images
> strikes the reader as a strange,
> vague, long-dormant heritage of his
> straight-laced Puritan heritage.[97]

This suspicion of the amoral-sensual experience is one
of the major themes in *The Marble Faun*. As much as
Hawthorne disapproved of the intoxicating sensuality
symbolized by Donatello, he recognized it as an
inevitable by-product of the corrupt social milieu of
Rome. The tension between Hawthorne's moral and sensual
faculties surfaces repeatedly in the novel:

> In a word, the Pincian garden is one
> of the things that reconcile the
> stranger (since he fully appreciates
> the enjoyment, and feels nothing of
> the cost) to the rule of an
> irresponsible dynasty of Holy
> Fathers, who seemed to have aimed at
> making life as agreeable an affair
> as it can well be.[98]

Hawthorne's parenthetical remark about the human cost of
the Pincian garden is his way of reminding himself and
the reader that his moral faculties have not been
totally coopted by the Roman Church. To his Puritan
sensibility, it is incomprehensible that human
sensuality could be incorporated into a complementary
relationship with a religious vision.

Hilda, the blonde and virginal New England innocent, functions throughout the novel as Hawthorne's moral norm. During a discourse in which she gives her reasons for disapproving of nudity in art, Hilda provides a good example of what Henry James thought to be the key to Hawthorne's aesthetics.

> An artist . . . as you must candidly confess, cannot sculpture nudity with a pure heart, if only because he is compelled to steal guilty glimpses at hired models. The marble inevitably loses its chastity under such circumstances.[99]

She concludes that she would prefer "as many heaps of quicklime" to any nude statue. Such absolutism is the product of an innocent and untested moral faculty. After Hilda sees Donatello killing Miriam's mysterious assailant, she discovers that experience alters one's capacity to make judgments—she does not wish to bear witness against her friends, and as a result, she becomes an accessory to the murder.

The murder radically changes Donatello from an amoral and sensual Italian nobleman into a brooding, introspective man who is haunted by his own actions. Donatello achieves stature through the awakening of his conscience, because for Hawthorne the *felix culpa* is the beginning of one's humanity. Likewise, Hilda's moral absolutism is tempered by her exposure to the complexity of human behavior. Her sense of guilt, born of the irreconcilable tensions between her sense of duty and her sense of friendship, is expiated when she goes to confession in Saint Peter's. As Hugo McPherson observes in *Hawthorne as Myth-Maker*:

> . . . if the Roman church, so to
> speak, 'keeps the devil alive'--
> keeps reminding man of his fallen
> nature--it also, unlike the Puritan
> faith, offers him a means of working
> out his salvation. Donatello and
> Miriam must suffer sorely for their
> humanity, but in the end they will
> receive the blessing of a benign
> Father, symbolized by the statue of
> Pope Julius.[100]

Any doubts concerning Hawthorne's attitude toward
Catholicism are clarified in the following passage from
The Marble Faun, in which Hawthorne reminds the reader
that the Roman Church

> . . . supplies a multitude of
> external forms, in which the
> spiritual may be clothed and
> manifested; it has many painted
> windows, as it were, through which
> the celestial sunshine, else
> disregarded, may make itself
> gloriously perceptible in visions of
> beauty and splendor.[101]

Hawthorne admired Catholicism for acknowledging man's
imperfections, and for providing *institutional* means of
working toward one's salvation--the expiation of guilt
through the confessional and the practice of good
works--but, as McPherson has observed, Hawthorne
essentially perceived "Roman Catholicism as a *European*
pattern, the product of centuries of human weakness and
need. Hilda can find solace and safety in this
communion, but she cannot join it."[102]

Despite its institutional excellence, Hawthorne
notes in an aside to the reader that the Roman Church is

flawed by the clergy who preside over it. He uses the image of machinery to describe these feelings about Catholicism, which

> . . . is such a miracle of fitness for its own ends, many of which might seem to be admirable ones, that it is difficult to imagine it a contrivance of mere men . . . . If there were but angels to work it, instead of the very different class of engineers who now manage its cranks and safety valves, the system would soon vindicate the dignity and holiness of its origin.[103]

Hawthorne's own attraction to Roman Catholicism was based upon both its healing theology which acknowledged mankind's sinful nature and the aesthetic dimension which allowed for the human celebration of the Divine, but the price demanded of "this system" was too high for Hawthorne's Protestant temperament.

Three decades later, in *A Mortal Antipathy*, Oliver Wendell Holmes echoed Hawthorne's evaluation of Roman Catholicism. Holmes juxtaposed a neurotic New Englander, Maurice Kirkwood, with his Italian servant Paul, whose physical and psychic health make him the antithesis of his master. Paul's well-being is purportedly a natural by-product of the twin influences of the Italian climate and the Roman Catholic Church.[104] It is Holmes' thesis that Kirkwood's neuresthenia is partly traceable to the failure of Protestantism to provide sufficient therapeutic outlets for personality disorders. As one character in the novel observes: "What a pity that Protestantism does not make special provision for all the freaks of individual character!"[105]

222

Maurice Kirkwood is afraid of people in general, and women in particular, because of a childhood accident in which he was severely lacerated when a seventeen-year old female cousin dropped him into a thorn bush. The traumatic reason for Maurice's antipathy to women is unknown to him, because he has successfully repressed the memory of the event, but he shudders uncontrollably when in the immediate vicinity of young women. As a result of this disorder, he lives a life of rural isolation with a faithful servant. The isolation from society diffuses Maurice's nervous attacks but leaves him terribly lonely, and it is his growing loneliness which leads him to consider, very briefly, one of the Catholic contemplative orders. He is still, however, enough of a Protestant to be unwilling to submit individual conscience to the authority of the papacy. Maurice Kirkwood, in his initial attraction to, and final repudiation of Roman Catholicism, repeats the theme sounded in *The Marble Faun* when he observes:

> . . . accustomed as I had become to the forms of the Roman Church, and impressed as I was with the purity and excellence of many of its young members with whom I was acquainted, my early training rendered it impossible for me to accept the credentials which it offered to me as authoritative.[106]

Maurice's psychic equilibrium is finally restored when he is rescued from a burning building by the beautiful and Amazon-like Euthymia. Rather than attempting to treat the symptoms of his sickness through conversion to Roman Catholicism, Maurice is cured through Euthymia's bravery.

The image of Catholicism in Frederic's *The Damnation of Theron Ware* is a more complicated affair.

Frederic uses the character of Father Forbes, the Catholic pastor of Octavius, to prophesy the future interaction of an expanding Catholic church with existing American institutions. Forbes, an extraordinary priest whose religious convictions are tempered by his acceptance of scientific skepticism and new biblical criticism, introduces Theron Ware to the question of Abraham's historical authenticity and raises doubts in Ware's mind as to the historicity of both the Old and the New Testaments. Forbes also predicts the ascendency of Irish-Catholicism in America because the Irish immigrants here are becoming lager-drinkers, and will therefore escape the historical yoke of addiction to whiskey. Once freed of this burden they will, according to Forbes, exemplify a new type of humanity:

> . . . the Kelt at his best. He will
> dominate America. He will be the
> American. And his church--with the
> Italian element thrown clean out of
> it, and its Pope living, say, in
> Baltimore or Georgetown--will be the
> Church of America.[107]

In describing an American Catholic Church dominated by the Irish, Frederic is not describing the Roman Church which Holmes and Hawthorne so admired for its skillful handling of complex human needs. In fact, this "new Kelt" is just the old Puritan in disguise, with the old energy to work for the glory of money, the rigid moral posture, and a suspicion and impatience with aesthetics.

The Irish immigrants to America were much closer to the American Protestant tradition than to the mainstream of European Catholicism. When Austin Briggs, Jr., suggests, in his fine study *The Novels of Harold Frederic*, that the conversation at the picnic between Forbes and Ware is just a joke on the priest's part, he credits Forbes with a lightness that is not justified by his subsequent shoddy treatment of Ware.[108] While the tone of their conversation is jocular, it has a deadly-serious and sectarian edge to it. There is a note of triumph in Forbes' dealings with Theron Ware, and as he looks out at the multitude of loyal parishioners, he can't resist a prophesy:

> In the end, it [Roman Catholicism] will embrace them all, and be modified by them, and in turn influence their development, till you have a new nation and a new national church, each representative of the other.[109]

In the novel, Frederic's emphasis upon Catholicism's apparent immutability provides a vivid contrast to the rapidly disintegrating fundamentalism of Theron Ware, and it implicitly raises fears--Forbes' prediction being a distillation of Nativist nightmares--regarding the future of American institutions.

Mark Twain: Fear of Catholic Authoritarianism

One of the most devastating attacks on Roman Catholicism in American fiction is found in Twain's *A Connecticut Yankee in King Arthur's Court* (1889). Twain had grown up on anti-Catholic literature such as Samuel F. B. Morse's *Foreign Conspiracy*, and he openly admitted in *Innocents Abroad* that his early exposure to Nativist propaganda continued to color his attitude toward the Roman Church: "I have been educated to enmity toward everything that is Catholic, in consequence of this, I find it much easier to discover Catholic faults than

Catholic merits."[110] In *A Connecticut Yankee*, Twain's observations on the sixth-century Roman Church are thinly veiled criticisms of Roman Catholicism as a continuing enemy of mankind. Part of this hostility can be traced to his early Nativist upbringing, but Twain was also fearful of all well-organized religions, as he demonstrated in his later attacks on Christian Science. When Henry Morgan, in *A Connecticut Yankee*, blames the Roman Church for the appalling stupidity of the poor people in Arthurian England, the nineteenth-century reader could draw his own conclusions regarding the Church's responsibility for the abysmal status of the Catholic immigrants arriving in America. Morgan describes the deleterious effects of Catholicism's power:

> In two or three centuries it had converted a nation of men to a nation of worms. Before the day of the Church's supremacy in the world, men were men . . . . But then the Church came to the front, with an ax to grind . . . she invented 'divine right of things,' and propped it all around, brick by brick, with the Beatitudes . . . and she introduced heritable ranks and aristocracies, and taught all the Christian populations of the earth to bow down to them and worship them. Even down to my birth-century that poison was still in the blood of Christendom.[111]

Morgan's implications are clear. If it took the church two or three centuries to subdue the Anglo-Saxons, how long would it take this abhorrent institution to undermine the even more delicate balance of a new democratic society?

For Twain the great danger of Roman Catholicism was not in any of its doctrinal or religious values but in its authoritarian structure, which was the real threat to democracy. As Henry Morgan states the case: "It being my conviction that any Established Church is an established crime, an established slave-pen, I had no scruples, but was willing to assail it in any way or with any weapon that promised to hurt it."[112] This speech justifying any means of attack on the Roman Church may also be read as Twain's rationalization for his own attacks on Catholicism in *A Connecticut Yankee*. The alternative to an established church is the proliferation of religious sects, for as Morgan tells us:

> We must have a religion—it goes
> without saying—but my idea is, to
> have it cut up into forty free
> sects, so that they will police each
> other, as had been the case in the
> United States in my time.
> Concentration of power in a
> political machine is bad; and an
> Established Church is only a
> political machine; it was invented
> for that; it is an enemy to human
> liberty, and does no good which it
> could not better do in a split-up
> and scattered condition. That
> wasn't law; it wasn't gospel: it
> was only an opinion—my opinion, and
> I was only a man, one man: so it
> wasn't worth any more than the
> pope's—or any less, for that
> matter.[113]

Twain is satirizing the hypocrisies of his own age
through the convention of historical burlesque. When he
mocks the relationship between the aristocracy and the
Church, he sounds Marxian. The tone is clearly sardonic
when Morgan observes:

> I will say this much for the
> nobility: that, tyrannical,
> murderous, rapacious, and morally
> rotten as they were, they were
> deeply and enthusiastically
> religious. Nothing could divert
> them from regular and faithful
> performance of the pieties enjoined
> by the Church.[114]

We are reminded once again that Mr. Dudley in *Esther*
and, later, David Levinsky also realized that the
pragmatism of the ruling classes dictated their
formalistic ties to an established church as an
efficient way of maintaining stability and order. A
distinction must be made, however, between Twain's
hostility to religious institutions and his enthusiasm
for Christianity, because this dichotomy of feelings is
consistent with his Protestant imagination. King Arthur
transcends the repressive influence of the corrupt
Church when he willingly exposes himself to smallpox
contagion in order to relieve human suffering. To be a
Christian, Arthur must ignore a Church ban on entering
an infected household; by ignoring the ban, as well as
Morgan's common-sense pleas against such exposure,
Arthur embodies a more humane Christianity. The
quixotic nature of his behavior bears witness to the
power of an idealism which can transcend corrupt
institutions.

Throughout the novel, Twain develops parallels
between sixth-century England and nineteenth-century
America: the peasant class is the equivalent of the

industrial working class; the knights of the round table are equated with the members of the New York Stock Exchange; the aristocratic class is likened to the capitalist class. But Twain's viewpoint on these parallels confuses the satire. Is he satirizing the encroachment of sixth-century institutions such as the Roman Church on nineteenth-century America, or is he showing us that very little has changed since the sixth century? Henry Morgan is an amusing character through whom we perceive the idiocies of life in another period of history, but he is also a damned fool himself whose final gift to Arthurian England is the ability to kill on a greater and more effective scale than any "fool" of that period could ever conceive. At the end of the novel, Henry observes the fruit of his labor:

> Within ten short minutes after we had opened fire [with Gatling guns], armed resistance was totally annihilated, the campaign [between Morgan and the Knights] was ended, we fifty-four were masters of England! Twenty-five thousand men lay dead around us.[115]

Henry Morgan, so pleased with the carnage before him, is the same person who clearly perceives the corruptions of an established Church which, for all its rottenness, never achieves the height of barbarism realized by Henry himself. His insane behavior at the end of the novel might be viewed as giving an ironic dimension to his criticism of sixth-century England, but it does not lessen the harsh judgments directed against the Roman Church. The ambiguity of Twain's satire throughout this novel is rooted in his own confusion, which eventually developed into the embittered misanthropy of his last years.

Twain's fear of Catholic power as a threat to American institutions was deep-seated, but what he and even less hostile nineteenth-century observers failed to anticipate was the impact of the Americanization process on the Catholic immigrant. By the second and third generation, these immigrants were more American than Catholic. In 1962, the sociologist David O. Moberg observed that:

> The national differences brought by various Catholic groups to America are diminishing, although Irish and German influences remain dominant . . . . A new general Catholic culture is emerging in America as its ethnic elements merge and Catholics rise into the middle classes. Since the models of behavior in the American middle class have always been Protestant, the dominant religion of the United States increasingly threatens the distinctives [sic] of the Catholic religion.[116]

This new Catholic culture Moberg describes is a nominal one, for it is characterized by imitation of the dominant Protestant majority and class aspirations. As David Levinsky realized early in his career, one must assume the manners and values of the dominant class in order to achieve success in the world which that class controls. The authoritarian structures of the Catholic Church, which caused so much concern among the Protestant novelists of the nineteenth century, proved to have a diminishing impact upon American Catholics as they were exposed to the principles of participatory democracy.

* *

Assimilation of religious sects into the values of the dominant Protestant majority is a matter of history in American life. In 1783, St. John Crevecoeur made the following prophetic comments on the viability of sectarianism in the benign environment of a democratic society:

> Thus all sects are mixed as well as all nations; thus religious indifference is imperceptibly disseminated from one end of the continent to the other; which is at present one of the strongest characteristics of the Americans. Where this will reach no one can tell, perhaps it may leave a vacuum fit to receive other systems. Persecution, religious pride, the love of contradiction, are the food of what the world commonly calls religion. These motives have ceased here: zeal in Europe is confined; here it evaporates in the great distance it has to travel; there it is a grain of powder enclosed, here it burns away in the open air, and consumes without effect.[117]

Crevecoeur's statement does indeed anticipate a good deal of the American religious experience in the nineteenth and twentieth centuries. When, as in the cases of the Mennonites, Amish, and Shakers, sectarian doctrines inhibit the processes of accomodation or assimilation, the sect must either isolate itself or face extinction. The more common occurence, however, is the evolution of the radical sect into a traditional church--the Christian Science movement vilified by Eggleston and Twain evolves into a "respectable" Protestant church whose membership is indistinguishable from that of other churches.

The emergence of a predominantly secular society in twentieth-century America has stimulated a re-evaluation of the cultural significance connected to the decline of religious sects. When Crevecoeur described the levelling process, he attempted to explain it as a function of increased freedom and lower population density, but he also speculated that the break with religious orthodoxy might eventually result in the need for another value system. This dilemma was most acute for Jewish immigrants, whose religious experiences in America are perhaps the most complex of all. The tensions created within the Jew who puts aside his Jewishness in order to achieve success in the Gentile society is still the primary theme of American Jewish novelists. As Roth, Malamud, Bellow, and Heller have demonstrated in their fiction, a price must be paid for buying the American dream. A variety of cultural and religious heritages were abandoned in the pursuit of Americanization; with the notable exception of Jewish and black literature, little attention has been given to this transmutation process.

It has become the commonplace assumption that secularism is the prevailing value system of contemporary America, but the more interesting question is the role assumed by institutional churches in disseminating the amorphous ideology of secularism. The Catholic Church has not usurped our democratic ideals, as some nineteenth-century novelists predicted. Whether it be labeled secularism or civil religion, it tends to level sectarian differences rather then the feared consolidation of Catholicism. The distinguished sociologist, Byron Wilson, concludes his analysis of secularization in *Religion in Secular Society* with this observation:

> Whether indeed our own type of society will effectively maintain public order, without institutional coercion, once the still persisting influence of past religion wanes even further, remains to be seen. It may be, that in response to the growing institutionalism, impersonality, and bureaucracy of modern society, religion will find new functions to perform--but that, perhaps, would be not the religion which accepts the values of the new institutionalism, the religion of ecumenism, but the religion of sects.[118]

The continued presence of storefront churches, fundamentalist sects, and experimental groups within established churches seems to support Wilson's observation on the viability of sects as opposed to institutional churches. Their appeal resides not in any "new functions," but in their ability to give a communal setting for religious expression.[119]

CHAPTER IV

RELIGION AND REFORM LITERATURE

Utopian communities flourished in America throughout the nineteenth century, and it has been said that the entire American experience has been an attempt to realize some ideal social concept, whether it be the Puritan vision of the "City on the Hill," the Marxist vision of economic equality, or the behaviorist vision of psychologist B.F. Skinner in *Walden Two*. This quest for a perfect social order has taken two forms: first, the various utopian experiments which have ventured to give social reality to some model of an ideal communal existence; and second, because reality so often disappoints, the creation of an idealized social order in fiction.[1] Nineteenth-century American social history is cluttered with the remnants of failed attempts to establish utopian communities from Brook Farm in Massachusetts to the Franciscan mission settlement in California, but this study is concerned with the equally real, and ultimately perhaps more significant, rise of utopian models in American fiction. To appreciate this development in literary history it is necessary to understand the social and historical forces which were reshaping America from a rural-agrarian society into an urban-industrial one. The inevitable frustrations flowing from this radical transformation in American life captured the attention of a generation of American writers. Whether employing the format of reform fiction or utopian fiction, they engaged their imaginations to create better worlds than the one they knew.

Utopias are in the strictest sense non-spatial and purely ideological. As Karl Mannheim has described it:

> A state of mind is utopian when it is incongruous with the state of reality within which it occurs. This incongruence is always evident in the fact that such a state of mind in experience, in thought, and in practice, is oriented towards objects which do not exist in the actual situation. However, we should not regard as Utopian every state of mind which is incongruous with and transcends the immediate situation (and in this sense, "departs from reality"). Only those orientations transcending reality will be referred to by us as utopian which, when they pass over into conduct, tend to shatter, either partially or wholly, the order of things prevailing at the time.[2]

Although Mannheim asserts rightly that the utopian vision is incongruous with the state of reality, he does not make clear that the intellectual basis for a utopian vision is in values already present in society. The utopian writer does not create the concept of justice, but the particular way in which he perceives and applies such concepts as "justice" or "charity" may distinguish him from others. He is a social engineer whose laboratory is his imagination, and his motivation is two-fold. His immediate concern is the successful translation of his ideas into fiction, but as a utopian propagandist, his ultimate goal is to disseminate those ideas which will ultimately affect and transform the social order.

Although there were occasional literary renderings of utopias prior to the Civil War, such as Cooper's *The Crater* (1847) and Hawthorne's *The Blithedale Romance* (1852), utopian literature was not a significant factor in American fiction until the problems and frustrations of industrialization had become so acute that they could no longer be ignored. The hundreds of utopian novels written between 1880 and 1920 sprang from a recognition that the social and political institutions which had complemented the Ante-Bellum agrarian world on both sides of the Mason-Dixon line were inadequate to the challenges of industrialization.[3] In *Looking Backward* and other novels which imitated it, there is a wearisome uniformity in the citation of social problems and the demands for redress: first, the inequitable distribution of the new industrial wealth; second, the deplorable living conditions endured by the working classes in the cities; and third, the brutalizing effects of industrial labor on the personality and character of the workingman. For most of the utopian writers, hope for the future lay in redirecting industrial productivity into more humane results. Although they continued to believe in the efficacy of reason and in man's capacity to rearrange his social environment, utopianists espoused the simplistic notion that once man understood his problems, there would be little difficulty in devising and implementing the right solutions.

The simple faith of the secular utopian writers did not differ greatly from that of the Social Gospel theologians whose vision of a Christian social order was the new dogma emanating from various Protestant seminaries at the end of the nineteenth century.

> Turning away from the traditional
> emphasis on spiritual and moral
> concerns, the new gospel stressed
> the social and pragmatic
> implications of Christian ethics and
> called for good works in social
> reform and betterment.[4]

There were various shades of reformism in this Social Gospel movement. Washington Gladden (1836-1918) sought to forestall the excesses of European socialism by co-opting its more acceptable principles into a Christian, and hopefully peaceful, reform movement; William Dwight Porter Bliss (1856-1926) spoke for a more radical socialism in his publication, *Dawn*; and Walter Rauschenbusch (1861-1918), perhaps the most influential voice in the movement, felt that the very future of institutional Christianity was yoked to reform theology. Although there were differences of opinion on how best to realize the needed improvements, all the Social Gospel clergy rejected the anti-social ideology implicit in the competitive model of Manchesterian economics and Spenserian sociology. Christian ethics were viewed as a necessary counterbalance for muting the competitive principles which gave sanction to the social and human failings of the new industrial society.

The critical convergence of opinion-shaping forces--novelists, muckrakers, theologians, politicians, intellectuals--provided the necessary blueprint for reform. The particular importance of Social Gospel theology is that it provided a religious imprimatur to this reform movement. By wedding a Christian vocabulary of justice to the rational model of socialism, the Social Gospel theology gave legitimacy to what otherwise might have been dismissed as European radicalism. Richard Hofstadter has appraised this phenomenon with the following observation:

> A current of criticism frequently
> neglected and underrated by
> historians of American social
> literature, it supplied several
> religious bodies with a lasting
> reform orientation, and paved the
> way for all socially-minded
> Protestant movements of a later day.
> Not the least of its accomplishments
> was to break ground for the
> Progressive era.[5]

In several of the novels examined in this chapter—Tourgee's *Murvale Eastman* (1889), Sheldon's *In His Steps* (1899), and Churchill's *The Inside of the Cup* (1913)—a theology of reform, individual and/or social, provides a resolution to social problems presented in the narrative. These reform novels give expression to both traditional and Social Gospel theology, whereas such utopian fiction as Howells' *A Traveller from Altruria* (1894) and *Through the Eye of a Needle* (1907), and Bellamy's *Looking Backward* (1887) present the same moral protest by creating imaginary states in which the principles of the Social Gospel are firmly established.

The protagonists in reform novels usually attempt to implement a Social Gospel vision, even though that vision, to use Mannheim's phrase, is "incongruous with the state of reality" in American society. After the protagonists are themselves enlightened by this visionary theology, they proselytize and attempt to effect change, and each novel concludes with the notion, frequently expressed in Christian symbols, that a new order is coming. Even Upton Sinclair in *The Jungle* (1905) used Christian metaphors at the end of his otherwise secular reform novel to give additional authority to his own vision, and by so doing he perhaps unwittingly placed his novel in the religious-redemptive tradition. Toward the conclusion of *The Jungle*, the

239

revolutionary socialist Lucas who had earlier castigated institutional religion as the enemy of reason and as the propagandist for capitalism's traditional virtues—frugality, humility, and obedience—he uses the historical Jesus to give credibility to his political platform by identifying Christian with proletarian aspirations.

> This Jesus of Nazareth! . . . This class conscious workingman! This union carpenter! This agitator, lawbreaker, firebrand, anarchist! He, the sovereign lord and master of a world which grinds the bodies and souls of human beings into dollars—if he would come into the world this day and see the things that men have made in his name, would it not blast his soul with horror? Would he not go mad at the sight of it, he the prince of Mercy and Love![6]

Although the use of Christ and his teachings to support socialist arguments was a common rhetorical device, the new Social Gospel theology gave explicit legitimacy to the role of organized religion as an agent of reform.

Although it is extremely difficult to identify precise levels of interaction, the relationship between Social Gospel theology, reform literature, and utopian literature may best be described as a complementary interaction inspired by the prevailing *Zeitgeist*. Reform novels, such as *The Jungle*, usually end with a prophecy for the future of society which the reader has been prepared to accept because it is reasonable and persuasive. On the other hand, the typical utopian novel portrays a society in which drastic reforms have already taken place, with the focus on the benefits flowing from such reforms. In *Looking Backward*, for example, Julian West describes his wonder at twentieth-century Boston functioning under Bellamy's Nationalism; in Howells' Altrurian novels, Mr. Homos bewilders his nineteenth-century listeners when he describes the charity and justice of his native land Altruria. With their commitment to verisimilitude, reform novelists sacrifice ideological symmetry in order to provide a more realistic portrait of society in a state of flux, whereas the utopian writers appear more concerned with the presentation of an idea no matter how fanciful the time-place metaphor. More important than such differences, however, were the religo-ethical values shared by reform and utopian novelists. The Progressive Era was informed by a pietism that perceived economic power struggles as battles between the forces of good and evil, and this simple moral landscape permeates both reform and utopian fiction.

Naturally, not *all* churches and churchmen at the end of the nineteenth century were advocates of Christian Socialism. Father John J. Ming, a Catholic theolgian, described Christian Socialism as an international conspiracy "turning to evil use the Gospel itself so as to deceive more readily the unwary."[7] The Reverend Mr. Henry Ward Beecher's wealthy congregation took comfort from his harangues against the evil of trade unionism, and he dismissed the workingman's grievances with a memorable admonishment:

> I do not say that a dollar a day is
> enough to support . . . a man and
> five children if a man would insist
> on smoking and drinking beer . . . .
> But the man who cannot live on bread
> and water is not fit to live.[8]

Beecher's ministry was devoted to convincing the rich that theirs was the kingdom of heaven, and, as Harvey

Wish notes, Beecher's success rested on the solid foundations of bourgeois complacency and self-congratulation:

> At a time when severe social dislocations had been let loose by industrialism and crowded cities, he [Beecher] diverted the Christian doctrine of social responsibility into the irresponsibility of Spencerian *laissez-faire* and the uncritical acceptance of the inevitability of social progress.[9]

Reactionary voices such as Ming and Beecher were unfortunately representative of a significant portion of church-affiliated Americans, but as the bleak consequences of such apologetics became obvious, this theology of the status-quo became intolerable.

By 1920, the major American religious groups had adopted official positions endorsing social reform programs: in 1908, the Protestant Federal Council of Churches adopted "A Social Creed of the Churches;" in 1918, the Central Conference of American Rabbis issued a statement that the ideal of social justice had always been an integral part of Judaism; and in 1919, the Administrative Committee of the National Catholic War Council adopted the Bishop's Program of Social Reconstruction which reiterated the principles already enunciated in the papal encyclical, *Rerum Novarum*.[10] Rapid adoption of social reform models by the major religions verified the respectability achieved by the reformers. It would have been institutional suicide for the churches to continue ignoring the legitimate aspirations of their memberships for a better standard of living. Walter Rauschenbusch had described the dangers awaiting organized religions' failure to participate in a reform movement.

> Religion must keep pace. The church must pass the burning torch of religious experience from age to age . . . . Its inspiring teaching must meet the new social problems so effectively that no evil can last long or grow beyond remedy. In every new age religion must stand the test of social efficiency . . . . Religion is a bond of social coherence . . . . Society changes . . . . Religion, by its very virtues of loyalty and reverence, may fall behind and lose its full social efficiency. It must be geared to the big live issues today if it is to manifest its full saving energies.[11]

In a similar vein, Cardinal Gibbons of Baltimore had cautioned the Vatican that its apparent intention to denounce the efforts of the Knights of Labor would have serious repercussions in the largely working class American Catholic Church. "To lose the heart of the people," he warned, "would be a misfortune for which the friendship of the few rich and powerful would be no compensation."[12] Both Rauschenbusch and Gibbons shared forebodings on the consequences facing their respective churches, and their theology was partly a defensive reaction to preserve the religious institutions which they served.

The dramatic confrontations in many of the novels to be studied in this chapter mirror the class conflict between establishment power brokers and reform theorists, and the novelists describe the role of the churches as crucial to the adoption of radical social changes. In his preface to *Caesar's Column*, Ignatius

Donnelly made a direct appeal for the churches to assume an active role in reversing the trend toward bloody revolution that he imagined in the futuristic world of his novel. Donnelly felt the churches must "assume [their] ancient station as crowned mistress of the souls of men . . . the champion and defender of mankind against all oppressors."[13] In *Caesar's Column*, the failure of the churches to bear witness against injustice is presented as the primary cause leading to the bloody revolution which concludes the novel. Shortly before the revolution occurs, Donnelly makes ironic use of a reactionary clergyman, in the mode of Beecher and Ming, delivering a sermon on the need for Christian humility and forbearance:

> This world is only a place of temporary trial, to prepare us for another and a better world. This existence consists of a few troubled and painful years, at best, but there [in heaven] you will enjoy eternal happiness in the company of the angels of God.[14]

In his parody of the reactionary clergyman delivering a gospel of Christian passivity, Donnelly is providing a textbook sample of the Marxian indictment that religion is the opiate of the people. The narrative of *Caesar's Column* concludes with an apocalyptic revolution which is Donnelly's prognosis of what inevitably flows from such establishmentarian theology.

The novels inspired by Social Gospel values are not uniform in their visions of reform, nor are they necessarily aesthetically satisfying, but they do reflect the aspirations, preoccupations, and creative energies of a generation of writers who felt that social justice could not be achieved unless the churches took an active role in accomplishing it. In making such an appeal to institutional churches, the novelists provided a program for justice in the social order which also made the churches more relevant. For all interested in how America moved from the simple assumptions of an agrarian world to the complex relationships of an urban-industrial society, the novelists examined in this chapter played a principal educational and propagandizing role.

Albion Tourgee: Journey to Christian Socialism

Albion Tourgee was a nineteenth-century social critic who advocated many reform issues which were eventually assumed into the Progressive Movement. He used fiction to champion various causes and his two most famous novels, *A Fool's Errand* and *Bricks Without Straw*, plead for racial justice in the South. When Tourgee turned his attention to the economic injustice and wage slavery which accompanied the industrialization of the North, he once again used the novel as a platform to express his concern. Although his reformism was eclectic--he supported high tariffs, Henry George's single tax, government ownership of communications, while opposing civil service reform--Tourgee never lost his sense of injustice.[15] His novel, *Murvale Eastman: Christian Socialist* (1889) contains a systematic condemnation of the human failings endemic to the emerging industrialism. Tourgee indicts the institutional church and its membership for failing to participate in alleviating the suffering of the industrial working class.

The novel opens with the Reverend Mr. Murvale Eastman presiding over a wealthy Chicago congregation with the picturesque name--the Church of the Golden Lilies. The name suggests an effete religious sensibility. Eastman devotes himself to assuring his congregation of their righteousness and that theirs is the path to eternal happiness. In return for the gospel of self-satisfaction, the Reverend Mr. Eastman receives the enthusiastic material support of his congregation. The Church of the Golden Lilies is a smashing financial success; by the prevailing standards of the time, it is "an outfit with a future." Nevertheless, Eastman is dissatisfied with his success because he suspects that, somewhere along the way, he has lost sight of his vocation. His vague stirrings of discontent initiate Eastman's spiritual journey, in the course of which he discovers that he must repudiate everything connected with the spiritually bankrupt Church of the Golden Lilies. As he disengages from this institutional affiliation, he experiences the renaissance of his Protestant sensibility--his new moral consciousness is rightly appalled by the inequities which have become the norm.

Since the Social Gospel was an ethical revivalism which demanded the commitment of its followers, Murvale Eastman's departure from an establishment church is not unusual. Many late nineteenth-century religions experienced a similar dislodgment as Gayrand S. Wilmore noted in *The Secular Relevance of the Church*:

> Some [ministers and seminary professors] could not remain in the church and found their way into the Socialist Party, the trade-union movement, and other social action groups. These men saw that the social gospel, for all its theological deficiencies which, of course, did not concern them, demanded a radical new social and political ethos for the church. But the turn in the road from orthodoxy,

which had been engineered by Rauschenbusch and others, had not been sharp enough to lead in a new direction. It could not bring an authentic reconstruction of the social order, nor a new relationship between the church and American culture.[16]

Murvale Eastman is representative of that group of ministers who could not reconcile their commitment to reform with continuing participation in the institutional church; the required reforms were too extensive and, as Eastman perceived, these changes were for the most part unacceptable to the majority of traditional worshippers whose religious concerns were private rather than social.

Early in the novel, Tourgee draws a prophetic outline of the inevitable confrontation which will take place between Eastman and his congregation.

The giants who wielded the material forces of civilization, the culture which molded its literature, and the fashion which shaped society, were all there, waiting eagerly for his teaching. Or was it teaching which they sought? If not, what was the desire that impelled this assembly? Worship? What was it, and what was his relation to it? Was Christianity only a form of worship, and he a mere figure in that form?[17]

While deriving a vainglorious pleasure from the presence of the wealthy and powerful in his congregation, he is nevertheless puzzled by their attendance. His curious ambivalence between social prestige and sound theology provides the dramatic tension in the novel. The implicit cynicism of the congregation is embodied in the character of Wilton Kishu, whose use of the church is devoid of any religious significance. One need only consult a standard social history of the period to find the historical models for Kishu.

> [He] was the chief factotum of the church of the Golden Lilies. He managed the finances; engineered the Sabbath-school; looked after the Mission, and, generally, took care that the Golden Lilies was in the van of all good and worthy works . . . . He did not pay as high wages as some, but invariably gave each of his employees a present at Christmas which was nearly equal to the deficit in his salary . . . . His favorite among his clerks were employed as ushers, and were liberally paid by the church as they deserved to be, for their services were very nearly faultless.[18]

To be indifferent to the substantive doctrines of Christianity is one thing, but to use the church as a means of granting fringe benefits for one's private enterprise reflects a level of cynicism unacceptable to Eastman's new consciousness.

Tourgee believed that the prevailing institutions of a society were no more than reflections of that society's idea of Christianity. With such a notion, Tourgee seemed to anticipate Josiah Royce's concept of the world as a self-interpreting community:

> A process of interpretation involves, of necessity, an infinite

248

> sequence of acts of interpretation
> . . . . These selves, in all their
> variety constitute the life of a
> single Community of Interpretation
> . . . . The universe is a community
> of interpretation whose life
> comprises and unifies all the social
> varieties and all the social
> communities.[20]

Royce was attempting to synthesize all diverse activities into a logical continuum which he called the Universal Community, but a less optimistic conclusion was drawn by Tourgee--that a community immersed in greed and selfishness has a kind of unity which can only be dealt with by repudiation.

Tourgee expressed in this novel, and throughout his public life, his belief that America was turning away from its professed ideals. Not only did the nation fail to protect the constitutional rights of its citizens (cf. *Bricks Without Straw*), but the churches failed to assert the Christian values of the gospels. For Tourgee, to be a Christian required a willingness to function outside of society's institutions, just as Christ had. In *Murvale Eastman*, Christ is described as an outcast: "The Romans despised him. The poor revered but distrusted him. A lover of pelf betrayed him; religion esteemed him a scoffer; politically he was regarded as a 'dangerous character.'"[21] By establishing the concept that Christian action is almost of necessity radical, Tourgee is shaping his protagonist's eventual destiny.

Eastman's shadowy speculations are given voice in his sermons, which are increasingly influenced by his new-found theological perspective:

> Christianity is emphatically the
> religion of humanity. Earth and man
> are its themes. Justice for the
> strong and mercy for the weak—these
> were the lessons Christ inculcated.
> He was not concerned with its forms
> and ceremonies. He established no
> church; he organized no cult; he
> prescribed no forms of worship.[22]

Eastman concludes this sermon by asserting that Christ's
purpose on earth was primarily aimed at the "betterment
of human conditions." Such views make Eastman
increasingly suspect to his establishmentarian
congregation, and as the narrative unfolds, Tourgee uses
his character as a convention for the increasingly
didactic tone of the novel reminiscent of Howells' use
of ministerial voices for similar purposes in *The
Minister's Charge* and *Annie Kilburn*. In both cases, the
novelists employ a clerical persona for their own
sermons to the reader. When Eastman informs his
congregation that a Christian's belief can only be
measured by the fruit of his actions, Eastman and
Tourgee have become one.

The novel disintegrates into a series of sermons,
a social tract which, while purporting to be a record of
Eastman's spiritual journey, barely maintains its
pretense to fiction. In the first sermon, Eastman
informs his congregation of the corrupting influence
which monied interests have had on all the churches
(p.187). In a subsequent sermon he asserts that church
ceremonies and rituals detract from the Christian way,
and in his most forthright sermon, he makes an attack on
the inequitable distribution of wealth. Eastman argues
that poverty and wealth are the real enemies of man, the
former creating temptations which can only be satisfied
through thievery, and the latter creating gluttonous

needs which can be satisfied only by avarice. Men are no longer virtuous he asserts, because they are distracted by such preoccupations.

His concern with the corrupting impact of capitalism becomes the major topic of his sermons: "The function of the Church is only to inspire action, to provide impulse, to exalt and purify motive, to incline man to apply the Christ-spirit to collective human relations."[23] With his conversion to Christian Socialism, Eastman discovers that his congregation is not empathetic to his new beliefs. His status with this membership was based upon his facility to mirror from his pulpit the existing values and prejudices of his congregation, and in the course of his transformation, he unfolds the answer to the question he posed himself at the beginning of the novel. No, they did not want him as a teacher, and yes, he was only the figure of formalized Christianity which had little meaning in the day-to-day lives of the members of the Church of the Golden Lilies.

When Murvale Eastman joins the League of Christian Socialists, he further incurs the wrath of Wilton Kishu, who has interpreted Eastman's sermons as personal attacks. Tourgee makes it clear that a Christian witness is unacceptable to well-to-do churchgoers, because Christianity is revolutionary and revolution is not favored by such a class. Kishu's character becomes increasingly villainous as Tourgee reveals the layers of his lying, cheating, and thieving behavior. Kishu, the defender of institutional churches and persecutor of Murvale Eastman, becomes a caricature of villainy while Eastman increases in virtue--the gospel tale is reenacted with Kishu playing Judas to Eastman's Christ. Finally, Kishu brings charges against Eastman for misuse of the pulpit and he asks the Association of Ministers to deprive him of his clerical status. An ecclesiastical trial ends in Eastman's favor, but by the end of the trial, he is indifferent to the verdict; his sole interest is Christian Socialism. He explains his break with the church and his new commitment in these terms:

> When Christianity does not impel the believer to recognize the rights, interests, and welfare of others as the measure of individual and collective duty, then, so far as concerns those who are wronged and weakened and debased in consequence, Christianity is no better than the cult of the Ammonite.[24]

Thus, as the Association of Ministers rules Eastman innocent, he ironically finds the church guilty of failure to bear witness to Christ.

This novel contains the quintessential Protestant theme--the individual conscience asserting a moral position and making a judgment against a corrupt institution. Tourgee articulates this premise in the preface to *Murvale Eastman*:

> The individual is the pivot of progress. Personal independence is the test of social forces. A nation may grow rich beyond all precedent, and at the same time individual opportunity be constantly restricted and the area of self-direction and control be rapidly diminished.[25]

If the individual's capacity to function as a moral agent is restricted by a powerful oligarchy in control of institutions, even churches, then the individual who seeks to lead a moral existence must break free of such encumbrances. By leaving the restrictions of a corrupt church and joining the League of Christian Socialists,

Murvale Eastman asserts his independence and his new faith in human progress. Prior to his journey to the city and his ministry in the Church of the Golden Lilies, Reverend Mr. Murvale Eastman had enjoyed a successful ministry in a rural church where a simple gospel met the spiritual needs of his congregation. By novel's end, his spiritual journey has led him to recognize that his simple rural faith is no longer adequate to express Christian concerns.

There are some potential problems with Eastman's commitment to the League of Christian Socialists, but Tourgee chooses not to explore them. Like any organization, the League will eventually impinge upon his individuality just as the church had. Further, if a communitarian vision is realized through the work of the League, what will be the role of the individual in such a society? Tourgee does not deal with such problems such as personal vs. communal values, nor does he answer the question as to who would arbitrate between conflicting interests. Still, despite Tourgee's failure to anticipate some of the possible conflicts inherent in his vision, *Murvale Eastman* offers an interesting analysis of the church's changing role in an early industrial society.

Charles M. Sheldon: Reform in Orthodox Garb

Seven years after Tourgee's novel was published, the Reverend Mr. Charles Monroe Sheldon, a Congregational minister from Topeka, Kansas, published one of the most popular novels in American literary history--*In His Steps: "What Would Jesus Do?"* (1896).[26] The novel developed from a series of sermons delivered by Sheldon:

> [In order] to keep up attendance at
> the Sunday evening service, he
> discovered a device for filling the
> pews . . . . Instead of delivering
> a second sermon he read to his
> congregation a chapter of a
> religious novel [i.e., *In His
> Steps*]. He ended each reading with
> a scene so full of suspense that
> everyone had to come back for the
> next installment.[27]

The general idea for his religious novels was probably
derived from the English journalist W. T. Stead's *If
Christ Came to Chicago* (1894); Part V of Stead's book--
"What Would Christ Do In Chicago?"--was probably the
structural model used by Sheldon for the fictional
sermons which evolved into *In His Steps*.

The novel opens with the Reverend Mr. Henry
Maxwell lamenting the lack of fervor in the Raymond
Church congregation, an indifference easily measured by
the poor attendance at Sunday services. This problem
was very real to Sheldon, whose activity as a writer was
inspired by a similar attendance problem in his own
church, although there the similarity between author and
protagonist ends. Maxwell is portrayed as not only
indifferent to Social Gospel theology, but positively
jubilant over the financial success of his church. "It
had the best choir. It had a membership composed of the
leading people, representatives of the wealth, society,
and intelligence of Raymond."[28] The annoyance over poor
attendance is based on the fact that Maxwell's sermons
seem to suffer if he does not have a full house.
Maxwell's vanity and shallowness are further amplified
by portraying his ministry as little more than a vehicle
for realizing a comfortable bourgeois existence in which
one of his major concerns is plotting his three-month
vacation touring Europe.

The catalyst for Maxwell re-examining the character and quality of his religious life is a seedy young man who interrupts one of his Sunday morning services by asking the minister and his congregation some questions regarding the nature of their religious commitments:

> What do Christians mean by following the steps of Jesus? I've tramped through this city for three days trying to find a job and in all that time I've not had a word of sympathy or comfort except from your minister here, who said he was sorry for me and hoped I would find a job somewhere.[29]

Unlike Lemuel Barker in Howells' *The Minister's Charge*, Sheldon's young man is an assertive and articulate spokesman for the disenfranchised. His challenge to the minister and his prosperous congregation is clear and uncompromising:

> Somehow I get puzzled when I see so many Christians living in luxury and singing, 'Jesus, I my cross have taken, all to leave and follow Thee,' . . . I understand that Christian people own a good many of the tenements. A member of a church was the owner of the one where my wife died, and I have wondered if following Jesus all the way was true in his case . . . . It seems to me there's an awful lot of trouble in the world that somehow wouldn't

> exist if all the people who sing
> such songs went and lived them
> out.[30]

After speaking out against what he perceives to be the hypocrisy of Christian church-goers, the young man collapses, and with his dying breath, he thanks Maxwell for his kindness.

The young man's impassioned speech and his sudden death produce a radical and improbable change in Maxwell's ministry. He resolves to form a league of people who will try to live strictly Christian lives. On the Sunday following the young man's death, the minister asks for

> . . . volunteers from the First
> Church who will pledge themselves
> earnestly and honestly for an entire
> year not to do anything without
> first asking the question 'What
> would Jesus do?' And after asking
> that question, each one will follow
> Jesus as exactly as he knows how, no
> matter what the results may be.[31]

Maxwell's appeal for volunteers is taken up by diverse members of the congregation, and the action of the novel is a series of vignettes showing individual characters attempting to do as Jesus would. The results are occasionally unintentionally amusing, for when the members of the community act out their applied Christianity, their behavior becomes a caricature of small town provincialism. Ed Norman, the local newspaper editor, accepts the challenge by refusing to report prizefight results, rejecting advertisements for whiskey and tobacco, and discontinuing his Sunday edition, a course of action which leads him toward bankruptcy. Rachel Winslow, a young and beautiful woman who plans on a singing career, turns down a lucrative job with a comic opera company because, she declares straightforwardly: "Jesus wouldn't sing opera!" And so it goes. The remaining vignettes are not quite so ludicrous, although there is a pitiful spiritual impoverishment in tale after tale.

In his provocative critique of *In His Steps*, Paul S. Boyer rejects the idea that the novel is primarily concerned with reform because the only explicit legislation it argues for is Prohibition:

> The destruction of the saloon is *the* theme of *In His Steps*, when the novel is read as a conservative reform tract. This is the one—the only—legislative reform which Sheldon tirelessly, unqualifiedly and passionately espouses.[32]

It seems unfair to categorize Sheldon simply as a temperance fanatic, for his commitment to Christian principles extends far beyond the issue of Prohibition. Milton Wright, for example, a prominent businessman in the town of Raymond, tells of one person's radical change. Wright adopts six principles under the title, "What Jesus Would Probably Do in Milton Wright's Place as a Businessman." The first and all-encompassing principle is: "He would engage in business for the purpose of glorifying God and not for the primary purpose of making money."[33] Wright swears never to think of profits as anything more than a trust fund for humanity and to pursue a life of selflessness and devotion to his fellowman. By the end of the novel, Wright has become the beloved idol of the Raymond working class, but all this is accomplished without any major reforms to social institutions. Wright is still a capitalist, albeit a humane and decent one. In the Wright episode, Sheldon has demonstrated that individual reform is the necessary and singular precondition for a better society. By resurrecting the traditional Calvinist doctrine of stewardship, Sheldon produces reform in his fictional world without disrupting the existing order of things.

One of the most interesting conversions is that of the local college president, Donald Marsh, who decides to abandon the congenial life of academe to join the fight for political and social change in Raymond. Even though public life is foreign to Marsh's temperament, it is the most expediential means to create needed reform. At one point, Marsh notes that one of the great failings in America has been the withdrawal of the educated and privileged classes into patrician privatism:

> Maxwell, you and I belong to a class of professional men who have always avoided the duties of citizenship. We have lived in a little world of scholarly seclusion, doing work we have enjoyed, and shrinking from the disagreeable duties that belong to the life of the citizen . . . . But the call has come to me so plainly that I cannot escape: 'Donald Marsh, follow me. Do your duty as a citizen of Raymond . . . . Help to cleanse this great municipal stable, even if you do have to soil your aristocratic feelings a little.' Maxwell, This is my cross. I must take it on or deny my lord.[34]

Beneath President Marsh's cumbersome rhetoric, Sheldon is expressing one of the period's most critical problems--the failure of the American upper class to provide leadership in a period of social transition.[35]

The social, economic, political and religious aspects of life in Raymond begin to reflect the consequences of the Jesus pledge in an ever-widening circle. Those taking the pledge produce changes in the lives of others. Word of the pledge reaches the Reverend Mr. Calvin Bruce, rector of the Nazareth Avenue Church in Chicago, and he communicates his enthusiasm to his old friend, the Bishop of Chicago. The Bishop's response, cautious and bureaucratic, is a moderate warning on the consequences arising from the Jesus pledge:

> I do not see how a perfect upheaval
> of Christianity, as we now know it,
> can be prevented if the ministry and
> churches generally take the Raymond
> pledge and live it out . . . . Now,
> in my church . . . it would be a
> difficult matter, I fear to find
> very many people who would take a
> pledge like that and live up to it.
> Martyrdom is a lost art with us.
> Our Christianity loves its ease and
> comfort too well to take up anything
> so rough and heavy as a cross.[36]

The Bishop's genteel cynicism about his fellow Christians is reminiscent of similar admonitions Eggleston had directed against his Methodist contemporaries.

Later in the novel the Bishop is impelled to make a decision regarding his own Christianity, when his friend, the Reverend Mr. Bruce, is forced to resign from Nazareth Church. Bruce so impresses the Bishop with his unworldly fervor that the older man also resigns his post, and together they start to build a settlement house in Chicago's worst slum. Thus, the speech, followed by the untimely death of the young tramp early in the novel, continues to have startling repercussions. But these events are so unlikely that the novel becomes absurd. Sheldon's characters are never in conflict with the society around them—they simply change the society through the force of the Jesus pledge.

If there are any doubts regarding the conservative theology of Reverend Sheldon, they are clarified by the villainous characteristics assigned to the novel's only Socialist, Carlsen. It is Carlsen who speaks of an inevitable workers' revolution, who calls American civilization "rotten to the core," and most importantly, it is Carlsen who asserts that this new urban-industrial civilization is incapable of correcting its ills. He points accusingly to Christianity's failures and tells an audience of workers:

> This city, and every other big city
> in this country, has its thousands
> of professed Christians who have all
> the luxuries and comfort, and who go
> to church Sundays and sing their
> hymns about giving all to Jesus and
> bearing the cross and following Him
> all the way and being saved.[37]

Carlsen echoes the young tramp in his attack on bourgeois religion, but he contends that the single tax remedy suggested by Henry George in *Progress and Poverty* is a more viable remedy for social ills than the Jesus pledge. He also observes, more accurately than Sheldon may have intended, that a wealthy congregation would "laugh at him for a fool or a crank or a fanatic" if he suggested the Jesus pledge to them.

Although George's single tax theory was both an inequitable and inappropriate instrument for social justice, compared to the Jesus pledge, it was a monument to common sense. In Sheldon's schema, Carlsen is the devil-figure who threatens to win the hearts of the poor and overturn our social institutions if Christians do not behave in a Christian manner (i.e., passive and forbearing). The fact that the socialists attacked the same foes—poverty, disease, and human suffering—is not as important as the threat which they posed to a congenital conservative like Charles Sheldon. Since the problems of society, by Sheldon's perceptions, were individual and *not* institutional, assaulting existing institutions would not only be misguided but unpatriotic. Maxwell, in rebuttal to Carlsen's demand for legislation, explains:

> . . . 'the gift, without the giver, is bare.' The Christianity that attempts to suffer by proxy is not the Christianity of Christ. Each individual Christian, business man, citizen, needs to follow in His steps along the path of personal sacrifice for Him . . . . Nothing but a discipleship of this kind can face the destructive selfishness of the age, with any hope of overcoming it.[38]

Perhaps Sheldon suspected that his Christian vision was nonsensical when he decided to conclude the novel with a dream sequence.[39] As Maxwell ponders the possibility of the entire world following in the steps of the Raymond congregation, he falls asleep and "dreamed of the regeneration of Christendom and saw in his dream a church of Jesus 'without spot or wrinkle or any such thing,' following Him all the way, walking obediently In His Steps."[40] For the Reverend Mr. Charles Sheldon, the individual Christian bearing witness to Christ is the only viable answer to social problems. Although the individual Christian must be awakened to the social implications of his Christianity, he nevertheless should not satisfy his witness by attempting to legislate justice as the socialists were suggesting. Sheldon's manner of dealing with social problems is to dream of a heavenly city on earth in which all men would become angelic disciples of Christ. Such a dream is, in Mannheim's phrase, "incongruous with reality," and Sheldon's is implicitly a reactionary voice because he makes clear that the changes suggested by radicals like Carlsen are even more terrible than the existing injustices. *In His Steps* is a curious blend of Christian Reformism and political conservatism, and where a conflict exists between the two, Sheldon comes down on the side of the status quo. The novel ends on an orthodox note, with a vision of a heavenly social order achieved without tinkering with the structure and character of America's social institutions.

Winston Churchill: The Patrician Reformer

The novelist Winston Churchill was very much a man of his age, and thus he was caught in the dilemma of resolving his own comfortable status in society with the obvious need for changes. As Charles Child Walcutt noted: "Churchill's dilemma is interesting because it is so open. While he reverenced gentility, social position, old homes, and fine manners, he strongly believed in social justice and a good life that depended on finer things than material decorations and snobbishness."[41]

In the same year that he published *The Inside of the Cup* (1913), Churchill wrote an article on the modern quest for religion in which he asserted that the traditional faiths were dead, and the time had come for a new religion. He proposed a positive righteousness to be called "the New Patriotism." The five principles for the new religion were taken from the gospels, and a close reading reveals Churchill's program to be little more than Social Gospel with a new, perhaps less threatening, label. The New Patriotism consists of:

1. The motivating force for all men shall be service.

2. Militant righteousness seeking to put into government, the Maxim: 'I am my brother's keeper.'

3. Open-mindedness and hence a capacity for growth.

4. The principle of individual worth, and this leads logically, through universal suffrage, to individual responsibility and democracy.

5. Acknowledging that man does not live by bread alone. Art, literature, science, music, and philosophy have their place,--yes, and religion.[42]

These principles are vague enough in character so that one can accurately anticipate the indecisive reformism which Churchill proposed. Like Sheldon, his investment in the status quo tempered any genuine desire for change in society.

The protagonist in *The Inside of the Cup* is once again a clergyman arriving in an urban setting (i.e., Chicago) after a distinguished ministry in the rural community of Bremerton. The Reverend Mr. John Hodder quickly comes to realize that the religious system and values which served his Bremerton congregation are inadequate to the social chaos of an industrial metropolis. The principal problem facing the Reverend Mr. Hodder in St. John's Church is the control exercised

263

by the upper classes over church policies. The most powerful voice in church affairs is once again the wealthiest member of the church--Eldon Parr--who has deliberately isolated St. John's from any contact with the social problems of the surrounding urban environs.

The education of the Reverend Mr. Hodder is initiated by Eldon Parr's daughter Alison, who is disillusioned with her father's use of power. Alison convinces the minister of his impotence in church matters, and she also brings up the possibilities of the Social Gospel. Although she is not a Christian herself, she confesses her belief that if "there is one element in Christianity which distinguishes it, it is the brotherhood of man.   That's pure nitroglycerin . . . ."[43] The explosive metaphor is prophetic, for as Alison observes:

> If Christians were logical, they should be Socialists. The brotherhood of man, cooperation--all that is Socialism, isn't it? It's opposed to the principle of the survival of the fittest, which so many of these so-called Christians [e.g., her own father] practice.[44]

Hodder responds limply to Alison's theorizing--"I'm afraid there is a great deal of truth in what you said." Although he appears unmoved from his conservative orthodoxy, Alison has planted the seed of a consciousness which moves him inexorably to a radical repudiation of all institutions.

Once begun, Hodder's conversion to the Social Gospel is swift. The building of a settlement house, which is presented as a noble endeavor in Sheldon's *In His Steps*, is opposed in principle by Hodder because such individual philanthropy obfuscates the need for

264

real reforms. Eldon Parr wants to build the settlement house, as Churchill presents it, as a means of buttressing the status quo. This leads Hodder to dramatically repudiate the whole notion of charity as a crime against civilization, calling it

> . . . this system of legalized or semi-legalized robbery and the distribution of largesse to the victims. The Church is doing wrong, is stultifying herself in encouraging it. She should set her face rigidly against it, stand for morality and justice and Christianity in government, not for pauperizing. It is her mission to enlighten these people.[45]

The reforms outlined in Churchill's novel are institutional and political, and in this respect, it is considerably more sophisticated than the Christian Socialism in *Murvale Eastman* or the religious individualism of *In His Steps*. Hodder envisions the true function of the Church as the education of the poor so that they may liberate themselves through political action and alter the foundations of society. The final solution to all social problems will be accomplished when "Christianity in government" becomes a fact of public life. On that day of "New Patriotism," philanthropy and charity will pass away because no individual man will have the wealth or power to act as a charitable agent. Society will take care of all its members because its political institutions will be Christianized.

The radical change in Hodder's thinking produces a series of crises in beliefs, but he finally decides against leaving the Church. In a conversation with the local librarian Engel (a significant name), Hodder explains his obstinate commitment to the church because it

> . . . has a large future . . . . In spite of the fact that truth has gradually been revealed to the world by what may be called an Apostolic Succession of Personalities-- Augustine . . . Francis of Assisi . . . our own Lincoln and Phillips Brooks,--to mention only a few,--the Church as a whole has been blind to it . . . she has never recognized that growth is the secret of life, that the clothes of one man are binding on another.[46]

Since Hodder sees himself as a part of this "Apostolic Succession," it would be self-defeating for him to leave the church. He is convinced that the radical vanguard, of which he is a member, is in the process of mobilizing the church as an instrument for massive social reform.

In conversations with McCrae, his Assistant Pastor, Hodder further reveals that he now rejects many of the church's doctrinal positions. He no longer believes in episcopal authority, nor does he believe in the virgin birth of Christ. The apparent inconsistency in his rejection of church doctrine and the retention of his faith is explained by Hodder as:

> . . . the extreme Protestant position . . . . It was this doctrine of Paul's of redemption by faith . . . of rebirth, if you will--that Luther and the Protestant reformers revived and recognized, rightly, as the vital element of

266

> Christ's teachings . . . . It is
> the leaven which has changed
> governments, and which in the end I
> am firmly convinced, will make true
> democracy inevitable. And those who
> oppose democracy inherently dread
> its workings.[47]

Although the battle which the minister will wage against
Eldon Parr and other members of the establishment is
essentially an economic and political one, he does not
use the vocabulary of class struggle but the vocabulary
of religion—good vs. evil.

Churchill uses Hodder's sermons to explicate the
principles of his own New Patriotism theory. The union
of Christianity and democracy is seen as essential to
the future of a healthy society, and the upper classes
must reform and cease the mockery of their charities
which inhibit necessary institutional reform. Hodder
creates a high standard of achievement for the
congregation that can only be satisfied through
institutionalized social justice.[48] Predictably, the
congregation of St. John's is less than enthusiastic
with the increasing "unreasonableness" of their
minister, and Eldon Parr brings charges against him as
the first step toward his dismissal. But Hodder
discovers an ally in Asa Waring, a wealthy trustee whose
dormant religious feelings have been awakened by the
young minister's idealism. Waring, functioning as a
moral commentator, describes the battle for Hodder's
position in the church in terms of good and evil. He
sees Hodder as a courageous witness for the spirit of
Christ.

> . . . the mission of the Church is
> to disseminate that spirit. The
> Church is the champion on which we
> have to rely, or give up all hope of

victory. The Church must train the
recruits. And if the Church herself
is betrayed into the hands of the
enemy, the battle is lost.[49]

Hodder has stirred Waring's hope that the corrupt power
of Eldon Parr may yet be defeated.

Churchill defuses the doomsday imagery by
introducing a powerful and articulate ally in the
character of Asa Waring while reaffirming the nobility
and power of the church to redress the ills of society.
Through the recruitment of idealistic and committed
youth, the church will successfully end human
oppression, and simultaneously absorb, in peaceful
fashion, the growing demand for political revolution and
social upheaval. Thus Churchill, who earlier in the
novel had established the need for political action as a
prerequisite for reform, delivers a more cautious
prescription for society's ills. By the end of the
novel he is no more in favor of real change than was
Charles Sheldon. The Reverend Mr. Hodder, following his
vindication by the trustees, begins to talk of
moderation rather than reform. He assures Eldon Parr
that they really are not too far apart:

The public conscience of which I
speak is the leaven of Christianity
at work. And we must be content to
work with it, to await its
fulfillment, to realize that no one
can change the world, but can only
do his part in making it better.[50]

In the "Afterword" to the novel, Churchill states that
Hodder's beliefs are his own, which would classify him
as a conservative Social Gospel adherent who affirms the
primacy of the church as an instrument of social change.

The conclusion of the novel on such a tentative note brings an abrupt and untimely halt to the development of Hodder's character. As Charles Walcutt has observed: "For four hundred and fifty pages we have been backing up, like the hero of a melodrama, for a forward rush that does not take place."[51] After Hodder has launched a convincing attack on the seamier aspects of charity and philanthropy, Churchill defuses him. The sidetracking of this embryonic radical develops out of the trustee's support for his ministry and his engagement to Alison Parr, whose own radicalism has also mysteriously disappeared. Although the reader is unprepared for the final cooptation of Hodder, it would have been extraordinary had Churchill ended the novel on a revolutionary note considering that Churchill continued his membership in the ranks of America's privileged class. After flirting with the radical vision in the opening section of *The Inside of the Cup*, he came down on the side of moderation, historical gradualism, and the preservation of existing institutions. Judging on a class basis alone, Churchill's version of social reform was a predictable one; it is also perhaps the best fictional rendering of the inevitable tensions between revolutionary principles and the institutional church. The problem of resolving antithetical value systems was familiar to a sympathetic middle-class readership, because Churchill's dilemma was also faced by millions of people who supported the Social Gospel but who didn't know how to integrate the realities of church life with this new theology.

Robert Herrick: Critic of Social Gospel

The novelist Robert Herrick was a New Englander by birth and a graduate of Harvard who settled in Chicago and taught at the University of Chicago for thirty years. Herrick had a sensitive moral perspective that differed profoundly from the perspectives of those novelists who wrote from the Social Gospel viewpoint. As one critic has noted, he was a man primarily concerned with the individual's exercise of will.

> Like his puritan ancestors, Herrick insists that the individual will, rightly organized and directed, is the means by which man attains the knowledge of ultimate reality . . . . It is the corruption and eventual rehabilitation of the will . . . which from the very beginning provides the dominant interest in his novels.[52]

He addressed himself to the specific need for a literature which would speak to "the American ideal, the American will, the American character." Herrick had little use for the reform novelists who failed to deal with what he considered to be the sources of injustice and tyranny, and in his view the hope for the future rested with

> . . . that splendid sense of will-- the power to mould our destiny as we would have it, to create afresh the forms and conditions of our social life . . . . We shall hear less, let us hope, about the 'captain of industry.'[53]

It was Herrick's opinion that those Social Gospel novels which made the "captain of industry" mankind's chief enemy were simplistic in their analyses of society's ills, and that from such literature, one could expect only foolish answers to serious problems.

The problems of American society at the end of the nineteenth century were, according to Robert Herrick, much more fundamental than the institutional prognosis presented by Progressives, Social Gospel theologians, or reform novelists. Selfish materialism was the critical flaw in our national life, and Herrick believed that it must be repudiated by all classes of society in order to restore health to the American character. To tamper with our basic institutions was to deal with symptoms rather than causes. Rather than social legislation, Herrick wanted a renaissance of individual responsibility. Unlike Sheldon and Churchill, Herrick did not articulate a political position from which he would have to retreat. From the beginning, he repudiated the Social Gospel and championed individual responsibility. But the inevitable question arises: can the traditional concept of individual responsibility be applied to the problems of an urban-industrial society? Herrick never provides the reader with an alternative value system, and, as Granville Hicks has noted, his literature is in fact a repudiation of the industrial civilization: "Withdrawal from the world, a life completely free from every taint of commercialism, such a life he describes in *The Master of the Inn*, that was the only way for the man who prized his integrity."[54]

The protagonist of *The Master of the Inn* (1916) is a healer of souls who presides over an isolated inn where human wreckage from the urban-industrial world comes to be restored. A former medical doctor who had forsaken his career, the Master preaches the healing powers of *Work*. Sounding like a disciple of Carlyle, he describes to his patients his foolproof formula: "Trouble evaporates being properly aired . . . . For you must learn to forget . . . forget day by day until the recording soul beneath your mind is clean. Therefore—work, forget, be new!"[55] Whether an ailment is physical, psychic, or social, the same stoic formula

271

applies: "The best way to forget pain was through labor. Not labor merely for oneself; but also something for others." Herrick held the fatalistic attitude that there were no cures for the massive social problems of his day, so it was logical for him to prescribe withdrawal into personally meaningful activity as a means of overcoming the helplessness of the individual. Through such a course of action, the individual achieves a spiritual awakening which is the foundation of real social change. A major flaw in Herrick's theorizing is that he projected his Puritan consciousness on the mass of his fellowman who did not all have the spiritual aspirations waiting to be awakened and guided. Herrick's confused feelings about the great possibilities of the human will vs. man's helplessness in the face of massive social ills would evolve into misanthropy in later life as his dream vision of a reformed people never was realized.

Herrick wrote his most important fiction during the first decade of the twentieth century--*The Common Lot* (1904), *The Memoirs of an American Citizen* (1905) and *Together* (1908). The realism with which he invested these novels is inseparable from the moralizing, but it is a curiously atypical morality which goes against the grain of the public morality of the age. In *The Memoirs of an American Citizen*, Herrick sympathetically traces the economic rise of an American businessman, Edward Van Harrington, in the bustling Chicago meat industry. Harrington's journey from poor boy to successful entrepreneur is marked by many hollow victories, because Herrick's intent is to show him as the victim of a shoddy, materialistic dream. Insofar as Harrington is a capitalist, he is a unique hero for a social reform novel. Consistent with his inversion of the reform fiction cliches, Herrick reserves his severest criticism for a Social Gospel minister, the Reverend Mr. Hardman, to whom Sarah Harrington gravitates against her husband's wishes. "I wanted Sarah to try a new minister, who had sense enough to stick to his Bible, but she was loyal to Hardman, and even thought there might be something in his ideas."[56]

Impending confrontation between Hardman and Harrington is described from the latter's point of view. Herrick is clearly more sympathetic to the businessman, who is credited with helping society through the creation of jobs. He is presented as a man of affairs who tolerates, with some amusement, the minister's harebrained ideas, because "women and clergy, they were both alike, made for some other kind of earth than this. I was made for just this earth, good and bad as it is,-- and I must go my way to my end."[57] The antipathy between the two men later surfaces when Hardman delivers to his congregation a thinly-veiled sermon against Harrington, who has recently been accused by the newspapers of nefarious business practices. As Herrick describes the business deal, it is neither truly wicked nor perfectly innocent, but rather ethically marginal and typical for the time. There is nothing marginal about Hardman's self-righteousness, however, as he points accusingly at Harrington and his wife and shouts to the congregation:

> And I say when such men come into our churches, when they have the effrontery to mingle with God-fearing people, and, unrepentant of their crimes, desecrate this sanctuary, yea, partake of the Holy Body . . . . I'll tell you, my people, that here in our very midst one of them comes--a man who has defied the laws of man and God.[58]

Angered by this attack, Harrington rises to leave the church, and his wife, overcome with humiliation, faints.

Herrick has orchestrated his own attack on the Social Gospel theology in this dramatic scene. An unrepentant Harrington turns to chastise the minister. "So this is the gospel you preach! Let her alone! You have hit her hard enough already. Another time when you understand this kind of business, you had better know what you are talking about." With the aid of an usher, Harrington carries his wife to the vestibule and delivers a parting shot at Hardman. "I have had enough of *your* gospel, my friend! I am going where I shall hear religion and not newspaper scandal."[59] In arranging the conflict between businessman and Social Gospel minister, Herrick dismisses the newspapers as a source of information reducing muckraking journalism to little more than scandal mongering which injures innocent parties such as Sarah Harrington. The implications are clear that sermons should be based on the Bible and not on the newspapers, and that Hardman has made judgments in areas where his knowledge and experience are pitifully inadequate, and for the first time in the novels examined, the minister is the voice of a self-serving ignorance.

Herrick is not satisfied to show Hardman as merely self-righteous and simplistic; he later depicts him trying to make money through investments, and not being "man enough" to accept the consequences when the investments begin to fail. Both Harrington and Hardman stand to lose all their capital, but only the minister behaves badly under the stress, and it is Harrington who describes his shabby behavior:

> He stammered out his story. Some one had told him that I was in a bad shape . . . . It had not occurred to him to sell his bonds before he preached that little sermon at me; but, now that my sins were

apparently about to overtake me, he
wished to save his property from
destruction.[60]

Thus, Hardman is both hypocritical and cowardly about
capitalism, wanting the easy money and yet frightened of
the risk.

In bold contrast, Harrington commits himself to
the repayment of all the money he borrowed. He even
assumes responsibility for the whining minister's bad
investment, writing Hardman a personal check for the
entire amount. Hardman's acceptance of the check proves
his own greed to be the equal of any he has sermonized
about, and Harrington remarks half ironically, "Gold's
the things these days!" Hardman misses the irony, as
Harrington later discovers. "The cashier at the bank
told me afterward that Hardman made such a fuss when he
went to cash his check that they actually had to hand
him out six thousand dollars in gold coin."[61] In this
scene of money-worship, Herrick reverses completely the
cliches of reform literature making the Social Gospel
minister a caricature of avarice, while the capitalist
is a man of honor who stands on his record of
achievement:

> In all the forty years of my life
> there had been no evil as I know
> evil. No man could say that he had
> harm from me . . . and for thousands
> of . . . workers as live from day to
> day, depending on men like me to
> give them their chance to earn bread
> for their wives and children, I had
> made the world better rather than
> worse. Unthinking thousands lived
> and had children and got what good
> there was in life because of me and
> my will.[62]

275

There is a moral and class arrogance in Harrington's posture, especially when he hides behind the phrase "as I know evil," or interprets his own climb to power and wealth as beneficial to "unthinking thousands." Given a choice between Hardman and Harrington, it is the businessman who is at least a man of personal integrity. As Vernon L. Parrington had observed, it is amazing that he has been able to retain these values:

> The competitive order, he perceives,
> requires an ethics different from
> the Christian ideal. The survival
> of the fittest means the survival of
> the strongest, the most cunning and
> unscrupulous. The realist who deals
> with facts discovers that he lives
> in a world with pigs—little pigs of
> the village, larger hogs of the
> city. To get in the trough a man
> must have fingers and toes and use
> them. The world belongs to the
> strong.[63]

Arthur Hobson Quinn thought *The Memoirs of an American Citizen* one of Herrick's best novels, and he has argued that "Herrick has also been able in a masterly way to indicate through Harrington's narrative his lack of any real understanding of right and wrong. The picture of life in Chicago is accurate, and the inter-relations of politics and business are sufficiently indicated."[64] According to this view, Herrick's intent in tracing his character's rise from the farm, through industry, to the senate, was ironic, but if such is the case then he has provided a very poor alternative in the character of a weak and ignorant clergyman. Regarding this dilemma, which Herrick could not solve, Granville Hicks has suggested that:

> Herrick refused to deceive himself:
> individual integrity was more
> important than wealth and power,
> than industrialism itself. No
> puritan in the narrow sense, he
> voiced what was probably
> Puritanism's last protest against a
> social order that . . . it did much
> to make possible.[65]

Such a posture anticipates the escape theme of *The Master of The Inn* (1916) and the eventual misanthropy of *Waste* (1924), in which American life has taken on an utterly hopeless quality after the Great War. By repudiating the possibility of change envisioned in Social Gospel teachings, Herrick was forced in upon his own world of moral absolutes, and like Howells' Squire Gaylord in *A Modern Instance*, the Puritan vision proved to be self-consuming as mankind inevitably failed to fulfill its demanding strictures.

Edward Bellamy: The Gospel of Nationalism

The religious values given explicit statement in the reform novels, thus far covered, are also found in the secular utopian literature popular during this same period. As Jay Martin observes: "In some senses, the utopian novel became for a brief time the true National Novel. The American discourse was conducted as the clash of alternate utopias, each asserting its right to shape the future."[66] Edward Bellamy was a pivotal figure in the literary utopian debate, and a good deal of the discussion among the utopians focused upon Bellamy's futuristic vision in *Looking Backward*. Not only was this novel the germ of the Nationalist movement, but it gave programatic definition to all who shared the dream for a more just social system. Bellamy's basic plan called for the conversion of private capitalism into national capitalism presided over by a government bureaucracy. A new ruling class structured along military-civil service models would appropriate power to the most productive citizens while guaranteeing that all citizens had equal access to the wealth produced.

It has been observed by more than one critic that the underlying assumptions of Bellamy's secular state were religious, even though Bellamy claimed to be an unaffiliated Christian who did not accept the beliefs of his father's Baptist ministry. Merle Curti has described Bellamy's application of religious values as nevertheless implicit throughout *Looking Backward*: "His underlying philosophy . . . resembled one of the basic assumptions of social Christianity. The idea that Christian duty requires the application of the law of love to everyday relations."[67] Bellamy claimed that his intention in writing this book was to protest the rapidly deteriorating state of America from "the heart of all religion and the express meaning of Christ."[68] The secular nationalist state described in *Looking Backward* was Bellamy's attempt to institutionalize the fundamental teachings of Christ.

Not only is the intent of this utopia the realization of religious values, but the justification for the work ethic supporting Bellamy's futuristic state is derived from the Bible:

> Every man shall serve the nation for a fixed period . . . . With the exception of this fundamental law, which is, indeed, merely a codification of the law of nature-- the edict of Eden--our system depends in no particular upon

legislation, but is entirely
voluntary, the logical outcome of
the operation of human nature under
national conditions.[69]

Bellamy rejected the notion of competition and the
concept of private property, although he found it
necessary to retain a quasi-religious work ethic. The
better world envisioned by Bellamy is an amalgam of
nineteenth-century ideologies incorporating Marxian
income distribution with a new found enthusiasm for the
military as a model of rational bureaucratic efficiency.
The cornerstone for Bellamy's better world was an
undiminished faith in that old-fashioned capitalist
commodity--the work ethic.

The idea of reshaping society so that it reflects
basic Christian teaching was, as we have seen, a
prevailing theological concept in Bellamy's day. The
notion that such an idea could be realized was another
index of American optimism:

> For [Bellamy], as for Emerson,
> nothing was fixed in human nature,
> everything lent itself to
> transformation; men were naturally
> good, the will was able to work
> miracles, and, if mankind desired a
> reasonable world, why should it not
> obtain one overnight? This American
> faith, which outlived Bellamy, had
> actuated the Brook Farmers. All the
> revivalists shared it,--sudden
> changes, for them, were a matter of
> course; and it sprang from the age-
> old belief in the millennium that
> had always lurked in the depths of
> the Yankee mind.[70]

The need to transform society was obvious, and Bellamy shared with the Social Gospel theologians a distress with the failure of Christian churches to bear witness against social injustice. In *Looking Backward*, he conveys his displeasure through a sermon delivered by the Reverend Mr. Barton in the year 2000:

> It must not be forgotten that the nineteenth century was in name Christian, and the fact that the entire commercial and industrial frame of society was the embodiment of anti-Christian spirit must have had some weight, though I admit it was strangely little, with the nominal followers of Jesus Christ.[71]

This complaint is identical to the one sounded in the novels of Tourgee, Sheldon, Churchill, and Herrick, all of whom agreed with the inadequacy of existing church institutions to function meaningfully in the new industrial society.

Later in the novel, Bellamy speculates on the causes for the decline in religious belief during the nineteenth century. The Reverend Mr. Barton describes the bleakness of nineteenth-century living which robbed men of all sense of joy and as a result made them dissatisfied not only with their own broken lives but with everything about them. In the same sermon, Barton describes the prevailing pessimism of the age:

> Despising themselves, they despised their Creator. There was a general decay of religious belief. Pale and watery gleams, from skies thickly veiled by doubt and dread, alone lighted up the chaos of earth. That men should doubt Him whose breath is

in their nostrils . . . seems to us
a pitiable insanity . . . . The
dawn has come since then. It's very
easy to believe in the fatherhood of
God in the twentieth century.[72]

Bellamy is formulating a questionable thesis here—that
men's faith in God will be restored when their material
needs are satisfied, and the contemporary reader with
twentieth-century hindsight may be forgiven a malevolent
chortle at such unfounded optimism.

The idea that men will renew their religious
beliefs when all of society prospers is a prophecy which
runs counter to the observations of most novelists
covered in this study. Generally, these novelists
portray a middle-class which supports the church because
it reflects middle class values; church affiliation is
better described as nominal or formal, rather than as
the dawn of a new era. Bellamy would have been closer
to the truth about religious attitudes if he had said
that any intensity of belief would tend to dissipate
with prosperity. The psychological and social factors
which give impetus to intense religious convictions are
usually not found in comfortable societies shaped by
secular institutions such as the benevolent and
omnipresent Nationalist government of Bellamy's future
world.

As the details of Nationalism unfold, the reader
is confronted with not only a new and more just
relationship between labor and economic rewards, but the
emergence of a revolutionary collectivist model which
alters human behavior. The new order of society will be
the ultimate benefit to the generations yet to come, and
as described by Barton, it is a paradisical future:

The way stretches far before us, but
the end is lost in light. For

281

> twofold is the return of man to God
> 'who is our home,' . . . The long
> and weary winter of the race is
> ended.   Its summer has begun.
> Humanity has burst the chrysalis.
> The heavens are before it.[73]

Throughout the concluding section, Barton speaks for
Bellamy, a fact made evident by the similarity in style
and content of the "Postscript," in which Bellamy
addresses the reader directly.

> Not only are the toilers of the
> world engaged in something like a
> world-wide insurrection, but true
> and humane men and women, of every
> degree, in a mood of exasperation,
> verging on absolute revolt, against
> social conditions that reduce life
> to a brutal struggle for existence,
> mock every dictate of ethics and
> religion, and render well-nigh
> futile   the   efforts   of
> philanthropy.[74]

By creating a utopia in which the state assumes
responsibility for the well-being of every citizen,
Bellamy anticipated, by two decades, Churchill's
criticism of philanthropy as a mere stopgap measure.

For some modern readers, the benefits of Bellamy's
economic egalitarianism are an inadequate compensation
for the many totalitarian aspects of Nationalist
society. As Northrop Frye has observed:

> *Looking Backward* had, in its day, a
> stimulating and emancipating
> influence on the social thinking of
> the time in a way that very few

books in the history of literature
have ever had. Yet most of us today
would tend to read it as a sinister
blueprint of tyranny, with its
industrial 'army,' its stentorian
propaganda delivered over the
'telephone' to the homes of its
citizens, and the like.[75]

Reading this novel with the hindsight of the multifarious totalitarian debacles of the twentieth century, both facist and communist, one can become angry or amused by Bellamy's political naivete. His intentions, filled with the noblest sentiments, were given a particular political application which contained what Frye described as a "blueprint for tyranny." Bellamy's centralized and collectivist system of governance proved to be a prescription with disastrous side effects.

Looking Backward is filled with the metaphors of the millenium which Bellamy borrowed from religious sources and incorporated into his secular novel, so that its long-range intent is a revival of religious interest. Bellamy stated that his underlying belief in writing *Looking Backward* was "that the Golden Age lies before us and not behind us, and is not far away. Our children will surely see it, and we, too, who are already men and women if we deserve it by our faith and works."[76] This concept of a reward based on "faith and works" suggests that Bellamy's vision is another kind of heavenly metaphor, a heaven which can be achieved through the institution of social justice for all. The ultimate glory awaiting mankind is a new beginning in which "The heavens are before it," and with such heavenly city images for society's future, Bellamy is the agent of the Enlightenment undaunted by the complex and harsh realities of urban-industrial America.

The millenial vision implicit in *Looking Backward* is also found in Howells' Altrurian romances--*A Traveler from Altruria* (1894) and *Through the Eye of the Needle* (1907). Although thirteen years passed between the publication of the two Altrurian romances, they are companion pieces which contain the substance of Howells' matured vision for social reform. As noted earlier, Howells' fiction evolved in the 1880's from a reflection of bourgeois manners and morals to a didactic literature of reform. His earlier economic novels--*The Minister's Charge, Annie Kilburn,* and *A Hazard of New Fortunes*-- dealt with social injustice, but it is the later utopian fiction that offers specific recommendations for reform. In 1888, Howells credited the New Testament as the inspiration for a generation of reform writers. "Christ and the life of Christ is at this moment inspiring the literature of the world as never before."[77] What he too broadly assigned to world literature was certainly true of his own work, and in the following year he returned to Boston and began associating with the Christian Socialists, who counted in their number such men as Edward Bellamy, Hamlin Garland, Richard T. Ely, W.D.P. Bliss, and Vidu Scudder, and their companionship was to effect dramatic changes in Howells' perspective.[78]

There is some dispute as to what had been the dominant influence on Howells in his creation of Altruria. Daniel Aaron has asserted that both romances were "most certainly derived from *Looking Backward* as well as from William Morris, Mazzini, Campanella, Ruskin, and Plato."[79] One difficulty with this theory is that it ignores Tolstoi's influence as a Christian Socialist and the effect of the Boston intellectual milieu to which Howells had attached himself. Clara Marburg Kirk speculates that the utopian romances might be read as Howells' response to the urgent pleas of

W. D. P. Bliss for a Christian Socialist literature, which appeared regularly in his journal, *Dawn*. Kirk also views the Altrurian romances as a logical step in the continuum of Howells' evolving social sensibility:

> . . . the reader [of the Altrurian novels] was carried one step further toward Christian Socialism . . . [and] introduced to an actual community of Christian Socialists expressing its belief in communal living in a remote land called Altruria.[80]

In the opening passage of *A Traveler from Altruria*, Howells makes explicit the relationship between the Christian tradition and the land of Altruria when Aristides Homos notes that his "civilization is strictly Christian . . . that of the first Christian commune after Christ." Even though Howells' own confidence in the supernatural dimension of Christianity had declined, he still used this tradition to create a personally meaningful structure in which Christian ethics were applied to social institutions.

> His practical social religion brought him a greater sense of security and real achievement. He conceived of it as an application of Christian ethics to democratic life. It was a Christianity shorn of its creed, dogmas, and orthodoxies, a religion whose purpose was to establish here and now the principles of human brotherhood.[81]

Howells projects his Christian Socialism into the altruism which humanizes Altruria, but as sympathetic as he was to Christian Socialism, he did have reservations because as a doctrine it was "loaded with the creed of the church, the very terms of which revolted me."[82]

The principles of Christian Socialism form the basic tenets of Altrurian life, but Homos, like his creator, speaks of Christianity as an ethical system. Unlike Bellamy, Howells repudiated the machine as a potential factor in freeing man. Aristides Homos is not a spokesman for a new world order: he is an ironic commentator who "is unable to value our devotion to the spirit of Christianity amid the practices which seem to deny it; but he evidently wishes to recognize the possibility of such a thing."[83] The passage is characteristic of Howells' technique of ironic counterpoint, with Homos always functioning as an ethical observer who measures the variance between professed ideals and actual social and political practices. Altruria is a real utopia because its ethical beliefs are woven into the fabric of society.

The two main characters in *A Traveler from Altruria* are the respectable author Mr. Twelvemough and the Altrurian Mr. Homos. Each reflects a dimension of Howells' own character: the established author in his early career and the increasingly concerned idealist. In the last decade of the nineteenth century, the dominant aspect of Howells' personality was clearly Homos, whose ethical perspective sharply contrasts with Twelvemough's shallow and venal attitudes. As Homos goes about helping railroad porters carry baggage and waitresses carry their trays, his genial interaction with the serving classes suggests Howells' own egalitarian disposition formed in the Ohio Territory of his childhood which is in dramatic contrast with the stuffy, supercilious New Englander Mr. Twelvemough. The novel's regional dialectic suggests that Howells' early values eventually triumphed over the adopted Brahmin persona of the Boston years.

The conflict between Altrurian and American values is given particular focus in the different attitudes manifested toward service people. Homos has come to America expecting to find a society similar to his native Altruria based on his reading of the Declaration of Independence, the Bill of Rights, and the Constitution. These documents contain the ideals which have shaped his homeland Altruria, but Homos soon discovers that these historical documents contain ideas no longer considered practical in the new industrial America. The contemporary deities are wealth, private property, and rugged individualism. The conservative Mr. Twelvemough is a rhapsodic apologist for the status quo when he declares:

> I consider it a perfect system. It is based upon individuality, and we believe that individuality is the principle that differences civilized men from savages, from the lower animals, and makes us a nation instead of a tribe or a herd.[84]

He goes on to justify the right of a man to destroy woodland by explaining to Homos that: "The woods were his; he had the right to do what he pleased with his own." The rights of private property are ultimate and inviolable in the new America which no longer gives even lip-service to the concept of stewardship, and what Homos finds most astonishing is the failure of his American acquaintances to perceive the violent abuses carried on in the name of property rights. Even more disturbing is their failure to understand the debilitating effect of their beliefs on their own humanity.

At one point, Homos explains to his American hosts that they should not have such difficulty believing in the efficacy of the Altrurian system, since it emulates the altruism common to the early followers of Christ. Altruria has organized a "national polity and a working economy" based on these Christian principles, and Homos notes ironically that Americans should certainly understand such concepts.[85] Howells lingers over the stark contrast between Christian Altruria and materialistic America by having the American Mrs. Makely dismiss the altruism of the early Christians as fanatical. She tells Homos that

> . . . they had to drop that. It was
> a dead failure. They found that
> they couldn't make it go at all,
> among cultivated people, and that,
> if Christianity was to advance, they
> would have to give up all that
> crankish kind of idolatry of the
> mere letter.[86]

Mrs. Makely, the voice of institutional Christianity, sounds the familiar arguments already reviewed in this chapter, and Howells repeats Tourgee's judgment that the institutional churches of America had been coopted to serve the ends of a capitalist class.

Later in the novel, Howells underscores the worldly character of the American Christian churches when Homos asks a minister how many workingmen are in his congregation, and the minister, slightly embarrassed about his congregation's social composition, sputters out the following apologia:

> I suppose they have their own
> churches. I have never thought that
> such a separation of the classes was
> right; and I have had some of the
> very best people--socially and
> financially--with me in the wish
> that there might be more

288

brotherliness between the rich and
the poor among us. But as yet--[87]

The minister's ineffective casuistry provides emphasis
to the absurd idea of a "Christian" community being
shaped by the economic status of its membership.

Nowhere in either of the two Altrurian romances
does Howells give a satisfactory explanation for the
successful evolution of Altruria. There is a statement
in Chapter Eleven of *A Traveler from Altruria* about its
people rejecting the notion of accumulation based on
private property, as a result of which social priorities
underwent a radical change. Although this revolutionary
break with the notion of accumulation remains
unexplained, the subsequent evolution in social
attitudes is compared to the cycle of life, and Howells
uses explicitly religious imagery to describe the
process: "The truth itself must perish to our senses
before it can live to our soul; the Son of Man must
suffer upon the cross before we can know the Son of
God."[88] The secret of Altruria's evolution remains
hidden in the mystical language of Mr. Homos, who like
his creator is unprepared for more specific
descriptions. A Christian ethic prevails in Altruria
without benefit of churches because, as earlier noted,
Howells had little patience with the specific creeds of
individual denominations. As Mr. Homos notes:

> We have several forms of ritual, but
> no form of creed, and our religious
> differences may be said to be
> aesthetic and temperamental rather
> than theological and essential . . .
> we look at the life of a man rather
> than the profession for proof that
> he is a religious man.[89]

Howells employs various representative professionals as the spokespersons for the conventional bourgeois beliefs of the age. Members of this class-- bankers, ministers, professors, industrialists--consider Homos an initially amusing curiosity whose ideas become increasingly irritating, while the working classes grow quite fond of him after their initial surprise at his egalitarian behavior. The pattern of Homos' relationship with Twelvemough reflects the tensions created by his constant measuring of Altrurian ideals against American realities. Twelvemough informs the reader

> . . . his acquaintance has become more and more difficult, and I was not sorry to part with him. That taste of his for low company was incurable . . . . I think he remained very popular with the classes he most affected.[90]

The effete Twelvemough has learned little from Mr. Homos, except perhaps to avoid further involvement with men like him. Since the novel ends on this note, one wonders whether Howells intends to convey the hopelessness of changing attitudes among the ruling classes, or whether one should read Twelvemough simply as an object-lesson in the kind of rude insensitivity which the middle-class readers of the period would wish to avoid. If this was Howells' intent, he was using a very clever form of propaganda for his social ideas. Twelvemough was a novelist whose sentimental fiction was in all likelihood read by the same type of people who would be reading *A Traveler from Altruria*. The business of changing the tastes and values of that reading public was the job that Howells took upon himself to accomplish, and ridiculing the popular literature which supported the status quo was one of the weapons he used throughout the Altrurian romances. Twelvemough, clearly a fool when measured against the humane and ethical Homos, is a symbol from which sensible readers would undoubtedly draw the right conclusions.

Despite the thirteen-year lapse between *A Traveler from Altruria* and its sequel, *Through the Eye of the Needle*, there was no new inspiration. As the critic George N. Bennett noted: "Howells simply eked out some old material already published in magazine form. He was by that time seventy years old, and his best work was behind him."[91] In preparing a library copy for these two books, Howells wrote in the preface that he considered the two utopian romances as born "of one blood" containing the abiding conviction "that emulation, rather than competition, is the only solution of our economic problems."[92]

One theme emphasized in the second Altrurian romance is the destructive consequences of egotism. Homos sees that the preoccupation with self at the expense of others can only result in a fragmented social order. He tells some dinner companions that:

> [Americans] must understand that the essential vice of a system which concentrates a human being's thoughts upon his own interests . . . colors and qualifies every motive with egotism.[93]

In others words, a society in which the individual ego is given pre-eminent status can never achieve the

Christian character of an Altruria. Homos' American hostess answers him with the practical wisdom of the day:

> Oh, people *never* do the charity that Christ meant . . . . Who would dream

> of dividing half her frocks and
> wraps with poor women, or selling
> *all* and giving to the poor . . . .
> We know that Christ was perfectly
> right, and that He was perfectly
> sincere in what He said to the good
> young millionaire but we all go away
> exceedingly sorrowful, just as the
> good young millionaire did.[94]

Howells conveys the sense that Christ is an impractical
visionary in the minds of nineteenth-century Americans.
But the final irony is the perception of the man of
wealth as "the good young millionaire," based, no doubt,
on his assets rather than his virtues. The inversion of
the Christian tradition by a materialistic society which
persists in defining itself as Christian was a puzzle
which confounded Howells and many other social
commentators of the period.

Howells' ambivalent attitude toward Christianity
was in evidence throughout both Altrurian romances.
Although he felt revulsion toward certain creeds and
toward ritualistic adherence to Christianity, he
nevertheless measured all experience by a Christian
ethic. His insistence on describing Altruria as a truly
Christian land might be interpreted as a simple
rhetorical device to legitimize this Marxist idyll for
his middle-class readers. Howells did not believe that
the world would be changed by a feverish wave of
conversions to Christian Socialism, and he conveyed
these sentiments in his portrait of the callous moral
sensibility of the American ruling class. Hope for
America rested in legislating the ideas set forth in
both the utopian novels and the reform novels. In 1890,
Howells noted in a letter to his father: "By and by
labor will be so pinched that the politicians will have
to put a socialistic plank into a platform, and then the
party that stands on it will win."[95]

By 1912, the Progressive Party had absorbed into its platform most of the principles for which the leaders of the Social Gospel and Christian Socialism had been campaigning. Theology became politically possible in that year.

> The party convention had as its theme song 'Onward Christian Soldiers,' and Theodore Roosevelt closed his acceptance speech with the ringing challenge, 'We stand at Armageddon and we battle for the Lord.' Ministers campaigned openly from the pulpit for the party . . . [because] the principles of the Progressive party should guide the nation for the next four years.[96]

Although the Progressives were defeated in 1912, the principles enunciated in the radical visions of the Social Gospel reformers and utopianists were to become the basis for such legislation as : anti-trust laws, binding arbitration, welfare and relief payments, unemployment compensation, government-financed housing, and the graduated income tax.

* *

The reform novelists and utopian novelists suggested similar remedies for America's social and political problems. Both reformers and utopianists believed that the literal application of Christian principles would serve to redress widespread economic injustices, and they held the naive notion that human misery would be resolved through the equitable distribution of wealth. The history of man is cluttered with ideological panaceas which promised the dawning of a new age. Christopher Dawson has noted that the fusion of religion with social movements is futile and destructive because

> . . . the religious impulse behind these social movements is not a constructive one . . . . As soon as the victory is gained and the phase of destruction and revolution is ended, the inspiration fades away before the tasks of practical realization.[97]

Dawson never explains what a constructive religious impulse might be, but his observation on the transitory nature of the union between religion and reform appears historically valid, and the prevailing theology in the twentieth century, profoundly influenced by existential concerns, gives further credibility to his thesis.

As noted earlier in the discussion of *Looking Backward*, a utopianist was subject to colossal errors in political and social judgment in the course of imagining a better world. The more thoughtful utopianists, such as Howells, were extremely wary of collectivist models. Howells was always fearful that utopian life would destroy man's freedom to practice the traditional virtues--bravery, constancy, self-denial, and self-assertion--because these virtues would be meaningless and unnecessary in a static society which has assumed responsibility for caring for all the needs of its citizenry. Jay Martin has extended the implications of this dialectic by noting:

> Thus for Howells the vision of utopia inevitably brings with it the dystopian nightmare he vaguely felt. The abundance of utopias in the late nineteenth century has resulted, for

this reason, in not only the
existence, but even the popularity
of the dystopia in our own day, of
which Orwell's *1984* and Huxley's
Brave New World are obvious
examples.[98]

As noted earlier in this chapter, it is unfair to
dismiss a utopia without understanding the motivation
behind its creation. Reform and utopian novels were
born of the same frustrations with the real economic
injustices of America's new industrialism. For a brief
moment in history, ministers, novelists, economists, and
finally politicians joined under the banners of reform
to attempt to redress the injustices that seemed to be
engulfing society. Ministers used the novel to preach
sermons, while novelists preached sermons in their
fiction. For both, Christ was the model of justice and
charity by which our social and economic institutions
should be guided.

The campaign by the Progressive Party in 1912 was
not the beginning of the movement, as many thought, but
rather its apex. As its ideas were absorbed into the
platforms of the two major political parties, the need
for the Progressive Party declined. A similar fate
awaited the Social Gospel movement, for as time passed
it looked more and more curious and quaintly innocent.
The Social Gospel was a theology to meet the problems of
a particular age. Prominent Protestant theologians such
as Reinhold Niebuhr and Paul Tillich were to assert a
more orthodox Christian vision which repudiated the
possibility that the Kingdom of God could be realized in
any conceivable socialist society.[99] This new vision,
called liberal realism, took into account the historical
patterns of man's behavior which argued against the
viability of any future universal brotherhood. As
Neibuhr wrote:

> A too simple social radicalism does
> not recognize how quickly the poor,
> the weak, the despised of yesterday,
> may . . . exhibit the same arrogance
> and the same will-to-power . . .
> which they were inclined to regard
> as a congenital sin of their
> enemies. Every victim of injustice
> makes the mistake of supposing that
> the sin from which he suffers is a
> peculiar vice of his oppressor.[100]

Niebuhr's reflections on the transitory character of social theology is a representative response of many twentieth-century neo-orthodox theologians who have contributed to a revisionist interpretation of Social Gospel theology. It is difficult to dispute the theoretical limitations of any political theology which links itself to specific programs of social reform, but it seems improper to dismiss such theologies which have contributed to the improvement of the human condition.[101] The Social Gospel theologians and their secular allies participated in a social revolution which harnessed the raw energy of industrialism and redirected its potency to the service of mankind.

296

EPILOGUE

The religious theme with its many variations has continued to be a significant factor in American fiction. Even the moribund reform novel had a brief renaissance during the Depressions years, and, once again, it was the institutional church which was portrayed as opposed to any attempts to achieve social justice. There was one major difference between the Depression novels and earlier reform fiction—the reactionary church was no longer always Protestant. In *Jews Without Money* (1930), Michael Gold resolves his protagonist's awakening to social issues by having him reject his Judaism in favor of Marxism. The novel ends with his revolutionary hope and exultation: "O workers' Revolution, you brought hope to me, a lonely, suicidal boy. You are the true Messiah. You will destroy the East Side when you come, and build there a garden for the human spirit."[1] James T. Farrell concludes *Studs Lonigan* (1932-1935) on a similar note of impending revolution. Studs is portrayed as the hapless victim of a spiritually impoverished Roman Catholicism, and on the day that he dies, workers are marching in the streets bearing signs of the new creed—"We'll Starve No More," "No Work No Rent," "We Demand Unemployment Insurance." In such a context the death of Studs Lonigan seems to herald a new social order, in which men will no longer be victimized by a religion which demands passivity in exchange for salvation.

The social reform theme is also present in John Steinbeck's *The Grapes of Wrath* (1939). Jim Casey abandons his fundamentalist religion for a social activism which echoes the ideas of Social Gospel theology. When Casey dies, suggesting a Christ-like sacrifice, Tom Joad assumes the role of an apostle who is totally committed to fighting economic oppression:

> Wherever they's a fight so hungry
> people can eat, I'll be there.
> Wherever they's a cop beatin' up a
> guy, I'll be there . . . . An' when
> our folks eat the stuff they raise
> an' live in the houses they build--
> why, I'll be there. See? God, I'm
> talkin' like Casey. Comes of
> thinkin' about him so much.[2]

Justice is the unifying creed of Joad's new faith; the new eucharist will be men enjoying the fruits of their labors.

Throughout the twentieth century, novelists continued to examine the collapse of religious orthodoxy. Jewish and Catholic novelists describe the loss of faith in a manner reminiscent of the nineteenth-century Protestant authors. The recession of the old orthodoxies before the tide of modernism was noted by George Santayana in 1913: "the civilization characteristic of Christendom has not disappeared, yet another civilization has begun to take its place."[3] It is this undefined civilization displacing the old faiths which creates an ideological tension in a number of contemporary novels. Although F. Scott Fitzgerald and Ernest Hemingway did not make extensive use of their religious backgrounds in their fiction, they did use it as a counterpoint to the newer consciousness. In *This Side of Paradise* (1920), Amory Blaine chafes against his Catholic upbringing:

> The idea was strong in him that
> there was a certain intrinsic lack
> in those to whom orthodox religion
> was necessary, and religion to Amory
> meant the Church of Rome. Quite
> conceivably it was an empty ritual
> but it was seemingly the only
> assimilative, traditional bulwark
> against the decay of morals . . . .
> Yet any acceptance was, for the
> present, impossible. He wanted time
> and the absence of ulterior
> pressure.[4]

Amory's pursuit of a new consciousness makes Catholicism
impossible because, for all its harmony and apparent
moral rightness, it limits his possibilities. In
contrast, Jake Barnes in *The Sun Also Rises* (1926)
continues to identify himself as a Catholic, although
religion affords him little comfort in his frustrating
relationship with Lady Brett. He reflects bitterly that
"The Catholic Church had an awfully good way of handling
all that. Good advice, anyway. Not to think about it.
Oh, it was swell advice. Try and take it sometime. Try
and take it."[5] Jake's stoicism is ultimately more
meaningful than his nominal Catholicism, and one
suspects that Studs Lonigan might have escaped his
sterile environment if he also had been capable of
putting his Catholicism aside.

The Catholic experience in America still awaits a
full treatment in fiction. Novels such as J. F. Powers'
Morte D'Urban (1962), Tom McHale's *Farragan's Retreat*
(1971), and John Gregory Dunne's *True Confessions* (1977)
incorporate Catholic experience into fictive form, but
the American Catholic is still more likely to find his
religious experiences reflected in Joyce's *A Portrait of
the Artist as a Young Man* than in any novel written by
an American. As more than one commentator has noted,

the defensiveness of the Catholic writer about his
background has vanished and "by escape from pretended
beliefs, Catholic writers have gained maneuvering room:
a fictive belief collapses into believable fiction
. . . . [Catholic novelists] can [now] talk of their
strange upbringing because they have (partially) escaped
it."[6]

Jewish novelists have made extensive use of the
tension between prevailing American secular values and
Jewish religious and cultural traditions. The question
raised by Abraham Cahan in *The Rise of David Levinsky* is
still the question raised by Jewish novelists: What
price does the Jew pay for assimilation into American
life? In *Goodbye, Columbus* (1958), Phillip Roth
satirizes a middle-class Jewish family who have put
aside their heritage in favor of a vulgar consumerism.
Bernard Malamud, in *The Assistant* (1957), presents a
failing Jewish shopkeeper whose dignity can be measured
by his stubborn adherence to Jewish law, especially when
other Jews desert the law to pursue worldly success.
The law by which Bober the shopkeeper abides is simple:

> [It] means to do what is right, to
> be honest, to be good . . . . Our
> life is hard enough. Why should we
> hurt somebody else? For everybody
> should be the best, not only for you
> or me. We ain't animals. This is
> why we need the Law. This is what a
> Jew believes.[7]

Malamud's character is anachronistic, for he continues
to believe what his Jewish neighbors have long since
disregarded. A sense of displacement and disorientation
in a hostile environment is a recurring problem for the
protagonists of Saul Bellow's novels. Asa Leventhal in
The Victim (1947) is representative; he is a second
generation Jew isolated from his past, alienated in the

300

urban present, and hounded by a WASP named Allbee who demands that Asa confess to an act of which he is not guilty. Leventhal's dilemma mirrors the pressures on the Jew in America to conform to the prevailing values of the dominant culture, even when acquiescence is absurd.

Although Jewish novelists have expressed the most concern with the decline of religiously inspired culture, various aspects of Protestantism continue to be scrutinized by novelists whose roots are in the Protestant tradition. With *Elmer Gantry* (1927), Sinclair Lewis analyzed evangelism with the same sharp eye Howells had used in *The Leatherwood God*. The still dominant Protestant culture receives additional fictional post-mortems in Santayana's *The Last Puritan* (1936), and, more recently, in John Updike's Rabbit Trilogy--*Rabbit, Run* (1960), *Rabbit Redux* (1972), and *Rabbit is Rich* (1982). Rabbit Angstrom is burdened by his loss of belief, and his desperate need for order surfaces in the occasional brief prayers which punctuate the narrative of *Rabbit, Run*. Lying in bed with his mistress on a Sunday morning, watching the churchgoers through a window, Rabbit prays: "Help me, Christ. Forgive me. Take me down the way. Bless Ruth, Janice, Nelson, my mother and father, Mr. and Mrs. Springer, and the unborn baby. Forgive Tothero and all the others. Amen."[8] The spiritual angst experienced by the young man is eventually blunted by his gradual absorption into the bourgeois life, and through the character of Rabbit, Updike has illustrated the extraordinary power of material success in mollifying the traditional concerns of religion.

In William Styron's *Lie Down in Darkness* (1951), the loss of faith which helps to destroy a Southern Protestant family suggests the larger traumas of American life. Styron uses Ella Swain, a black servant, as a counterpoint of spiritual strength in a manner

301

reminiscent of Faulkner's use of Dilsey in *The Sound and
the Fury*. The central characters in Styron's novel are
casualties: Mr. Loftis, alcoholic and disillusioned;
Mrs. Loftis, filled with bitterness and hatred; and
Peyton, their oldest daughter, who commits suicide.
News of the bombing of Hiroshima acts as a catalyst for
the disintegration of the Loftis family. Peyton's
breakdown accelerates after she hears of the bombing on
the radio, and her thoughts take a decidedly religious
turn:

> Oh my God, why have I forsaken You?
> Have I through some evil inherited
> in a sad century cut myself off from
> you forever, and thus only by dying
> must take the final change: to walk
> into a dark closet and lie down
> there and dream away my sins, hoping
> to wake in another land, in a far
> fantastic dawn?[9]

Her final thoughts before her death are a desperate
prayer for hope. "Perhaps I shall rise at another time,
though I lie down in darkness and have my light in
ashes."[10] Styron concludes the novel with Ella Swain's
hopeful cries at a revival meeting: "Yes, Jesus! I
seen Him! Yeah! Yeah! . . . Yes. Jesus! Yeah!
Yeah!"[11] It would be foolish to conclude that Styron is
prescribing an evangelistic faith as a cure for modern
man's spiritual bankruptcy. But if we interpret Ella's
"Yeah! Yeah!" as an expression of man's need to assert
a faith in some transcendent meaning, the novel might be
read as a parable of hope.[12]

In *Modern Poetry and the Christian Tradition*, Amos
N. Wilder notes that "the artist takes on the role of
the seer and art tends toward religious ceremony,
especially in the wide use of myth."[13] American
novelists will undoubtedly continue to write about

churches and sects because they are the visible representations of interior tensions experienced by the artist, the tensions between spiritual aspirations and physical reality. As we have seen throughout this study, the novelist measures the success or failure of the churches by the ideals of the Judeo-Christian tradition. In so doing, he functions as a restorative agent for the spiritual life of his society. William Faulkner noted on the occasion of receiving his Nobel Prize that it is the privilege of the writer

> . . . to help man endure by lifting his heart, by reminding him of the courage and honor and hope and pride and compassion and pity and sacrifice which have been the glory of his past. The poet's voice need not merely be the record of man, it can be one of the props, the pillars to help him endure and prevail.[14]

To evaluate and to criticize religious institutions was, and continues to be, an important subject for the novelists concerned with the moral and spiritual climate of American life.

In this study, we have examined how several generations of American novelists described the changing character of American religious expression and their concern with this phenomenon. The decline of belief in traditional religions seemed to threaten the very order of the civilized world they had known. As Emily Dickinson had noted in her epigramatic verse:

> The abdication of Belief
> Makes the Behavior small—
> Better an ignis fatuus
> Than no illume at all

In recent years, there has been a spate of social science literature which has echoed and updated the earlier expressed concerns of the novelists covered in this study. Daniel Bell's *The Cultural Contradictions of Capitalism* (1976), Christopher Lasch's *The Culture of Narcissism* (1979), Richard Sennett's *The Fall of Public Man* (1976), and countless others describe, in sometimes strident terms, the negative consequences flowing from the excesses of material capitalism. The emergence of the self as an idol is read as an almost inevitable consequence of bourgeois consumerism, and this new idolatry shifts authority from society to the imperious self. In so doing, the Ideology of Self displaces the inhibiting and social functions of religious institutions by purging their authority and implicitly giving license to anti-social behavior. Robert Bellah with his Civil Religion thesis has given us an accurate description of the ritual and myths of contemporary America with their quasi-religious character, but what he and others are describing is not a substitute for the authority of traditional faiths whether they be Protestant, Catholic or Jew.

The search for belief has not abated with the passage of years. The novelists covered in this study anticipated in their fictive worlds the anguish which has come to be the haunting concern of thoughtful Americans in the twilight years of the twentieth century. The absence of religious belief appears to have the serious social and moral consequences feared, but the prescription seems even more cloudy than a hundred years ago. The search continues.

NOTES

INTRODUCTION

[1]*The American Vision* (New Haven: Yale Univ. Press, 1963), p. 5.

[2]Thomas C. Hall describes this tradition in *The Religious Background of American Culture* (Boston: Little Brown, 1930). "The historic priesthood lost all meaning (after the Reformation), for every Christian was a priest before God, and was under obligation so far as he had gifts and strength to proclaim the word of God. The forgiveness of sin . . . depended solely upon the calling of God to life and duty (p. 20)."

[3]Pietism and the American Character," *The American Experience*. ed. Hennig Cohen (Boston: Houghton Mifflin, 1968), pp. 57-58.

[4]"The Indignity Put Upon the Remains of George Holland by the Rev. Mr. Sabine," *Mark Twain's Contributions to the Galaxy* (Gainesville, Fla.: Florida State Univ. Press, 1961), pp. 128-129.

[5]*Modern Poetry and the Christian Tradition* (New York: Scribner, 1952), pp. xii-xiii.

[6]Forum, 10 (November, 1890), p. 286.

[7]"The Background of the American Novel," *Yale Review*, III (January, 1914), p. 214.

[8]*Theory of Literature* (New York: Harcourt, Brace 1949), pp. 99-100.

[9]*Novelist's America: Fiction as History* (Syracuse: Syracuse Univ. Press, 1969), pp. 4-5.

[10]*Critic*, 41 (December, 1902), p. 537.

[11]"The Responsibilities of the Novelist," *Critic*, 41 (December, 1902), p. 538.

[12]"Social History in American Literature," *Yale Review*, 18 (September, 1928), p. 147.

[13]*Culture and Anarchy* (Cambridge: Cambridge Univ. Press, 1961), pp. 206-207. Arnold concluded his analysis of his century's ills with the Following hopeful prophecy in *Culture and Anarchy*. "But, although those chiefly attracted by sweetness and light will probably always be the young and enthusiastic, and culture must not hope to take the mass of mankind by storm . . . . "yet" . . . . however great the changes to be accomplished (by the forces of Hebraism and Hellenism), and however dense the array of Barbarians, Philistines, and Populace, we will neither despair on the one hand, nor, on the other, threaten violent revolution and change. But we will look forward cheerfully and hopefully to 'a revolution,' as the Duke of Wellington said, 'by due course of law . . . .'"

[14]*The American Scene* (New York, 1907), p. 23.

[15]Jones writes: "Most of the religious novels I have looked into make their subject the education by life of a minister or a partisan of some form of Christian orthodoxy into a wider knowledge of, and

sympathy for, his fellow men. There are, doubtless, stories of a contrary tendency; in general, however, American fictionists tend to the view that sectarianism is a blind alley (*Belief and Disbelief in American Literature*, p. 71)." This generalization ignores the predominant ambivalence of most American fictionists toward sectarianism as a frequently narrowing but nevertheless very real spiritual and moral catalyst in the lives of their characters, an ambivalence found in the novels of Howells, Stowe, Eggleston, Howe, Tourgee, and Churchill.

[16]Arnold Smithline, *Natural Religion in American Literature* (New Haven: College and Univ. Press, 1966), p. 167.

[17]Stewart, p. 149.

[18]cf. *American Civil Religion*, eds. Russell E. Richey and Donald G. Jones (New York: Harper & Row, 1974). This text contains the original essay by Robert Bellah which appeared in *Daedalus* (Winter, 1967) along with a number of critical and supportive responses to Bellah's thesis. Of particular interest are the following essays in this collection: Will Herberg's "America's Civil Religion: What It Is and When It Comes," Martin E. Marty's "Two Kinds of Civil Religion," and Leo Marx's "The Uncivil Response of American Writers to Civil Religion in America."

CHAPTER I–THE NOVELIST AND THE NEW ENGLAND TRADITION

[1]Two novels dealing with the spiritual cults in New England after the Civil War--Elizabeth Stuart Phelps' *The Gates Ajar* and Henry James' *The Bostonians*--will be discussed later in this study.

[2]*The American Vision* (New Haven: Yale Univ. Press, 1963), p.70.

[3]John T. Frederick, *The Darkened Sky* (South Bend, Indiana: Notre Dame Univ. Press, 1969), p. 48.

[4]*The Blithedale Romance* (New York: Norton, 1958), p. 156.

[5]The discord between orthodoxy and liberalism dates back to the seventeenth century and to the debate which preceded the adoption of the Half-Way Covenant (1662). William Haller observes in *The Puritan Town-Planting in New England Colonial Development, 1630-1660.* (New York: Columbia Univ. Press, 1951) that the cause for the dissolution Puritan orthodoxy can ultimately be traced to Puritan dogma. "The Puritans' great failure was in their attempt to maintain social unity through orthodoxy. At the beginning they did not doubt that they had the means of discovering the truth, and the power and the duty to suppress deviations from it. But their philosophical method itself tended toward diversity and intellectual individualism, and the conditions of frontier life gave the individualism the means of survival (p. 110)."

[6]Joseph Haroutunian, *Piety Versus Moralism: The Passing of New England Theology* (New York: H. Holt & Co., 1932), p. xxii. For more recent interpretations of American religious developments in the period from the Great Awakening to the American Revolution see: "The Socialization of Piety" in Perry Miller's *The New England Mind: From Colony to Province* (Cambridge: Harvard Univ. Press, 1953), Alan Heimert's *Religion and the American Mind* (Cambridge: Harvard Univ. Press, 1966), and Conrad Wright's *The Beginnings of Unitarianism in America* (Boston, 1955).

[7]*Piety Versus Moralism*, pp. 89-90.

[8]*Religion in America: Past and Present* (Englewood Cliffs, N.J.: Prentice-Hall, 1961), p. 75.

[9] In strong reaction against the theocratic interpretation of New England Puritanism, Clifford K. Shipton has written a number of articles: "A Plea for Puritanism," *American Historical Review* 60 1935), 460-467; "Puritanism and Modern Democracy," *New England Historical and Geneological Register*, 101 (1947), 181-198; and "The New England Clergy in the 'Glacial Age'," *Publications of the Colonial Society of Massachusetts*, 31 (1933). Shipton has categorically denied the existence of any Puritan orthodoxy such as is posited by Perry Miller. Other modifications of Miller's thesis may be found in Edmund S. Morgan's *Visible Saints* (New York, 1963), Darrett B. Rutman's *Winthrop's Boston* (Chapel Hill, N.C., 1965) and in Larzer Ziff's *The Career of John Cotton* (Princeton, N.J., 1962). While contemporary historians may argue the very existence of Puritan orthodoxy in the seventeenth century, there can be little doubt that orthodoxy existed in the fiction of the nineteenth century as an historical reality with which the fictionists measured the religious beliefs of his own age.

[10]*Henry Wadsworth Longfellow* (New York: Twayne, 1964) p. 123.

[11]*Longfellow: A Full Length Portrait* (New York: Oxford Univ. Press, 1955), p. 296.

[12]Henry Wadsworth Longfellow, *Kavanagh: A Tale* (New Haven: College & Univ. Press, 1965), p. 43.

[13]*Kavanagh*, p. 49.

[14]*Kavanagh*, p. 78.

[15]*Kavanagh*, p. 80.

[16]*American Poets: From the Puritans to the Present* (Boston: Houghton-Mifflin, 1968), p.42.

[17]For a religiously orthodox interpretation of American writers such as Holmes, one should read Augustus Hopkins Strong's *American Poets and Their Theology* (Freeport, N.Y.: Books for Libraries Press, 1968), esp. pp. 320-345. It is Strong's thesis that Holmes was rebelling against "hyper-Calvinism" rather than Calvinism.

[18]Oliver Wendell Holmes, *Elsie Venner* (Boston: Ticknor & Fields, 1861), I, 84.

[19]*Elsie Venner*, I, 85-86.

[20]*Elsie Venner*, I, 87.

[21]*Elsie Venner*, I, 87.

[22]*Elsie Venner*, I, 88.

[23]*Elsie Venner*, I, 88-89.

[24]*Elsie Venner*, I, 144.

[25]Regarding the impact of religious beliefs, Holmes wrote in *The Autocrat of the Breakfast Table* (1858): "We frequently see persons in insane hospitals, sent there in consequence of what are called religious mental disturbances. I confess I think better of them than of many who hold the same notions and keep their wits and appear to enjoy life very well, outside of the asylums. Any decent person ought to go mad if he really holds such or such opinions. It is very much to his discredit, in every point of view, if he does not."

[26]*Elsie Venner*, I, 283.
[27]*Elsie Venner*, II, 10.

[28]*Elsie Venner*, II, 23-24.

[29]*Elsie Venner*, II, 27.

[30]*Elsie Venner*, II, 108.

[31]"Literature and Orthodoxy in Boston After the Civil War," *The American Culture*, ed. Hennig Cohen (New York: Houghlin Mifflin, 1968), p.355.

[32]"The Novel of Puritan Decay: From Mrs. Stowe to John Marquand," *NEQ*, 13 (December, 1940), p. 627.

[33]Harriet Beecher Stowe, *The Minister's Wooing* (Ridgewood, N.J.: Gregg Press, 1968), p. 23.

[34]*The Minister's Wooing*, pp. 72-73.

[35]*The Minister's Wooing*, p. 144.

[36]*The Minister's Wooing*, p. 163.

[37]*The Minister's Wooing*, p. 165.

[38]*The Minister's Wooing*, pp. 242-243.

[39]*The Minister's Wooing*, p. 333.

[40]*The Minister's Wooing*, p. 349.

[41]*The Minister's Wooing*, p. 431.

[42]*The Minister's Wooing*, p. 482.

[43]*The Minister's Wooing*, p. 553.

[44]Willard Thorp, "The Religious Novel as Best Seller in America," *Religious Perspectives in American Culture*, eds. James W. Smith and A. Leland Jamison (Princeton: Princeton Univ. Press, 1961), p. 221.

[45]Mary K. Ford, "Margaret Deland," *Bookman*, 25 (July, 1907), p. 54.

[46]Margaret Deland, *John Ward, Preacher* (Ridgewood, N.J.: Gregg Press, 1968), pp. 56-57.

[47]*John Ward, Preacher*, pp. 97-98.

[48]*John Ward, Preacher*, p. 98.

[49]*John Ward, Preacher*, p. 166.

[50]*John Ward, Preacher*, p. 189.

[51]*John Ward, Preacher*, p. 228.

[52]*John Ward, Preacher*, p. 140.

[53]*John Ward, Preacher*, p. 140.

[54]*John Ward, Preacher*, p. 427.

[55]Henry Adams (pseud. Frances Snow Compton), *Esther: A Novel*, introd. Robert E. Spiller. fac. ed. (N.Y., 1938), pp. 62-63.

[56]By setting the novel in New York and employing the pseudonym of Francis Snow Compton, Adams attempted to disguise his authorship, but his skillful portrait of Boston and its social environs betrayed his identity.

[57]*Esther*, p. 150.

[58]*Esther*, p. 155.

[59]*Esther*, pp. 171-172.

[60]*Esther*, p. 184.

[61]*Esther*, p. 207.

[62]*Esther*, p. 254.

[63]*Esther*, p. 297.

[64]*Esther*, pp. 301-302.

[65]*Symbol and Idea* in Henry Adams (Lincoln, Neb.: Nebraska Univ. Press, 1970), pp. 56-57.

[66]Cf. Ernest Samuels, *Henry Adams: The Middle Years* (Harvard Univ. Press, 1958), pp. 238-258.

[67]*Letters of Henry Adams*, 1858-1891, ed. Worthington C. Ford (Boston: Houghton Mifflin, 1930), p. 377.

[68]In New England church history, there are classic examples marking the failure of both liberal and orthodox measures to counteract religious indifference: the *Half-Way Covenant* (1662) was a quasi-liberal attempt to arrest the declining church membership and it failed, while the *Great Awakening* (1740's) was a quasi-conservative response to the accelerating secularization of the eighteenth century, and it too failed to reverse the historical forces which had spawned it.

[69]Arlo Bates, *The Puritans* (Ridgewood, N.J.: Gregg Press, 1967), p. 170.

[70]*The Puritans*, p. 211.

[71]*The Puritans*, p. 279.

[72]*The Puritans*, p. 321.

[73]*The Puritans,* p. 373.

[74]Gay Wilson Allen, *William James: A Biography* (New York: Viking Press, 1967), pp. 376-377.

[75]*The Puritans,* p. 422.

[76]*The Puritans,* p. 423.

[77]*The Puritans,* p. 42.

[78]*The Puritans,* p. 424.

[79]William Dean Howells, *A Modern Instance* (Boston: James R. Osgood & Co., 1909), p. 27.

[80]*A Modern Instance,* pp. 36-37.

[81]*The Road to Realism: The Early Years 1837-1885 of William Dean Howells* (Syracuse: Syracuse Univ. Press, 1956), p. 212.

[82]Kermit Vanderbilt, *The Achievement of William Dean Howells: A Reinterpretation* (Princeton: Princeton Univ. Press., 1968), p. 60.

[83]Edward Wagenknecht described the Boston milieu of this time as "an influence which makes for corruption" in *William Dean Howells: The Friendly Eye* (New York: Oxford Univ. Press, 1969), p. 185.

[84]*A Modern Instance,* p. 281.

[85]*A Modern Instance,* pp. 288-289.

[86]*The Achievement of William Dean Howells,* p. 62.

[87]*The Immense Complex Drama: The World and Art of the Howells Novel* (Columbus, Ohio: Ohio State Univ. Press, 1966), pp. 69-70.

[88]*The Realist at War: The Mature Years 1885-1920 of William Dean Howells* (Syracuse: Syracuse Univ. Press, 1958), p. 94.

[89]William Dean Howells, *The Minister's Charge: The Apprenticeship of Lemuel Barker* (Boston: Ticknor and Co., 1887), p. 199.

[90]*The Realist at War*, pp. 5-6.

[91]*The Minister's Charge*, p. 387.

[92]*The Minister's Charge*, p. 458.

[93]*The Minister's Charge*, p. 459.

[94]Cf. *W. D. Howells and Art in His Time* (New Brunswick, N.J.: Rutgers Univ. Press, 1965), p. 193.

[95]The reformer's zeal in this novel has generated hostile criticism such as Van Wyck Brooks' comments in *Howells: His Life and World*: "After *The Minister's Charge*,--in which Boston appeared in the policeman's phrase, as a 'bad place' for so many,--Howells published *Annie Kilburn*, a Tolstoian novel that showed how little moral convictions count for aesthetic righteousness. For, while this was full of happy touches and well-drawn minor characters, the protagonists were decidedly unconvincing (p. 182)."

[96]William Dean Howells, *Annie Kilburn: A Novel* (New York: Harper & Bros., 1889), p. 13.

[97]*Annie Kilburn*, p. 153.

[98]*Annie Kilburn*, p. 170.

[99]Edward Wagenknecht, *William Dean Howells: The Friendly Eye*, p. 45.

[100]*Annie Kilburn*, p. 240.

[101]*Annie Kilburn*, p. 273.

[102]*The Realist at War*, pp. 87-88.

[103]*Annie Kilburn*, p. 289.

[104]*The Life and Letters of William Dean Howells, I* (Boston, n.d.), p. 416.

[105]Van Wyck Brooks, *New England Indian Summer* (Cleveland: World, 1946), p. 409.

[106]George Santayana, *The Last Puritan: A Memoir in the Form of a Novel* (New York, 1936), p. 7.

[107]"The Novel of Puritan Decay: From Mrs. Stowe to John Marquand," *NEQ*, 13 (December, 1940), pp. 632-633.

[108]*The Last Puritan*, p. 159.

[109]*Society, Culture, and Personality: Their Structure and Dynamics* (New York: Harper, 1947), p. 709

[110]*The American Mind: An Interpretation of American Thought and Character Since the 1880's* (New Haven: Yale U.P., 1950), p. 165.

CHAPTER II—FRONTIER RELIGION AND THE NOVELIST

[1]*Culture on the Moving Frontier* (New York: Harper & Row, 1961), p. 168.

[2]*Puritanism and the Wilderness* (New York: Columbia University Press, 1969), pp. 120-121.

[3]The pervasiveness of religion in the lives of the settlers was also observed by Ralph Rusk in *The Literature of the Middle Western Border* (New York: Ungar, 1925), I, p. 38. Perhaps the best explanation for this dependency is found in Freud's *The Future of an Illusion* (New York, 1964), p. 30: "Religious ideas have arisen from the same need as have all other achievements of civilization: from the necessity of defending oneself against the crushingly superior force of nature."

[4]The transitional process of frontier settlement was described by H. Richard Niebuhr in *The Social Sources of Denominationalism* (Cleveland: World, 1957), as follows: "The frontier usually passes from the pioneer stage into a period of settled agricultural life. A relatively stable and homogeneous, rural population takes the place of the shifting early settlers. The folkways and modes of an older society reassert themselves; social institutions are established; . . . the early individualism in government, economics, morality, and religion makes way for trust in social institutions and forms. The frontier sect becomes a rural church in which sharply defined character, inherited from the pioneer days has been modified by the influence of social habit (p. 181)."

[5]*Society and Thought in Modern America* (New York: Longmans, Green, 1952), p. 87.

[6]"Instruments of Culture on the Frontier," *Yale Review*, 36 (1947), pp. 243-244.

[7]F. I. Moats described the itinerant ministry of the circuit rider as follows: "(It) reached out and carried the gospel to the remote hamlets and to the scattered rural population. Circuits were often three hundred to five hundred miles in circumference and each had many stations or appointments where classes had been organized. In a territory where money was scarce and where few men of means could be found to support the gospel ministry, the itinerating ministry was peculiarly suited to the condition." cf. "The Rise of Methodism in the Middle West," *Mississippi Valley Historical Review*, 15 (1928), p. 79.

[8]William Warren Sweet, *The Story of Religions in America* (New York: Harper & Bros., 1930), p. 315.

[9]*The Life of the Mind in America* (New York: Harcourt, Brace & World, 1965), p. 10.

[10]Moats, p. 88.

[11]*Edward Eggleston* (New York: Twayne, 1963), pp. 124-125.

[12]In the following quotation, Randel cautions the readers not to overstate Eggleston's assessment of Taine's influence. "Literary historians in their laudable quest for lines of influence, have gratefully followed his lead in giving Taine a major share of the credit. A little second thinking, however, produces the suggestion that not even so eminent an authority as Taine could supply the original idea of writing about humble people in humble settings. It is more reasonable to say that Taine renewed and underscored a tendency already present."

[13]*The Circuit Rider* (New York: J.B. Ford & Co., 1874), pp. vi-vii.

[14]*The Circuit Rider*, p. 99.

[15]*The Circuit Rider*, pp. 100-101

[16]Cf. Frederic L. Paxson, *History of the American Frontier*, 1763-1893 (Boston: Houghton Mifflin, 1924), pp. 117-119. At one point, Paxson describes the frontier ministry as follows: "The Methodists and Baptists laid stress less on a learned clergy and more on the power of exhortation. The rough and ready circuit rider was a natural democrat, with a message for every sinner . . . The frontier continued . . . to provide followers for any teacher who proclaimed a new Gospel or interpreted an old one in a language comprehensible to its spirit. The old ties were broken, the eternal needs of the human soul continued to prevail, but the common experiences of religion needed to be restated in terms of frontier life."

[17]*The Circuit Rider*, p. 101.

[18]*The Circuit Rider*, pp. 158-159.

[19]Vernon Loggins, "Introduction," *The Hoosier School-Master* (New York: Hill & Wang, 1961), p. ix.

[20]J.A. Rawley, "Some New Light on Eggleston," *AL*, 11 (January, 1940), p. 458.

[21]*The Hoosier School-Master*, p. 79.

[22]*The Hoosier School-Master*, p. 125.

[23]In her cruel treatment of the Thomson girl, Mrs. Means calls to mind Miss Havisham's cruelties to Pip in *Great Expectations*. Eggleston was a great admirer of Dickens, and it was not unlikely that his caricaturing was inspired by his reading of Dickens.

[24]*The Hoosier School-Master*, p. 161.

[25]*Culture on the Moving Frontier*, p. 182.

[26]Cf. John T. Flanagan, "The Novels of Edward Eggleston," *CE*, 5 (February, 1944), 250-254. In this brief critical survey of Eggleston's fiction, Flanagan dismissed The End of the World as having "little to recommend it save its sketches of religious dementia and its character of the Backwoods Philosopher . . . . " The portrait of religious dementia is central to the novel, and this is one of the best nineteenth-century fictional portraits of this all too frequent event in the early West. For this reason alone, one must disagree with Flanagan's evaluation.

[27]A *New Lighter* is a revivalist-oriented Congregationalist.

[28]*The End of the World: A Love Story* (New York: Orange Judd & Co., 1883), pp. 202-203.

[29]*The End of the World*, p. 39.

[30]*The End of the World*, p. 142.

[31]Cf. Arnold Smithline, *Natural Religion in American Literature* (New Haven: College and University Press, 1966).

[32]*The End of the World*, p. 144.

[33]*The End of the World*, p. 225.

[34]The following description of the Millerites is given by Clifton E. Olmstead in *Religion in America: Past and Present* (Englewood Cliffs, N.J., Prentice-Hall 1961), p. 87 "A leading exponent of premillenialism was William Miller (1782-1849). a Baptist preacher In 1838. he published lectures in which he predicted the second coming of Christ would take place about the year 1843. The work soon received nationwide publicity and numerous disciples appeared to lend support to the movement. During the summers of 1842 and 1843, more than 100 camp meetings were held in the United States to prepare the people for the advent of Christ. With the dawning of that keenly anticipated year, the tension mounted, for the second coming was expected to occur between March 1843 and March 1844. As the year waxed and waned, expectancy was turned into disappointment, and with the passing of the spring equinox in 1844 a gray pall of gloom settled over the Millerites."

[35]*The End of the World*, p. 257.

[36]*The End of the World*, p. 278.

[37]William Randel, *Edward Eggleston* (New Haven: College & University Press, 1963), p. 155.

[38]*The Leatherwood God* (New York: Harpers, 1916), p. 4.

[39]*The Ordeal of Faith: The Crisis of Church-Going in America*, 1865-1900 (New York: Philosophical Library, 1959), p. 7.

[40]William C. McLoughlin's, *Modern Revivalism: Charles Grandison Finney to Billy Graham* (New York: Ronald Press, 1959) provides an excellent survey of religious revivalism for a century and a half in its earlier benign stages. He did not anticipate the

nightmarish consequences implicit in the psychological dynamics of evangelism which could lead to the horrors perpetrated in Jonestown, Guyana.

[41]*The Leatherwood God*, p. 172.

[42]*The Road to Realism* (Syracuse: Syracuse Univ. Press, 1958), p. 267.

[43]*The Leatherwood God*, p. 232.

[44]*Zury: The Meanest Man in Spring County* (Urbana, Illinois: Univ. of Illinois Press, 1956), pp. 151-152.

[45]*Zury*, p. 260.

[46]*Zury*, p. 279.

[47]Eggleston and Kirkland are perhaps guilty of simplifying the hostility which the frontier settlers felt toward education. Ray A. Billington in *America's Frontier Heritage* (New York: Holt, Rinehart, and Winston, 1966) wrote: "The prevalence of these anti-cultural prejudices is attested particularly by those who dealt with the commonpeople on the more primitive agricultural frontiers. There, they reported, lack of learning bred hostility to learning, until men of above-average educational backgrounds found life unpleasant. 'Here the people despise knowledge,' observed a minister from the backcountry. One Tennessee promoter, seeking to attract settlers by assuring them that they would soon achieve 'Civilization, intelligence, comfort and health' if they settled on his lands, was rudely told that they had come west to escape civilization, and that if it caught up with them they would move on (p. 89)."

[48]Although his novels always contained sympathetic portraits of Southern characters, Albion Tourgèe was the target for many bitter attacks by Southern apologists,

and even Jay B. Hubbell in *The South in American Literature*, 1607-1900 (Durham. N.C.: Duke University Press. 1954). treats Tourgée in a critically biased manner Hubbell used a loyal daughter of the Confederacy. a Mrs. Spencer, to evaluate Tourgée's reconstruction novels. "Albion Tourgée, who had lived for some years in North Carolina used in *A Fool's Errand* (1879) and *Bricks Without Straw* (1880) some of his own experiences in trying to reconstruct the South. Mrs. Cornelia Spencer recorded in her diary a more judicial appraisal than most Southern readers were capable of making: "I have just read Tourgée's *Fool's Errand*. It is very smart, and the only book on this phase of the South and North that presents a true picture. He has done it well. Tells the truth as nearly as a carpetbagger and a Tourgée could be expected to do. I think he tried to be fair (p. 734)." This superficial evaluation appears without comment from Hubbell, and so one must assume that this judgment from Mrs. Spencer's diary is shared by Hubbell.

[49]*Bricks Without Straw* (Ridgewood, N.J.: Gregg Press, 1967), p. 133.

[50]*Bricks Without Straw*, p. 172.

[51]*Bricks Without Straw*, p. 184.

[52]*Bricks Without Straw*, pp. 184-185.

[53]This interpretation of the Civil War was given its first fictional rendering in John DeForest's *Miss Ravenel's Conversion* (1867). DeForest was still acting as a Reconstruction official in the Union army when he wrote his novel. Dr. Ravenel, the father of the heroine, gives the following interpretation of the war's historical significance: "The victory of the North is at bottom the triumph of laboring men living by their own industry, over non-laboring men who wanted to live

by the industry of others . . . . Slavery meant in reality to create an idle nobility. Liberty has established an industrious democracy. In working for our own living we are obeying the teachings of this war, the triumphant spirit of our country and age . . . . Yes, we must all go to work. That is, we must be useful and respectful." (New York: Holt, Rinehart, and Winston, 1965), p. 465.

[54]*Bricks Without Straw*, p. 452.

[55]The success of Dixon's effort in justifying revenge upon the emancipated Negro and in discrediting the Reconstruction Period may be observed in the great popular success of *Birth of a Nation*, the motion picture adaptation of *The Clansman*, and subsequent rise in the Klan's popularity throughout the United States culminating in its near success at controlling the Democratic Party Convention of 1924.

[56]*The Clansman: An Historical Romance of the Ku Klux Klan* (Ridgewood, N.J.: Gregg Press, 1967), pp. 46 -47.

[57]*The Clansman*, pp. 319-320.

[58]*The Clansman*, p. 374.

[59]Benjamin T. Spencer, *The Quest for Nationality* (Syracuse: Syracuse University Press, 1957), p. 261.

[60]*The Varieties of Religious Experience* (New York: Longmans, Green, 1928), p. 50.

[61]Charles L. Sanford, "An American Pilgrim's Progress," *The American Culture*, ed. Hennig Cohen (New York: Houghton, Mifflin, 1968), p. 82.

[62]The inability of the stoic personality to deal with success is beautifully summarized in the second stanza of Emily Dickinson"s Poem #252:

> Power is only Pain --
> Stranded, thro' Discipline,
> Till Weights -- will hang --
> Give Balm -- to Giants --
> And they'll wilt, like Men --
> Give Himmaleh --
> They'll Carry -- Him!

[63]*The Story of a Country Town* (Cambridge, Mass.: Belknap Press, 1961), p. 37.

[64]*The Story of a Country Town*, p. 121.

[65]*The Story of a Country Town*, p. 141.

[66]*The Story of a Country Town*, p. 197.

[67]*Babbitt* (New York: Harcourt, Brace & World), pp. 204-205.

[68]Nelson Klose, *A Concise Guide to the American Frontier* (Lincoln, Nebraska: Nebraska Univ. Press, 1964), pp. 58-59.

[69]Harry Williams, Richard N. Current, and Frank Freidel, *A History of the United States* (to 1876) (New York: Knopf, 1960), pp. 448-453.

[70]*Ramona: A Story* (Boston: Roberts Bros., 1884), I, p. 62.

[71]*Ramona*, I, p. 30.

[72]*Ramona*, I, p. 103.

[73]*Ramona: A Story* (Boston: Roberts Bros., 1884), II, p. 4.

[74]*Ramona*, II, p. 92.

[75]*Ramona*, II, p. 265.

[76]*Ramona*, II, pp. 281-282.

[77]*The Damnation of Theron Ware* (New York: Holt, Rinehart and Winston, 1963), pp. 28-29.

[78]*The Damnation of Theron Ware*, p. 326.

[79]*The Damnation of Theron Ware*, p. 327.

[80]*The Damnation of Theron Ware*, p. 210.

[81]*The American Mind: An Interpretation of American Thought and Character Since the 1880's* (New Haven: Yale Univ. Press, 1950), p. 168.

[82]The fundamentalist *Weltanschauung* has declined steadily throughout the twentieth century despite the Pyrrhic victory of the Scopes trial and the continuing success of some celebrated evangelists.

[83]Louis B. Wright, *Culture on the Moving Frontier*, p. 197.

CHAPTER III—THE NEW RELIGIONS:
NATIVE-BORN AND IMMIGRANT

[1]New England: *Indian Summer* (Cleveland: World, 1946), p. 414.

[2]*Religion in America: Past and Present* (Englewood Cliffs, N.J.: Prentice-Hall, 1961), pp. 120-121.

[3]"Literature and Orthodoxy in Boston after the Civil War," *The American Culture*, ed. Hennig Cohen (New York: Houghton Mifflin, 1968), p. 344.

[4]*A History of American Literature Since 1870* (New York: Cooper Square Publishing, (1968), pp. 222-223.

[5]*A History of American Literature since 1870*, p. 222.

[6]Elizabeth Stuart Phelps, *The Gates Ajar*, ed. Helen Sootin Smith (Cambridge, Mass.: Harvard Univ. Press, 1964), p. 46.

[7]Phelps, *The Gates Ajar*, pp. 110-111.

[8]Helen Sootin Smith, "Introduction," *The Gates Ajar*, pp. vi-vii.

[9]"Introduction," p. xxi.

[10]*The Growth of the American Mind*, 3rd ed. (New York: Harper & Row, 1964), p. 521.

[11]*American Fiction: An Historical Critical Survey* (New York: Appleton-Century, 1936), p. 195.

[12]*The Novels of Henry James* (New York: Macmillan, 1961), p. 137.

[13]*Henry James: The Middle Years* (New York: Lippincott, 1962), p. 141.

[14]"The Portrait of New England," *Nation*, 156 (December 1, 1945), p. 582.

[15]Henry James, *The Bostonians* (New York: Modern Library, 1956), p. 82.

[16]Philip Rahv, "Introduction," *The Bostonians* (New York, 1945), p. 584.

[17]"The Portrait of New England," p. 582.

[18]*The Bostonians*, p. 137.

[19]*The Bostonians*, p. 194.

[20]*The Bostonians*, p. 238.

[21]*The Bostonians*, p. 455.

[22]Bogan, "The Portrait of New England," p. 586.

[23]*The Novels of Henry James*, p. 137.

[24]*A Religious History of the American People* (New Haven: Yale Univ. Press., 1973), p. 1025.

[25]Henry Steele Commager, *The American Mind* (New Haven: Yale Univ. Press., 1950), pp. 186-187.

[26]"Christian Science," *North American Review*, 175 (December, 1902), p. 762.

[27]"Christian Science-III," *North American Review*, 176 (February, 1903), pp. 183-184.

[28]William Randel, *Edward Eggleston* (New Haven: Twayne, 1963), pp. 122-123.

[29]"Preface," *The Faith Doctor: A Story of New York* (New York: D. Appleton & Co., 1891), pp. 3-4.

[30]*The Growth of American Thought*, p. 537.

[31]*The Faith Doctor.* pp. 135-136.

[32]*The Faith Doctor*, p. 194.

[33]*The Faith Doctor*, p. 262.

[34]*The Faith Doctor*, pp. 287-288.

[35]*The Faith Doctor*, pp. 288-289.

[36]*The Faith Doctor*, p. 394.

[37]Two excellent critical studies of *The Undiscovered Country* may be found in the following books: George N. Bennett, *William Dean Howells: The Development of a Novelist* (Norman, Oklahoma: Univ. of Oklahoma Press, 1959), pp. 96-105, and Kermit Vanderbilt, *The Achievement of William Dean Howells* (Princeton: Princeton Univ. Press, 1968), pp. 11-49.

[38]William Dean Howells, *The Undiscovered Country* (Boston: Houghton, Mifflin, 1880), p. 18.

[39]*The Undiscovered Country*, p. 70.

[40]Edwin Cady, *The Road to Realism*, p. 197.

[41]*William Dean Howells: The Development of a Novelist*, p. 99.

[42]*The Undiscovered Country*, p. 113.

[43]*The Undiscovered Country*, pp. 125-126.

[44]*The Undiscovered Country*, p. 193.

[45]*The Undiscovered Country*, p. 216.

[46]*The Undiscovered Country*, pp. 235-236.

[47]Kermit Vanderbilt, *The Achievement of William Dean Howells*, p. 23.

[48]*The Undiscovered Country*, p. 365.

[49]*The Undiscovered Country*, p. 373.

[50]George Bennett, *William Dean Howells: The Development of a Novelist*, p. 103.

[51]*The Undiscovered Country*, p. 419.

[52]*William Dean Howells: The Friendly Eye* (New York: Oxford Univ. Press, 1969), p. 238.

[53]*The Day of Their Wedding* (New York: Harper & Bros., 1896), p. 9.

[54]*The Day of Their Wedding*, pp. 84-85.

[55]*The Day of Their Wedding*, pp. 152-153.

[56]*Protestant-Catholic-Jew*, rev. ed. (Garden City: Doubleday, 1960), p. 21.

[57]"American Backgrounds for Fiction: The Pennsylvania Dutch," *Bookman*, 38 (November, 1913), pp. 244-247.

[58]Helen Reimensnyder Martin, *Sabina: A Story of the Amish* (New York, 1905), p. 4.

[59]*Sabina*, p. 29.

[60]*Sabina*, p. 67.

[61]*Sabina*, p. 90.

[62]*Sabina*, pp. 145-146.

[63]Robert E. Spiller, ed., *Literary History of the United States* (New York: Macmillan, 1953), p. 684.

[64]Helen R. Martin, "American Backgrounds for Fiction: The Pennsylvania Dutch," *Bookman*, 38 (November, 1913), p. 245.

[65]*American Judaism* (Chicago: Univ. of Chicago Press, 1957), p. 6.

[66]The other Luska books are: *As It Was Written: A Jewish Musician's Story* (1885), *Mrs. Peixeida* (1886), *My Uncle Florimonde* (1888), *A Latin Quarter Courtship and Other Stories* (1890), and *Grandison Mather* (1890).

[67]*American Authors 1600-1900: A Biographical Dictionary of American Literature*, eds. Stanley J. Kunitz and Howard Haycraft (New York: H. W. Wilson, 1938), p. 336.

[68]*DAB*, VIII, p. 274.

[69]*The Jew in the American Novel* (New York: Herzl Institute, 1959), p. 16.

[70]This same theme is given a comic treatment in the recent Joseph Heller novel *Good as Gold* (New York: Simon and Schuster, 1979).

[71]*The Yoke of the Thorah*, p. 58.

[72]*The Yoke of the Thorah*, p. 83.

[73]*The Yoke of the Thorah*, p. 167.

[74]*The Yoke of the Thorah*, p. 171.

[75]*The Yoke of the Thorah*, p. 177.

[76]*The Yoke of the Thorah*, pp. 282-283.

[77]*American Judaism*, p. 69.

[78]Abraham Cahan, *The Rise of David Levinsky* (New York: Harper, 1960), p. 61.

[79]*The Rise of David Levinsky*, p. 75.

[80]*The Rise of David Levinsky*, p. 109.

[81]*The Rise of David Levinsky*, p. 110.

[82]*The Rise of David Levinsky*, p. 125.

[83]*The Rise of David Levinsky*, p. 169.

[84]*The Rise of David Levinsky*, p. 260.

[85]*The Rise of David Levinsky*, p. 282.

[86]Levinsky as a wealthy Jew seeking social acceptance in the Gentile upper-classes of America is reminiscent of Rosedale in Wharton's *The House of Mirth*.

[87]*The Rise of David Levinsky*, p. 379.

[88]*The Rise of David Levinsky*, p. 380.

[89]*The Rise of David Levinsky*, p. 530.

[90]Stephen J. Brown, S. J. and Thomas McDermott, *A Survey of Catholic Literature* (Milwaukee: Bruce Publishing, 1945), p. 142.

[91]"The Renascence in American Catholic Letters," *The Catholic Renascence*, ed. Norman Weyand, S. J. (Chicago: Loyolas Univ. Press, 1951), p. 172.

332

[92]*A History of American Civilation* (New York: Books for Libraries Press, 1968), p. 233.

[93]*Stanhope Burleigh: The Jesuits in Our Homes* (New York: Stringer & Townshend, 1855), p. xii.

[94]Henry James, *The American* (Boston: Houghton Mifflin, 1962), p. 327.

[95]*The American*, pp. 327-328.

[96]*The American*, p. 328.

[97]*Hawthorne* (Ithaca, N. Y.: Cornell Univ. Press, 1967), p. 127.

[98]Nathaniel Hawthorne, *The Marble Faun or The Romance of Monte Beni* (New York: Washington Square Press. 1958). p. 79

[99]*The Marble Faun*, p. 99.

[100]*Hawthorne as Myth-Maker* (Toronto: Toronto Univ. Press, 1969), p. 32.

[101]*The Marble Faun*, p. 285.

[102]*Hawthorne as Myth-Maker*, pp. 162-163.

[103]*The Marble Faun*, p. 285.

[104]cf. Oliver Wendell Holmes, *A Mortal Antipathy* (Boston: Houghton Mifflin, 1893), pp. 56-57.

[105]*A Mortal Antipathy*, p. 71.

[106]*A Mortal Antipathy*, p. 216.

[107]Harold Frederic, *The Damnation of Theron Ware* (New York: Holt, Rinehart, & Winston, 1963), p. 244.

[108]*The Novels of Harold Frederic* (Ithaca, N. Y.: Cornell Univ. Press, 1969), pp. 127-128.

[109]*The Damnation of Theron Ware*, p. 246.

[110]*Innocents Abroad* (New York, 1929), II, p. 39.

[111]*A Connecticut Yankee in King Arthur's Court* (New York: Collier, 1917), p. 65.

[112]*A Connecticut Yankee*, p. 128.

[113]*A Connecticut Yankee*, pp. 148-149.

[114]*A Connecticut Yankee*, p. 136.

[115]*A Connecticut Yankee*, p. 444.

[116]*The Church as a Social Institution* (Englewood Cliffs: Prentice Hall, 1962), p. 55.

[117]"Letter III," *Letters from an American Farmer* (Garden City, N. Y.: Doubleday, n.d.), pp. 56-57.

[118]*Religion in Secular Society* (Baltimore: Penguin Books, 1969), pp. 262-263.

[119]John Naisbitt in *Megatrends: Ten New Directions Transforming Our Lives* (New York: Warner Books, 1982) makes the following distinction between the continued vitality of sects as opposed to institutional churches. "The United States is today undergoing a revival in religious belief and church attendance. But except for the Southern Baptists, none of the major old-line denominations is benefiting; they all continue in a two-decade decline . . . . This should not be surprising.

During turbulent times many people need structure--not
ambiguity--in their lives. They need something to hang
on to, not something to debate. The demand for
structure will increase, supplied not by the old,
established denominations--Catholics, Episcopalians,
Methodists, Presbyterians, and Lutherans--but by the
Southern Baptists, the Mormons, the Seventh-Day
Adventists, and by the great array of the new, native-
grown fundamentalist faiths, by the charismatic
Christian movement and the youthful Jesus movement.
There are thousands of independent Christian churches
and communities in the United States today. The
Reverend Jerry Falwell's Thomas Road Baptist Church in
Lynchburg, Virginia, and the Reverend Robert Schuller's
Chrystal Cathedral in Garden Grove, California, are
well-known independent churches. Their congregations
are among the largest in the nation, but thousands of
others, many with fewer than 100 members, have sprung up
across the country. Since the 1960's there has also
been the widespread interest in Eastern religions, and
such groups as the Hare Krishnas are gaining a growing
number of followers (pp. 239-240)."

CHAPTER IV-RELIGION AND REFORM LITERATURE

[1]Mark Holloway, in his brief and literate survey of
American utopian communities titled *Heavens on Earth*,
describes the history of utopian movements in America
beginning with the earliest Labadists community at
Bohemia Manor in 1680 to John Humphrey Noyes' community
at Oneida in 1880. What becomes apparent in reading
about the historical development of these communities is
the failure of every attempt to establish a permanent
community based upon a utopian ideology. Not only did
these communities fail, but, with the rare exception of
some religious communities, the failure was usually
quite swift.

[2]*Ideology and Utopia: An Introduction to the Sociology of Literature* (New York: Harcourt, Brace & Co., 1936), p. 173.

[3]For further information refer to the bibliography compiled by Negley and J. Max Patrick "Selected List of Utopian Works 1850-1950," *The Quest for Utopia: An Anthology* (New York: H. Schuman, 1952).

[4]John M. Blum et al., *The National Experience* (New York: Harcourt, Brace & World, 1963), p. 454.

[5]*Social Darwinism in American Thought*, rev. ed. (Boston: Beacon Press, 1967), p. 110.

[6]*The Jungle* (New York: Viking, 1946), p. 331.

[7]*The Characteristics and Religions of Modern Socialism* (New York: Benziger Bros., 1909), pp. 336-337.

[8]Harvey Wish, *Society and Thought in Modern America* (New York: Longmans, Green, 1952), pp. 152-153.

[9]*Society and Thought in Modern America*, pp. 152-153.

[10]Edwin Scott Gaustad, *A Religious History of America* (New York: Harper & Row, 1966), pp. 252-254.

[11]*The Social Gospel in America: 1870-1920*, ed. Robert T. Handy (New York: Oxford Univ. Press, 1966), pp. 374-375.

[12]John Tracy Ellis, *American Catholicism* (Chicago: University of Chicago Press, 1955), pp. 104-105.

[13]"To the Public," *Caesar's Column: A Story of the Twentieth Century*, ed. Walter B. Rideout (Cambridge, Mass.: Harvard Univ. Press, 1960), p. 3.

[14]*Caesar's Column*, pp. 164-165.

[15]Otto H. Olsen, *Carpetbagger's Crusade: The Life of Albion Winegar Tourgèe* (Baltimore: Johns Hopkins Univ. Press, 1965), pp. 260-261.

[16]*The Secular Relevance of the Church* (Philadelphia: Westminster Press, 1962), p. 7.

[17]Albion Tourgee, *Murvale Eastman: Christian Socialist* (Ridgewood, N. J.: Gregg Press, 1968), p. 44.

[18]*Murvale Eastman*, p. 41.

[19]*Murvale Eastman.* p. 60.

[20]*The Problem of Christianity* (New York, 1913), II, pp. 272-273.

[21]*Murvale Eastman*, p. 61.

[22]*Murvale Eastman*, p. 116.

[23]*Murvale Eastman*, p. 273.

[24]*Murvale Eastman*, p. 472.

[25]*Murvale Eastman*, p. v.

[26]Fifty years after its publication, the sales for *In His Steps* had surpassed the six million mark, according to Frank Luther Mott in *Golden Multitudes: The Story of the Best Seller in the United States* (New York: Macmillian, 1947), p. 1971. Harvey Wish described its success in *Society and Thought in Modern America* as

follows: "No man in the entire Social Christian movement enjoyed so vast an audience as the Reverend Charles Monroe Sheldon of Topeka, Kansas, whose mass appeal as a novelist may justly be compared with that of Harriet Beecher Stowe (p. 165)."

[27]Willard Thorp, "The Religious Novel as Best Seller in America," *Religious Perspectives in American Culture*, eds. James W. Smith and A. Leland Jamison (Princeton: Princeton Univ. Press, 1961). pp. 223-234.

[28]Charles M. Sheldon, *In His Steps: "What Would Jesus Do?"* (Chicago, 1899), p. 6.

[29]*In His Steps*, p. 10.

[30]*In His Steps*, p. 11.

[31]*In His Steps*, p. 17.

[32]"*In His Steps*: A Reapprisal," *AQ*, 23 (Spring, 1971), p. 65.

[33]*In His Steps*, p. 87.

[34]*In His Steps*, pp. 103-104.

[35]The sociologist E. Digby Baltzell, in *The Protestant Establishment: Aristocracy and Caste in America* (London: Secker and Warburg, 1965), describes the same failures of the Protestant ruling class in America at the end of the nineteenth century, and Baltzell further notes that the energies of this class were transferred to creating a caste-like system to prevent contact with the people and problems of society at large.

[36]*In His Steps*, p. 205.

338

[37]*In His Steps*, p. 267.

[38]*In His Steps*, p. 277.

[39]Gayrand S. Wilmore in *The Secular Relevance of the Church* writes: "It is rare and not a particularly desirable turn of affairs when whole congregations suddenly change their image of the church and assume a witness of active engagement with the world. This is not likely to happen in any case . . . . The nominal membership and marginal faith of the majority will provide the main direction for what is done inside the building (p. 85)."

[40]*In His Steps*, p. 284.

[41]*American Literary Naturalism: A Divided Stream* (Minneapolis: Univ. of Minnesota Press, 1956), p. 179.

[42]"A Modern Quest for Religion," *Century Magazine*, 87 (1913). p. 172.

[43]Winston Churchill, *The Inside of the Cup* (New York: Macmillan, 1913), p. 121.

[44]*The Inside of the Cup*, p. 127.

[45]*The Inside of the Cup*, p. 167.

[46]*The Inside of the Cup*, p. 271.

[47]*The Inside of the Cup*, p. 323.

[48]*The Inside of the Cup*, p. 361.

[49]*The Inside of the Cup*, p. 423.

[50]*The Inside of the Cup*, p. 497.

[51]*American Literary Naturalism, A Divided Stream*, p. 163.

[52]Blake Nevius, "The Idealistic Novels of Robert Herrick," *AL*, 21 (March, 1949), p. 61.

[53]Robert Herrick, "The Background of the American Novel," *YR*, 3 (January, 1914), p. 233.

[54]*The Great Tradition* (New York: International Publishers, 1935), p. 184.

[55]*The Master of the Inn* (New York: Scribners, 1916), p. 24.

[56]*The Memoirs of an American Citizen* (New York: Macmillan, 1905), p. 205.

[57]*The Memoirs of an American Citizen*, p. 218.

[58]*The Memoirs of an American Citizen*, p. 213.

[59]*The Memoirs of an American Citizen*, p. 214.

[60]*The Memoirs of an American Citizen*, p. 273.

[61]*The Memoirs of an American Citizen*, p. 273.

[62]*The Memoirs of an American Citizen*, p. 250.

[63]*Main Currents in American Thought* (New York: Harcourt, Brace, 1930), III. p. 349.

[64]*American Fiction: An Historical and Critical Study*, p. 633.

[65]*The Great Tradition*, p. 186.

[66]*Harvests of Change: American Literature*, 1865-1914 (Englewood Cliffs, N. J.: Prentice-Hall, 1967), p. 225.

[67]*The Growth of American Thought* (New York: Harper & Bros., 1943), p. 629.

[68]Sylvia Bowman *et al. Edward Bellamy Abroad: An American Prophet's Influence* (New York: Twayne Pub., 1962), p. 40.

[69]Edward Bellamy, *Looking Backward*, 2000-1887 (Boston: Houghton Mifflin, 1966), p. 70.

[70]Van Wyck Brooks, *New England Indian Summer*: 1865-1915 (Cleveland: World, 1946), p. 388.

[71]*Looking Backward*, p. 169.

[72]*Looking Backward*, p. 170.

[73]*Looking Backward*, p. 175.

[74]*Looking Backward*, p. 202.

[75]"Varieties of Literary Utopias," *Utopias and Utopian Thought*, ed. Frank E. Manuel (Boston: Houghton Mifflin, 1966), p. 29.

[76]*Looking Backward*, p. 203.

[77]"The Editor's Study," *Harpers Monthly*, 78 (1888), p. 159.

[78]Clara Marburg Kirk, *W. D. Howells, A Traveler from Altruria* (New Brunswick, N. J.: Rutgers Univ. Press, 1962), p. 24.

79*Men of Good Hope: A Story of American Progressives* (New York: Oxford Univ. Press, 1951), p. 195

80*W. D. Howells, A Traveler from Altruria*, p. 29.

81Hannah Graham Belcher, "Howell's Opinions on the Religious Conflicts of His Age as Exhibited in Magazine Articles," *AL*, 15 (November, 1943), p. 265.

82*Life in Letters*, II, p. 3.

83William Dean Howells, "Introduction," *Through the Eye of a Needle: A Romance with an Introduction* (New York: Harper & Bros., 1907), p. vi.

84*A Traveler from Altruria* (New York: Hill & Wang, 1957), pp. 18-19.

85*A Traveler from Altruria*, p. 106.

86*A Traveler from Altruria*, p. 106.

87*A Traveler from Altruria*, p. 147.

88*A Traveler from Altruria*, p. 171.

89*A Traveler from Altruria*, p. 199.

90*A Traveler from Altruria*, p. 210.

91*William Dean Howells: The Development of a Novelist*, p. 205.

92*W. D. Howells, A Traveler from Altruria*, p. 143.

93*Through the Eye of a Needle*, p. 85.

94*Through the Eye of a Needle*, p. 89.

[95]Quoted by Edwin H. Cady in *The Realist at War: The Mature Years 1885-1920 of William Dean Howells* (Syracuse: Syracuse Univ. Press, 1965), p. 146.

[96]Winthrop S. Hudson, *Religion in America: Years of Midpassage*, 1860-1914 (New York: Scribner, 1965), p. 315.

[97]*Progress and Religion* (Garden City, N. Y.: Doubleday 1960), p. 182.

[98]*Harvests of Change*, p. 231.

[99]Albert T. Mollegan, "The Religious Basis of Western Socialism," *Socialism and American Life*, eds. Donald Drew Egbert and Stow Persons (Princeton: Princeton Univ. Press, 1952), I. p. 123.

[100]*The Nature and Destiny of Man: A Christian Interpretation* (New York: Scribners, 1953), I, p. 226.

[101]The dialectic continues, and in the recently published *Christian Realism and Liberation Theology* (Maryknoll, N. Y.: Orbis, 1981), Dennis McCann analyzes the new Liberation Theology as experiencing the historical theological problem of trying to resolve "salvation" and "liberation."

EPILOGUE

[1]*Jews Without Money* (New York: International Publishers, 1935), p. 309.

[2]*The Grapes of Wrath* (New York: Viking, 1958), p. 572.

[3]*Winds of Doctrine* (New York: Charles Scribner's Sons, 1913), p. 1.

[4]*This Side of Paradise* (New York: Scribners, 1970), p. 281.

[5]*The Sun Also Rises* (New York: Scribners, 1954), p. 31.

[6]Garry Wills, "Catholic Faith and Fiction," *The New York Times Book Review* (January 16, 1972), p. 16.

[7]*The Assistant* (New York: Signet, 1957), p. 99.

[8]*Rabbit, Run* (New York: Crest, 1965), p. 77.

[9]*Lie Down in Darkness* (New York: Bobbs-Merrill, 1951), p. 382.

[10]*Lie Down in Darkness, p. 386.*

[11]Lie Down in Darkness, p. 400.

[12]The title, *Lie Down in Darkness,* comes from Thomas Browne's *Urn Burial,* which is a study of man's mortality. The companion essay to *Urn Burial* was *The Garden of Cyrus,* which describes an act of faith based on an unusual application of the teleological proof for God's existence.

[13]*Modern Poetry and the Christian Tradition* (New York: Scribners, 1952), p. 267.

[14]*William Faulkner: Three Decades of Criticism,* eds. Frederick J. Hoffman and Olga W. Vickery (Michigan State Univ. Press, 1960), p. 348.

BIBLIOGRAPHY

LIST OF NOVELS CITED

Adams, Henry (pseud. Frances Snow Compton). *Esther: A Novel*. fac. ed. New York: Scholars Facsimiles and Reprints, 1938.

Anderson, Sherwood. *Winesburg, Ohio*. New York: Viking, 1965.

Bates, Arlo. *The Puritans*. 1898; rpt. Ridgewood, N. J.: Gregg Press, 1968.

Bellamy, Edward. *Looking Backward, 2000-1887*. Boston: Houghton Mifflin, 1966.

Cahan, Abraham. *The Rise of David Levinsky*. New York: Harper, 1960.

Churchill, Winston. *The Inside of the Cup*. New York: Macmillan, 1913.

Deland, Margaret. *John Ward, Preacher*. 1888; rpt. Ridgewood, N. J.: Gregg Press, 1968.

Dixon, Thomas. *The Clansman*. 1905; rpt. Ridgewood, N. J.: Gregg Press, 1967.

Donnelly, Ignatius. *Caesar's Column: A Story of the Twentieth Century*. ed. Walter B. Rideout. Cambridge: Harvard Univ. Press, 1960.

345

Dunne, John Gregory. *True Confessions.* New York: Dutton, 1977.

Eggleston, Edward. *The Circuit Rider.* New York: J. B. Ford & Co., 1874.

_____. *The End of the World: A Love Story.* New York: Orange Judd & Co., 1883.

_____. *The Faith Doctor: A Story of New York.* New York: D. Appleton & Co., 1883.

_____. *The Hoosier School Master.* Ed. Vernon Loggins. New York: Hill & Wang, 1961.

Farrell, James T. *Studs Lonigan.* New York: Modern Library, 1938.

Fitzgerald, F. Scott. *The Side of Paradise.* New York: Scribner's, 1970.

Frederic, Harold. *The Damnation of Theron Ware.* New York: Holt, Rinehart, & Winston, 1963.

Gold, Michael. *Jews Without Money.* New York: International Publishers, 1935.

Hawthorne, Nathaniel. *The Marble Faun or The Romance of Monte Beni.* New York: Washington Square Press, 1958.

Heller, Joseph. *Good as Gold.* New York: Simon and Schuster, 1979.

Hemingway, Ernest. *The Sun Also Rises.* New York: Scribner's, 1954.

Herrick, Robert. *The Master of the Inn.* New York: Scribner's, 1916.

346

_____, *The Memoirs of an American Citizen.* New York: Macmillan, 1905.

Holmes, Oliver Wendell. *Elsie Venner.* 2 vols. Boston: Ticknor & Fields, 1861.

_____, *A Mortal Antipathy.* Boston: Houghton Mifflin, 1893.

Howe, E. W. *The Story of a Country Town.* Cambridge: Harvard Univ. Press, 1961.

Howells, William Dean. *Annie Kilburn: A Novel.* New York: Harper Bros., 1889.

_____, *The Day of Their Wedding.* New York: Harper & Bros., 1916.

_____, *The Minister's Charge: The Apprenticeship of Lemuel Barker.* Boston: Ticknor & Fields, 1887.

_____, *A Modern Instance.* Boston: James R. Osgood, 1909.

_____, *Through the Eye of a Needle: A Romance with an Introduction.* New York: Harper & Bros., 1907.

_____, *A Traveler from Altruria.* New York: Hill & Wang, 1957.

_____, *The Undiscovered Country.* Boston: Houghton Mifflin, 1880.

Jackson, Helen Hunt. *Ramona: A Story.* 2 vols. Boston: Robert Bros., 1884.

James, Henry. *The American*. Boston: Houghton Mifflin, 1962.

——————————. *The Bostonians*. New York: Modern Library, 1956.

Kirkland, Joseph. *Zury: The Meanest Man in Spring County*. Urbana, Ill.: Univ. of Illinois Press, 1956.

Lewis, Sinclair. *Babbitt*. New York: Harcourt, Brace, & World, 1922.

——————————. *Main Street*. New York: Collier, 1920.

Longfellow, Henry Wadsworth. *Kavanagh: A Tale*. New Haven: College & Univ. Press, 1965.

Luska, Sidney. *The Yoke of the Thorah*. New York: Cassell & Co., 1887.

McHale, Tom. *Farragan's Retreat*. New York: Viking, 1971.

Malamud, Bernard. *The Assistant*. New York: Signet, 1957.

Martin, Helen Reimensnyder. *Sabina: A Story of the Amish*. New York: Century Co., 1905.

Phelps, Elizabeth Stuart. *The Gates Ajar*. ed. Helen Sootin Smith. Cambridge: Harvard Univ. Press, 1964.

Santayana, George. *The Last Puritan: A Memoir in the Form of a Novel*. New York: Scribner's, 1936.

Sheldon, Charles M. *In His Steps: What Would Jesus Do?*
Chicago, 1899.

Sinclair, Upton. *The Jungle*. New York: Viking, 1946.

Steinbeck, John. *The Grapes of Wrath*. New York:
Viking, 1958.

Stowe, Harriet Beecher. *The Minister's Wooing*. 1859;
rpt. Ridgewood, N. J.: Gregg Press, 1968.

Styron, William. *Lie Down in Darkness*. New York:
Bobbs-Merrill, 1951.

Tourgee, Albion. *Bricks Without Straw*. 1880; rpt.
Ridgewood, N. J.: Gregg Press, 1967.

——————————. *A Fool's Errand*. New York: Harper
& Row, 1966.

——————————. *Murvale Eastman: Christian
Socialist*. 1889; rpt. Ridgewood, N. J.: Gregg
Press, 1968.

Twain, Mark. *A Connecticut Yankee in King Arthur's
Court*. New York: Collier, 1917.

Updike, John. *Rabbit, Run*. New York: Crest, 1965.

——————————. *Rabbit Redux*. New York: B. Knopf,
1971.

——————————. *Rabbit is Rich*. New York: B.
Knopf, 1982.

ADDITIONAL SECONDARY SOURCES CONSULTED

Aaron, Daniel. *Men of Good Hope: A Story of American Progressives*. New York: Oxford Univ. Press, 1951.

Abell, Aaron Ignatius. *The Urban Impact on American Protestantism*. London: Archon, 1943.

Ahlstrom, Sidney. *A Religious History of the American People*. New Haven: Yale Univ. Press, 1973.

Allen, Gay Wilson. *William James: A Biography*. New York: Viking, 1967.

American Authors, 1600-1900: A Biographical Dictionary of American Literature. Eds. Stanley J. Kunitz and Howard Haycraft. New York: H. W. Wilson, 1938.

Arnold, Matthew. *Culture and Anarchy*. Cambridge: Cambridge Univ. Press, 1961.

Baltzell, E. Digby. *The Protestant Establishment: Aristocracy and Caste in America*. London: Secker & Warburg, 1965.

Belcher, Hannah Graham. "Howells's Opinions on the Religious Conflicts of His Age as Exhibited in Magazine Articles," *AL*, 15 (November, 1943), 262-278.

Bell, Daniel. *The Cultural Contradictions of Capitalism*. New York: Basic Books, 1976.

Bennett, George N. *William Dean Howells: The Development of a Novelist*. Norman, Okla.: Univ. of Oklahoma Press, 1959.

Bercovitch, Sacvan. *The Puritan Origins of the American Self*. New Haven: Yale Univ. Press, 1975.

Billington, Ray A. *America's Frontier Heritage*. New York: Holt, Rinehart, & Winston, 1966.

Blake, Nelson. *Novelist's America: Fiction as History*. Syracuse: Syracuse Univ. Press, 1969.

Blum, John M. *et al*. *The National Experience: A History of the United States*. New York: Harcourt, Brace, & World, 1963.

Bogan, Louise. "The Portrait of New England," *Nation*, 156 (December, 1945), 582+.

Bowman, Sylvia et al. *Edward Bellamy Abroad: An American Prophet's Influence*. New York: Twayne, 1962.

Boyer, Paul S. *"In His Steps*: A Reappraisal," *AQ*, 23 (Spring, 1971), 60-78.

Boynton, Percy H. "The Novel of Puritan Decay: From Mrs. Stowe to John Marquand," *NEQ*, 13 (December, 1940), 626-637.

Briggs, Austin. *The Novels of Harold Frederic*. Ithaca, N. Y.: Cornell Univ. Press, 1969.

Brooks, Van Wyck. *Howells: His Life and World*. New York: Dutton, 1959.

—————————. *New England: Indian Summer*. Cleveland: World, 1946.

Brown, Stephen J. and Thomas McDermott. *A Survey of Catholic Literature*. Milwaukee: Bruce Publishing, 1945.

Cady, Edwin H. *The Realist at War: The Mature Years 1885-1920 of William Dean Howells.* Syracuse: Syracuse Univ. Press, 1958.

——————————. *The Road to Realism: The Early Years 1837-1885 of William Dean Howells.* Syracuse: Syracuse Univ. Press, 1956.

Cargill, Oscar. *The Novels of Henry James.* New York: Macmillan, 1961.

Carnegie, Andrew. *The Gospel of Wealth and Other Timely Essays.* ed. Edward C. Kirkland. Cambridge: Harvard Univ. Press, 1962.

Carrington, George C. *The Immense Complex Drama: The World and Art of the Howells Novel.* Columbus: Ohio State Univ. Press, 1966.

Carroll, Peter N. *Puritanism and the Wilderness.* New York: Columbia Univ. Press, 1969.

Churchill, Winston. "A Modern Quest for Religion," *Century Magazine*, 87 (1913), 169-174.

Commager, Henry Steele. *The American Mind: An Interpretation of American Thought and Character Since the 1880's.* New Haven: Yale Univ. Press, 1950.

Curti, Merle. *A History of American Civilization.* New York: Books for Libraries Press, 1968.

——————————. *The Growth of the American Mind.* 3rd ed. New York: Harper & Row, 1964.

Dawson, Christopher. *Progress and Religion.* Garden City, N. Y.: Doubleday, 1960.

Dinnerstein, Leonard and David Reimers. *Ethnic Americans: A History of Immigration and Assimilation.* New York: Harper & Row, 1975.

Eddy, Mary Baker. *Science and Health.* 28th ed. rev. Boston: The Author, 1887.

Edel, Leon. *Henry James: The Middle Years.* New York: Lippincott, 1962.

Egbert, Donald Drew and Stow Persons, eds. *Socialism and American Life.* 2 vols. Princeton: Princeton Univ. Press, 1952.

Ellis, John Tracy. *American Catholicism.* Chicago: Chicago Univ. Press, 1955.

Fiedler, Leslie. *The Jew in the American Novel.* New York: Herzel Inst., 1959.

_____. *Love and Death in the American Novel.* New York: Criterion, 1960.

Flanagan, John T. "The Novels of Edward Eggleston," *CE,* 5 (1944), 250-254.

Ford, Mary K. "Margaret Deland," Bookman, 25 (July, 1907), 511-519.

Frederick, John T. *The Darkened Sky: Nineteenth-Century American Novelists and Religion.* South Bend: Notre Dame Univ. Press, 1969.

Freud, Sigmund. *The Future of an Illusion.* New York: Doubleday, 1964.

Gaustad, Edwin Scott. *A Religious History of America.* New York: Harper & Row, 1966.

Glazer, Nathan. *American Judaism*. Chicago: Univ. of Chicago Press, 1971.

Greeley, Andrew. *That Most Distressful Nation: The Taming of the American Irish*. Chicago: Quadrangle, 1972.

Griffin, Clifford S. *Their Brothers' Keeper: Moral Stewardship in the United States*, 1800-1865. New Brunswick: Rutgers Univ. Press, 1960.

Guttman, Allen. *The Jewish Writer in America: Assimilation and the Crisis of Identity*. New York: Oxford Univ. Press, 1971.

Hall, Thomas C. *The Religious Background of American Culture*. Boston: Little Brown, 1930.

Haller, William. *The Puritan Town-Planting in New England Colonial Development, 1630-1667*. New York: Columbia Univ. Press, 1951.

Handlin, Oscar. *The Uprooted: The Epic Story of the Great Migrations That Made the American People*. Boston: Little Brown, 1951.

Handy, Robert T., ed. *The Social Gospel in America: 1870-1920*. New York: Oxford Univ. Press, 1966.

Haroutunian, Joseph. *Piety Versus Moralism: The Passing of New England Theology*. New York: H. Holt, 1932.

Heimert, Alan. *Religion and the American Mind*. Cambridge: Harvard Univ. Press, 1953.

Herberg, Will. *Protestant-Catholic-Jew: An Essay in American Religious Sociology*. rev. ed. Garden City: Doubleday, 1960.

Herrick, Robert. "The Background of the American Novel," *YR*, 3 (January, 1914), 213-233.

Hicks, Granville. *The Great Tradition.* New York: International Publishers, 1935.

Higham, John. *Strangers in the Land: Patterns of American Nativism, 1860-1925.* New Brunswick: Rutgers Univ. Press, 1955.

Hofstadter, Richard. *Social Darwinism in American Thought.* rev. ed. Boston: Beacon Press, 1967.

Holloway, Mark. *Heavens on Earth: Utopian Communities in America, 1680-1880.* 2nd ed. New York: Dover, 1966.

Horton, Rod W. and Herbert W. Edwards. *Backgrounds of American Literary Thought.* New York: Appleton-Century, 1952.

Hubbell, Jay B. *The South in American Literature.* Durham, N. C.: Duke Univ. Press, 1954.

Hudson, Winthrop S. *American Protestantism.* Chicago: Univ. of Chicago Press, 1961.

_____. *Religion in America: Years of Mid-Passage, 1860-1914.* New York: Scribner's, 1965.

James, Henry. *The American Scene.* Bloomington: Indiana Univ. Press, 1968.

_____. *Hawthorne.* Ithaca, N. Y.: Cornell Univ. Press, 1967.

James, William. *The Varieties of Religious Experience.* New York: Longmans Green, 1928.

Jones, Howard Mumford. *Belief and Disbelief in American Literature*. Chicago: Univ. of Chicago Press, 1967.

————, "Literature and Orthodoxy in Boston after the Civil War," *The American Culture*. Ed. Hennig Cohen. New York: Houghton Mifflin, 1968.

Josephson, Matthew. *The Robber Barons: The Great American Capitalists, 1861-1901*. New York: Harcourt Brace, 1962.

Kaul, A. N. *The American Vision: Actual and Ideal Society in Nineteenth-Century Fiction*. New Haven: Yale Univ. Press, 1963.

Kazin, Alfred. *On Native Grounds: An Interpretation of Modern American Prose Literature*. New York: Reynal & Hitchcock, 1942.

Kirk, Clara M. *W. D. Howells and Art in His Times*. New Brunswick, N. J.: Rutgers Univ. Press, 1965.

Klose, Nelson. *A Concise Guide to the American Frontier*. Lincoln, Neb.: Univ. of Nebraska Press, 1964.

Lasch, Christopher. *The Culture of Narcissism: American Life in an Age of Diminishing Expectations*. New York: Norton, 1979.

Letters of Henry Adams, 1858-1891. ed. Worthington C. Ford. Boston: Houghton Mifflin, 1930.

Life and Letters of William Dean Howells. 2 vols. ed. Mildred Howells. Garden City: Doubleday, 1928.

Lyon, Melvin. *Symbol and Idea in Henry Adams*. Lincoln, Neb.: Univ. of Nebraska Press, 1970.

McLoughlin, William G. *Modern Revivalism: Charles Grandison Finney to Billy Graham*. New York: Ronald Press, 1959.

_____, "Pietism and the American Character," *The American Experience*. Ed. Hennig Cohen. Boston: Houghton Mifflin, 1968.

McPherson, Hugo. *Hawthorne as Myth-Maker*. Toronto: Toronto Univ. Press, 1969.

Mannheim, Karl. *Ideology and Utopia: An Introduction to the Sociology of Literature*. New York: Harcourt Brace, & Co., 1936.

Manuel, Frank E., ed. *Utopias and Utopian Thought*. Boston: Houghton Mifflin, 1966.

Martin, Helen Reimensnyder. "American Backgrounds for Fiction: The Pennsylvania Dutch," *Bookman*, 38 (November, 1913), 244-247.

Martin, Jay. *Harvests of Change: American Literature, 1865-1914*. Englewood Cliffs, N. J.: Prentice-Hall, 1967.

Mather, Cotton. *Essays to Do Good*. 2nd ed. rev. George Burder. London: J. Dennett, 1808.

May, Henry F. *Protestant Churches and Industrial America*. New York: Harper & Row, 1949.

Miller, Perry. *The Life of the Mind in America*. New York: Harcourt Brace & World, 1965.

_____, *The New England Mind: From Colony to Providence*. Cambridge: Harvard Univ. Press, 1953.

_____, *The New England Mind: The Seventeenth Century*. Cambridge: Harvard Univ. Press, 1963.

Ming, John J. *The Characteristics and Religion of Modern Socialism*. New York: Benziger Bros., 1909.

Moats, F. I. "The Rise of Methodism in the Middle West," *Mississippi Valley Historical Review*, 15 (1928), 69-88.

Moberg, David O. *The Church as a Social Institution*. Englewood Cliffs, N. J.: Prentice-Hall, 1962.

Morgan, Edmund S. *Visible Saints*. New York: New York Univ. Press, 1963.

Mosier, Richard D. *The American Temper: Patterns of Our Intellectual Heritage*. Berkeley: Univ. of California Press, 1952.

Mott, Luther. *Golden Multitudes: The Story of the Best Seller in the United States*. New York: Macmillan, 1947.

Murdock, Kenneth B. *Literature and Theology in Colonial New England*. New York: Harper, 1963.

Naisbitt, John. *Megatrends: Ten New Directions Transforming Our Lives*. New York: Warner Books, 1982.

Negley, Glenn Robert and J. Max Patrick, eds. *The Quest for Utopia: An Anthology*. New York: H. Schuman, 1952.

Nevius, Blake. "The Idealistic Novels of Robert Herrick," *AL*, 21 (March, 1949), pp. 56-70.

Niebuhr, H. Richard. *The Kingdom of God in America.* New York: Harper, 1937.

_____. *The Social Sources of Denominationalism.* Cleveland: World, 1957.

_____. *Beyond Tragedy: Essays on the Christian Interpretation of History.* 1965; rpt. Freeport, N. Y.: Books for Libraries Press, 1971.

_____. *The Nature and Destiny of Man: A Christian Interpretation.* New York: Scribner's, 1953.

Norris, Frank. "The Responsibilities of the Novelist," *Critic,* 41 (December, 1902), 566-640.

Novak, Michael (ed.). *Capitalism and Socialism.* Washington: American Enterprise Institute for Public Policy Research, 1979.

Olmstead, Clifton E. *Religion in America: Past and Present.* Englewood Cliffs, N. J.: Prentice-Hall, 1961.

Olsen, Otto H. *Carpetbagger's Crusade: The Life of Albion Winegar Tourgee.* Baltimore: Johns Hopkins Univ. Press, 1965.

Parrington, Vernon Louis. *Main Currents in American Thought, 1860-1920: The Beginnings of Critical Realism in America.* Volume III. New York: Harcourt Brace, 1930.

Pattee, Fred Lewis. *A History of American Literature Since 1870.* 1943; rpt. New York: Cooper Square Publishing, 1968.

Paxson, Frederic L. *History of the American Frontier,* 1763-1893. Boston: Houghton Mifflin, 1924.

Pick, John. "The Renascence in American Catholic Letters," *The Catholic Renascence.* Ed. Norman Weyand, S. J. Chicago: Loyola Univ. Press, 1951.

Quinn, Arthur Hobson. *American Fiction: An Historical Critical Survey.* New York: Appleton Century, 1936.

Randel, William. *Edward Eggleston.* New York: Twayne, 1963.

Rawley, J. S. "Some New Light on Eggleston," *AL,* 11 (1940), 453-458.

Richey, Russell E. and Donald G. Jones, eds. *American Civil Religion.* New York: Harper & Row, 1974.

Rideout, Walter B. *The Radical Novel in the United States, 1900-1954.* Cambridge: Harvard Univ. Press, 1956.

Royce, Josiah. *The Problem of Christianity.* 2 vols. New York: Macmillan, 1913.

Rusk, Ralph. *The Literature of the Middle Western Border.* 2 vols. New York: Ungar, 1925.

Rutman, Darrett B. *Winthrop's Boston.* Chapel Hill, N. C.: Univ. of North Carolina Press, 1965.

Samuels, Ernest. *Henry Adams: The Middle Years.* Cambridge: Harvard Univ. Press, 1958.

Sanford, Charles L. "An American Pilgrim's Progress," *The American Culture.* Ed. Hennig Cohen. New York: Houghton Mifflin, 1968.

Santayana, George. *Character and Opinion in the United States*. New York: Doubleday, 1920.

Schlesinger, Arthur M. "Social History in American Literature," *YR*, 18 (September, 1928), 135-147.

Schneider, Herbert W. *A History of American Philosophy*. 2nd ed. New York: Columbia Univ. Press, 1963.

Sennett, Richard. *The Fall of Public Man*. New York: Knopf, 1976.

Shipton, Clifford K. "A Plea for Puritanism," *AHR*, 60 (1935), 460-467.

_____. "Puritanism and Modern Democracy," *New England Historical and Geneological Register*, 101 (1947), 181-198.

Smith, Henry Nash, ed. *Popular Culture and Industrialism, 1865-1890*. Garden City: Doubleday, 1967.

_____. *Virgin Land: The American West as Symbol and Myth*. Cambridge: Harvard Univ. Press, 1950.

Smith, James W. and A. Leland Jamison, eds. *Religious Perspectives in American Culture*. Princeton: Princeton Univ. Press, 1961.

Smithline, Arnold. *Natural Religion in American Literature*. New Haven: College and Univ. Press, 1966.

Sorokin, Pitrim A. *Society, Culture, and Personality: Their Structure and Dynamics*. New York: Harper, 1947.

Sowell, Thomas. *Ethnic America.* New York: Basic Books, 1981.

Spencer, Benjamin T. *The Quest for Nationality: An American Literary Campaign.* Syracuse: Syracuse Univ. Press, 1957.

Spiller, Robert E. *et al.*, eds. *Literary History of the United States.* 3rd. ed. rev. New York: Macmillan, 1963.

Stewart, Randall. *American Literature and Christian Doctrine.* Baton Rouge: Louisiana State Univ. Press, 1958.

Strong, Augustus Hopkins. *American Poets and Their Theology.* 1916; rpt. Freeport, N. Y.: Books for Libraries, 1968.

Sweet, William Warren. *The Story of Religions in America.* New York: Harper & Bros., 1930.

Tawney, R. H. *The Acquisitive Society.* New York: Harcourt Brace, 1948.

Tawney, R. H. *Religion and the Rise of Capitalism.* New York: Harcourt Brace, 1926.

Taylor, Walter Fuller. *The Economic Novel in America.* Chapel Hill: Univ. of North Carolina Press, 1942.

Twain, Mark. "Christian Science," *North American Review,* 175 (December, 1902), 756-768.

_____. "Christian Science—III," *North American Review,* 176 (February, 1903), 1-9, 173-184.

Vanderbilt, Kermit. *The Achievement of William Dean Howells*. Princeton: Princeton Univ. Press, 1968.

Wagenknecht, Edward. *Longfellow: A Full Length Portrait*. New York: Oxford Univ. Press, 1955.

_____, *William Dean Howells: The Friendly Eye*. New York: Oxford Univ. Press, 1969.

Waggoner, Hyatt. *American Poets: From the Puritans to the Present*. Boston: Houghton Mifflin, 1968.

Walcutt, Charles Child. *American Literary Naturalism: A Divided Stream*. Minneapolis: Univ. of Minnesota Press, 1956.

Wecter, Dixon. "Instruments of Culture on the Frontier," *YR*, 36 (1947), 242-256.

Weisenburger, Francis P. *The Ordeal of Faith: The Crisis of Church-Going in America, 1865-1900*. New York: Philosophical Library, 1959.

Wellek, Rene and Austin Warren. *Theory of Literature*. New York: Harcourt Brace, 1949.

Weyand, S. J., Norman (ed.). *The Catholic Renascence*. Chicago: Loyola Univ. Press, 1951.

Wilder, Amos N. *Modern Poetry and the Christian Tradition*. New York: Scribner's, 1952.

Williams, Cecil. *Henry Wadsworth Longfellow*. New York: Twayne, 1964.

Williams, T. Harry *et al*. *A History of the United States to 1876*. New York: Knopf, 1960.

Wilmore, Gayrand S. *The Secular Relevance of the Church*. Philadelphia: Westminster Press, 1962.

Wilson, Byron. *Religion in Secular Society*. Baltimore: Penguin, 1969.

Wish, Harvey. *Society and Thought in Modern America*. New York: Longmans, Green, 1952.

Wright, Conrad. *The Beginnings of Unitarianism in America*. Boston: Beacon Press, 1955.

Wright, Louis B. *Culture on the Moving Frontier*. New York: Harper & Row, 1961.

Ziff, Larzer. *The American 1890's: Life and Times of a Lost Generation*. New York: Viking Press, 1966.

——————————, *The Career of John Cotton*. Princeton: Princeton Univ. Press, 1962.